*WORLD WAR I*

*THROUGH*

*MY SIGHTS*

# WORLD WAR I
# THROUGH
# MY SIGHTS

HORATIO ROGERS

PRESIDIO PRESS
SAN RAFAEL, CALIFORNIA

1976

World War I through My Sights

Library of Congress Catalogue Card Number 74–31941

ISBN 0–89141–004–x

Printed in the United States of America by
The Stinehour Press, Lunenburg, Vermont

Published by Presidio Press
1114 Irwin Street
San Rafael, California 94901

A great peril escaped makes a great storyteller
of a common person enough

OLIVER WENDELL HOLMES

# FOREWORD

SINCE THE "COMMON MAN" has become fashionable as a subject of historical investigation, one hears frequent laments about the scarcity of sources. For good reason presidents wrote and kept more papers than postmen who simply carried them. Similarly generals and admirals have written more military narratives than soldiers and sailors. I was consequently delighted when my neighbor, Dr. Horatio Rogers, decided to print his recollections of World War I as an enlisted man in Battery A, 101st Field Artillery, Twenth-Sixth Division, American Expeditionary Force. During his service in France, Dr. Rogers had carried a vest-pocket notebook in which he jotted brief reminders of names, dates, and places. In 1928 he came upon this and, reflecting that parts of it were as illegible as his grandfather's Civil War diary, over which he had often puzzled, wrote the narrative that follows. In each chapter the quotation from the notebook is printed verbatim, followed by the recollections inspired by these laconic notes. The whole was then typed and bound. As Dr. Rogers had permitted me to read this narrative several years ago, I was delighted when he decided last autumn to have it printed. It appears in 1975 exactly as it was written forty-seven years earlier.

Although this artillery scout, who enlisted at twenty, describes World War I through the eyes of a corporal, this is not the diary of a "common man." Having entered Harvard College in 1915, Horatio Rogers enrolled in the R.O.T.C. and spent the summer of 1916 in the Student's Military Camp at Plattsburg, New York. The following summer, he went on his own to the Commonwealth Armory on

July ninth and enlisted in Battery A. By September he was in France. He came honestly by the feeling that it was the duty of an able-bodied young man to serve his country by bearing arms. One night in July 1918 when in the front lines, he received a letter from his father, the Reverend Lucian Waterman Rogers, rector of the Episcopal Church of the Redeemer in Chestnut Hill, Massachusetts, which said: "I wish to heaven that I were in your place. The great call came to you and it came to my father, but I am left behind to nibble around these trees like an old rat. . . . But what difference does it make! Let each man take the part assigned him, and not merely act it, but *be* it."

The narrative is vivid, for it is written in the English that comes from having grown up in a household supplied with books, where the cadences of the King James Bible and the (unrevised) Book of Common Prayer were an unconscious part of daily life. One follows Corporal Rogers through training, combat, cheerful shenanigans in France after the Armistice, to his return home and discharge at Camp Devens in April 1919. He then returned to Harvard College, where, thanks to credit benevolently given for conversational French and map reading, he completed his degree requirements in one rather than two years, receiving his A.B. in 1920, as of 1919. Three years later in 1923 he received a Harvard M.D. and began a career as a Boston surgeon at the Massachusetts General Hospital. He married Caroline Stevens of North Andover, who had served in France as a nurse's aide in a civilian hospital at Toul during the war.

In World War II Dr. Rogers returned to active duty as a medical officer with the Sixth General Hospital, a unit organized at the Massachusetts General, with which he served in the Mediterranean theatre at Casablanca, Rome, and Bologna. On retiring from practice Dr. Rogers moved to North Andover, where he has been an uncommonly helpful trustee of the Merrimack Valley Textile Museum, founded by his wife in 1960. His manual skill has been turned to woodworking, repairing looms, building pedestals, and painting signs; his literary skill has produced useful writing for the North Andover Historical Society. At Chatham on Cape Cod, where he and his wife enjoy the company of numerous descendants, Dr. Rogers traps and smokes eels of admirable flavor. I have greatly enjoyed his company, and am proud to have a hand in introducing this first-rate document of personal experience of American life in wartime.

WALTER MUIR WHITEHILL

North Andover, Massachusetts
February 8, 1975

# APOLOGY

ONE DAY IN 1928, I came across the notebook which I carried during the war. It was surprising how ten years had blurred the writing. Some of it was as illegible as parts of my grandfather's Civil War diary, over which I have often puzzled, wishing I knew the story hidden there. I stood in the attic, the notebook in my hand, idly turning the familiar pages, and wondering how long it would take for this story to be lost in its turn. It was then that the temptation came to write about the war. The same impulse, I guess, prompts people to return to a burning house for some article of no great value, but which represents a little part of their life to them. I have succumbed to the temptation, and now my old notebook can fall to pieces as fast as it will. If anyone in years to come should feel his curiosity stirred by the faded relic, it may be satisfied. Also he can discover how he himself might have felt.

# THE NOTEBOOK

THIS IS a little dark-red vest-pocket book with leather covers. When my father bought it for me he got the best he could find. On the flyleaf is written:

Horatio Rogers, Corp'l
Btry. A, 101st Regt. F.A.
26th Division
51st Brigade
A.E.F.

Most of the pages are covered with neat working notes: methods of figuring firing data, of determining the water a given stream will supply, of estimating the numbers of troops seen on a road, of stringing telephone wire, of interpreting the hieroglyphics on shellcases, of guessing the distance of a shot by flash and sound, and many others, useful and useless.

At the back are ten pages full of irregular words, spotted with rain, written on horseback, in shell holes, dugouts, and haylofts, on troop trains, camions, and ships. These are the landmarks for what follows, and I shall copy them verbatim at the head of each chapter.

# CONTENTS

# CHAPTER I

*Into the army. Battery A leaves Boston.*

"Com. Armory, July 25, 1917. drills; packing; horse smell;
misgivings; lonesomeness; trucks; L.W.R.
woebegone on corner; lump."

A BATTERY of field artillery is getting ready to leave the Commonwealth Armory in Boston. The men wear wide-brimmed Stetson
hats with red cords. The "oldtimers" who have been in the Massachusetts Volunteer Militia for several months or years have insignia on their blouse collars: a bronze disc on one side saying *A1* *
with crossed cannons, and *MVM*† on the other side; but no one is
wearing a blouse today, for the heat is overpowering in the noonday
sun that beats down on the paddock and gun ramp, and it is not cool
in the large indoor riding ring. The air is full of dust and the penetrating smell of horses. Orders are being shouted, crates nailed up,
blankets rolled, harness overhauled; a corporal can't find the breech
cover for the first piece and is noisy about it. I stand aside. These men
find it easier to do the work themselves than to show a recruit how to
do it. I did try to appear busy for a while but I didn't know what to
do and after getting yelled at for putting curry combs in the instrument chest, or spare stirrup leathers in the cook's bedding roll, I
stopped trying to be useful.

I did not know where we were going, and I didn't know anyone
to ask. Of the few men I had met doing foot drill in the ring on two
or three previous evenings, the only one whose name I remembered,
Spike Spiers, was not in sight.

I knew something about foot drill from the Harvard R.O.T.C.‡

* Battery A. First Regiment.
† Massachusetts Volunteer Militia.
‡ Reserve Officers' Training Corps.

It had started in the spring of my sophomore year and everybody joined. Tom Proctor came down from Dartmouth to be in it. Bradford Eddy's mother asked Aunt Emily to ask me if it was a good thing for him to join, and I said yes. Carl Morss, my roommate, was a lieutenant. The fellows I knew who were captains had acquired great dignity and importance. I was a corporal and had been assigned as bayonet instructor. We bought uniforms, attended lectures on trench warfare by French officers, drilled on Soldiers' Field in the afternoons, and were keen on military books, mapmaking, minor tactics, and Infantry Drill Regulations. It was all right while college held, as it offered an escape from the regular curriculum, but after college ended, we moved into the Freshman Dormitories as barracks and did R.O.T.C. all day. It was then that I began to wonder if I wanted to keep on with it.

I had been to the Students' Military Camp at Plattsburg in the summer of 1916 and probably stood a good chance of getting a commission in the R.O.T.C. But it looked like a long job. Already there were letters and reports from friends who had gone over in the Legion and Ambulance. Some had been killed. The papers were full of German atrocities and Allied unsuccess. Each "great drive" the Allies made seemed to accomplish nothing. Then Russia was overthrown, and I had visions of a Prussianized world. I had not been very serious when I entered the R.O.T.C. but I now began to think very seriously. At the same time, Ted Storer, who had gone to Country Day School with Carl Morss and was now top sergeant of A Battery, "the dude battery," began to come around to our room to talk enlistment.

I could ride, and I pictured the worst that could happen to an artilleryman as being blown up among his friends—a much nicer end than being bayonetted and left out in "no-man's-land." What a man my father was! How he must have suffered as he saw where it was all leading, and how wise and unselfish were his counsels. He asked the advice of everyone whose judgment he trusted. I was already vaguely interested in medicine, so he found out the possibilities of the Medical Corps. They amounted to sweeping the floor in some hospital ward. Dr. Scudder urged me to finish my college course and to enter the Medical School, and if the war was still going on then, it would be time enough to enter the Medical Corps. This appealed to my cowardice but left me somehow uncomfortable. I couldn't do it.

I see now that I was thinking mostly of my own moral comfort, and very little of my parents' anguish, which they kept to themselves. They never tried to influence me to their own advantage, but helped me in every way they could to make the decision which was so important to our family circle. I don't know what made me decide as I did; who can ever know himself truly enough to tell? I decided to join the Battery and went down to the armory the next night, the ninth of July, to enlist.

I remember looking around the room after my physical examination and enrollment. Here were the men I was going out with to war. Larry Williams was playing ragtime on the piano and singing. Someone told me his name. Everyone was talking and laughing. I felt a little thrill of emotion, and the phrase "comrades-in-arms" came into my head. A year later, on July 19th, Larry was killed by German shellfire on the edge of a thicket at Belleau Woods, and his parents received their telegram from the War Department.

At home we talked about the present and the immediate future. When should I leave Boston? What should I need to take? And how nice it was to be in a unit of the personnel and traditions of Battery A. My parents bravely kept their deepest thoughts to themselves, but I can guess now what they were. They had me photographed in my uniform; I didn't see why! I attended a few evening drills at the armory, with my parents watching from the gallery. (Polly was too small to come.) I learned a few men's names, and then the word came that the Massachusetts Militia was to be called out July 25th. I had been living in a mental fog, not thinking of anything, but feeling relieved that there was nothing more to be decided.

The packing-up was all Greek to me. I had never seen a gun close to, and I would have called it a cannon offhand. Someone told me to get on a truck piled high with packing boxes, and the truck jounced out of the paddock onto the macadam of Commonwealth Avenue. At the corner of the street stood a man on the sidewalk with a straw hat in his hand. He looked up. It was my father. He smiled, and I saw him still waving his hand as the truck turned the next corner. A great lump came into my throat and I winked back tears.

CHAPTER II

*Boxford and early training. Departure.*

"Boxford, July 25, 1917. Baldpate Inn; special detail; sick; drills; heat; slippery grass; junk."

I WAS LYING on a canvas cot, half-asleep, while the July sun beat down on the tightly stretched khaki-colored tent above my head, and the heat, like the breath of an oven, radiated down on my partly clad body. Every muscle ached. Moisture exuded from every pore. The day before was a bad dream, full of loading equipment on trains at the freight yard, a hot ride in a stuffy passenger car, with a crowd yelling on every station platform, hands reaching up to the car windows with gifts of sticky chocolate or defunct pie, and finally unloading freight cars at Boxford. Then across a half mile of field, and an afternoon of putting up tents in rows: great pyramidal brutes large enough to hold eight cots. At last a bugle had sounded, and I had grabbed my mess kit and lined up at the cook tent at the head of the Battery street. Stew, coffee, bread, and jam, and then a dip of the aluminum mess kit and cup in a tub of warm, greasy water before putting it away under my cot, and I had strolled down the Battery street to see where I was.

4

"They had me photographed in my uniform;
I didn't see why!"

Batteries B and C were arriving and setting their tents next to us, and I walked down their streets to see if they had their tents straight. Soon it got dark and I began to be lonely. I talked with anyone I remembered having seen before at the armory and felt as if I had known them a long time. At taps I had gone to bed on my cot, not knowing whether to undress or not. Some of the recruits had pajamas they put on. I had compromised by taking off my boots, leggings, and hat. I rolled my blouse up for a pillow and, in spite of the buttons on it, I was soon asleep. Reveille had seemed to blow not more than five minutes later and the sun was shining. During the night the horses had come up with the drivers over the road, and they were now tied to long ropes stretched between the tops of limber wheels behind the Battery street. After a breakfast of coffee, bread, and oatmeal with karo on it, eaten sitting on the ground, I had been put to sorting harness from the packing boxes, cleaning it with saddle soap, and grooming two horses. At last I was through, with twenty minutes for "bunk-fatigue" before dinner.

I looked around through half-closed eyes at the seven other cots containing limp figures. There was Spider Barnes, a thin, red-faced, black-haired boy with a high voice. He came from Arlington, Massachusetts, and proved a good neighbor as he had a mother who sent him cake every few days. He turned out to be a driver in France and I did not see much of him. There was Jack Cleary, a big, blond Irishman from West Roxbury, hard-fisted, strong as an ox, and very easy going. He had baby-blue eyes with a lurking twinkle in them. He also became a driver. Spike Speirs of Dorchester, he of the red hair, plump figure, freckles, and strident voice, was there too. He was early detached to Headquarters Company and was lost sight of. The fourth was Norbert Rigby from Brookline. He was a thin, pale boy with a slight Cockney accent. In France, he became a gunner, and was killed in April, near St. Julien. The fifth was Lyell Hale Ritchie, a Harvard freshman and a member of the Owl Club at Cambridge. He lived in Hinsdale, Illinois, but hadn't bothered to go home to enlist. Thin, stoop-shouldered, frail-looking, with expressive brown eyes and a quick sympathetic smile, "Pancakes" as he soon came to be called by Beck, and later by all his friends, was as green a rooky as I, so we hit it off from the start. At first I took him for a Harvard exquisite, but he proved a paladin when the bad times came. The two others were destined to play almost as large a part in my adventures as was Pancakes. Alfred Beck was brusque to a fault, and was feared and disliked by everyone who did not know him well. He had been a real-estate broker in Jamaica Plain. He was spare of figure, gruff of voice, picturesque and acrid of speech, and had a heart of gold. He had a nose like the beak of a hawk, bridged by metal-rimmed spectacles. He soon became "Spreckles" to his friends, but remained "Sergeant Beck" to others. Robert H. Ives Gammell was the eighth in the tent. He was an artist whose star was beginning to rise in Boston, and has since risen. He came of an old and proud family in Providence, Rhode Island. He had roamed the world, had studied art in Paris, spoke French, was a connoisseur of wines, cheeses, and landscapes, and had a coy wit and a dainty gift of expression. He was so small that every army uniform was too big for him, so he was an absurd sight with the seat of his breeches hanging almost as low as his knees, and his hands almost hidden in his sleeves. He wore a little mustache, spoke in a low voice, and nothing escaped the notice of his robin's eyes. Both he and Beck were to get commissions, and he was to serve in the Army Secret Service and perform exploits about which his lips are officially sealed.

Through the tent door I could see the heat waves shimmering above the horse lines. The intermittent drone of locusts filled the dead air. Around the tent pole the slickers and overcoats hung in a limp festoon. Overcoats! My God. I felt hotter for looking at them. Spider Barnes was snoring loudly while flies walked on his moist face. I got up slowly, put on my shirt and hat, and strolled down to the latrine.

At the foot of each battery street, in the space between the last tents and the beginning of the horse lines, a deep, narrow pit had been dug. A birch log was suspended over it on forked stakes at either end, and on this log we sat after breakfast like sparrows on a telegraph wire. Every day the latrine detail removed the log, threw straw down the latrine, poured kerosene on it, and burned out the latrine.

I remember the sensation caused by one Alcohol Johnson just after taps one night. He had returned from a convivial evening with his friends and did not notice that the birch log was insecurely attached at one end. When he sat down, it gave way. He was pulled out by members of the ninth section who had heard the sounds of the accident. I don't know where he slept that night, but I feel sure it was not in his squad tent.

Only a few special days stand out in my memory. For the rest, it is a blur of heat, drills, parched grass, and always new outfits coming in and new rows of tents springing up like the dragon's teeth in the story of Cadmus.

On Sundays, the camp was thronged with visitors, and through every tent fly we could see family reunions: a fat woman sitting on a cot, an oldish man examining everything with serious eyes while making jokes, and a self-conscious boy standing among piles of knitted socks, knitted helmets, knitted bellybands, knitted mufflers, cakes, pies, baskets of fruit, and wrapping paper everywhere. On Monday mornings, the camp looked like a fairground after the fair.

The big treat was to be taken to nearby Baldpate Inn by one's family for Sunday dinner. One or two friends were always asked to come along to keep the conversation impersonal, and I usually took Ritchie and Gammell because their friends never visited them. How we would eat. Those chicken dinners with Golden Bantam corn were angel food to us. Then we would stretch out on the grassy bank in the sun and talk to Ma and Pa as if we were just out for a school holiday. Too soon the sun would sink, and after goodbyes full of forced jollity, we would hike back towards camp, leaving two silent figures looking after us down the road. No one ever had much to say on the way back to camp.

It was usually on Mondays that I would look at the horse I was grooming and speculate on how I could make him kick me so as to break my leg without breaking my neck too. Well, he never did, and if one kicked I always seemed to dodge quickly enough.

Everyone was assigned to some job after the routine foot drill, mounted drill, and chores were done. Some worked on the guns, learning the exact drill by which six men loaded, aimed, and fired a gun with clocklike precision. Others practiced harnessing, hitching, and driving. Largely through the influence of Gammell, Beck, and Ritchie, I threw my lot in with the Special Detail, or Battery Commander's Detail as the drill book called it. We studied signalling with flags, both wigwagging with one big flag waved to right and left to form the dots and dashes of the Morse code, or semaphoring, with a flag in each hand held at arbitrary angles to form the different letters, or buzzing with an electric telegraph key. We spent hours drawing panoramic sketches showing various targets: houses, corners of fields, crossroads, etc., with their variation from "basic deflection." We exhausted all our mathematics in the study of firing data, elevations, parabolas, deflections, parallaxes, allowances for wind and shell lot, defilades, indirect fire, lateral observations, and "three-point problems." My father brought me books on algebra and trigonometry, with a slide rule and log. tables, which I tackled without hesitation. We rode out into the country and went through the pantomime of taking up position, picking up targets, laying in guns, and reporting firing data.

Many of the instruments were large and heavy, and these would bang against our shoulder blades and hip bones at every trot of the horse. Pancakes Ritchie was no horseman, and we had to laugh to see him go galloping around a corner with one foot out of the stirrup and a flurry of leather instrument cases flying around his neck.

Each day two privates were detailed to kitchen police.* One was

* "Police" is used in the army to mean clean or tidy, correct. "Policing the battery street" is picking up the rubbish on it. "Police that coat" means make it neat. The Military Police (MPs) were for preserving order.

8

to run the incinerator—a pit covered with an iron grating on which the swill and rubbish was consumed by a hot wood fire beneath—and one to peel potatoes and to scour greasy kettles. There wasn't much to choose between the jobs. I got the incinerator, and the combination of its heat and the August sun sent me to bed for two days. I wondered if they would excuse me from the army on the ground of weak health, but no one offered to. I really don't know whether I should have been glad or sorry then.

The heat was intense. The field where we had foot drill was uneven and carpeted with parched grass. The soles of our shoes became so slippery that it was like walking on ice, and it was almost impossible to run. My legs ached every night as if I'd been walking thirty miles.

Watering the horses was always interesting and sometimes very funny. We would line up, march to the picket line, and each untie two horses. If our detail was small, some would have to take four. Then holding the halter shanks, we would scramble onto a horse and move across the field to the road. Here we would form a procession, and a sedate lieutenant would lead us down to the pond, about half a mile from camp. On reaching the pond, the idea was to halt on the road while the lieutenant told off six or eight horses to drink at a time. After drinking, they were supposed to wait in line on the road till all were watered, before starting solemnly back to camp. Well, this programme was usually greatly varied by impromptu performances. I remember George Shepley, who weighed about one hundred pounds, leading a big wheel horse by a chain halter shank. The wheeler was thirsty and he ignored George's feeble tugs on the chain. The horse George was riding went slowly enough, so the time came when George had to choose which horse to stay with. He chose to hang onto the halter shank, and I saw him dragged over his horse's head and go bobbing along at the end of the chain, while the thirsty wheeler stampeded through the whole battery so fast that George's feet touched the ground only about every third jump.

Chester A. Soule was a youth who took himself very hard, wore spurs always, and claimed he was "born on a horse." One day his horse broke ranks and started to run away with him. The lieutenant and two sergeants, never suspecting his birthplace, took after him. He managed to stay on and beat them to the pond, and when they got there he was standing up to his neck in water, yelling, "Help, help, I can't swim!" We all called him "Ah Soule."

Then one day, coming back from water, the whole column stampeded, and there was a glorious cavalry charge that ended only when Lyell Ritchie's horse galloped into the captain's tent, plunged out the back end, tripped over a guy rope, and fell down, dragging the whole wreck after him. Why no one was hurt, I can't tell.

August fifth came, and the militia regiments were drafted into the Federal Service. There were inspections and endless standing in line. By this time there were only patches of grass left in the battery streets, and those were burned yellow by the sun.

I had taken my gunner's examination and passed, so I could wear a little cloth projectile sewed on my sleeve. I had made friends, and enemies—one corporal in particular, named Lloyd, seemed always to be at cross purposes, but we carried it no further than hard looks. There was also a man named Nyland, an affected, pushing sort whom I was supposed to like because he knew my godmother. Lloyd went crazy from the sound of the guns at the training camp in France and was sent home. Nyland I learned to tolerate but I never liked him. Some of the mechanics and farriers were much older men who had served terms in the regular army or were extra hard-boiled from some other cause. For these I felt respect tinged with dislike. Later on, after living at the front with them, I came to despise some and to admire others most heartily.

On August tenth I got my corporal's stripes, and learned that too much modesty was mistaken by some for weakness and that with certain types it paid to put on an appearance of being more hard-boiled than nature had intended.

"August tenth I got
my corporal's stripes."

The leather puttees and campaign hats
were discarded in France. Note the bulge
of the notebook in my shirt pocket.

"We knew we were going to leave Boxford."

There were occupations for spare time if anyone had the vitality to do more than lie on his back after hours. We used to go swimming in the pond half a mile behind the picket lines, and we built a shower bath at the foot of the Battery street after water had been piped into camp. Sometimes we took our horses swimming in the pond. There was a Y.M.C.A. tent behind the 101st Regiment camp, with writing materials and a store for chocolate, etc. Boxing matches were arranged by the chaplains in a natural amphitheatre between the regiments. On Sundays the regimental band played "Onward, Christian Soldiers" in a jazzy tempo for reveille march, and at church call, after watering and grooming, we lined up and marched to the place the boxing matches were held to hear the chaplain preach not very good sermons. He seemed to be trying to lower himself to what he considered was the soldiers' level, and he put it quite low. After supper on weekday nights the band played sad popular airs like "I want to go home" and "There's a long, long trail awinding." Some of these wretched tunes rang in my head all through the war.

One night in August there was a terrific thunderstorm. I was on guard at the picket line. Great sweeps of wind blew the rain in sheets against my slicker and down my neck. A crackling lightning flash would leave a picture of terrified horses crowded together, while one or two reared up and fell across a neighbor's halter shank. Another flash, and I saw the large canvas of the Y.M.C.A. tent go floating down the wind, while the tables, chairs, and piano were left naked to the rain. The next instant the darkness blotted it out. On top of a blinding glare came a thunderous crash that left me crouching against a caisson, weak and shaken. A bolt had struck a tent in the 102nd, and five men were laid out; one was killed.

A score of times my parents, one or both, made the long trip up to Boxford in the heat, and always brought a load of gifts. They became as familiar with our battery street as with my old room at college.

On September sixth reveille sounded as usual, the regimental band played a march as it circled the camp as usual, but after the customary work details were assigned, we were surprised to be put at packing harness and painting "A 101 FA 51–26" on the boxes. Then we drew barracks bags of blue denim bearing our battery number—mine was 146—in addition to our regiment, brigade, and division. We were told to pack these for a long trip.

The day was spent in striking tents and packing them, and cleaning and packing equipment. We knew we were going to leave Boxford and we hoped (and feared) it was for France. The work went on half the night—a bitterly cold night as September nights can be—and all packed up we tried to sleep close to big bonfires made mostly of the pajamas, bellybands, excess socks, books, and the mountains of non-portable truck which everyone had accumulated. It would have taken a dozen barracks bags to transport the junk that each of us thought he needed, and there were bitter moments when we had to choose what valued articles to leave behind. There is still a pair of good shoes buried in the field where my bed stood against a possible early return to Boxford. I looked for them after the war, but I couldn't find the place by a hundred yards.

At daybreak we marched down to the railroad track heavily loaded, and as I looked back to where our canvas city had been, I saw an empty field with not even a burnt match to show where we had lived for five weeks. I got aboard a passenger car and squeezed into a seat with all my equipment. There was no one around even to leave a message with. The train pulled out and we were gone.

A few hours later, my father walked through the field with his arms full of bundles, looking for my tent.

# CHAPTER III

## *Hoboken. We cross the ocean.*

"Hoboken, Sept. 7. Drizzle; bleak; warehouses; cobblestones; dock.
East River. Adriatic. Statue of Liberty."

EVIDENTLY the long slow train ride made little impression on my mind at the time and I can recall nothing about it now. Presumably I was hot, sleepy, and uncomfortable like everyone else and dozed most of the way, wedged between overcoats and blanket rolls.

I remember stumbling out of the lighted car into the rain and dark. I was in a train yard with cobblestones underfoot. I heard someone yelling "Squad 7 this way" and lined up between two bulging bunches of equipment that were Curtis and Gammell. I remember standing in the rain a long time. There were shouts of "Where do we go from here?" and "When do we eat?" but nothing came of them. The sky grew gray behind the black hulks of warehouses and brick sheds.

Troops were moving at the front end of the yard, silent shapes half-seen in the gray dark. A whistle blew. "Squads left!" I struggled along over the cobblestones, my blanket roll jostling against Allen's which was slung over the wrong shoulder. "Right by twos!" A halt, and onward again. We were entering a building. There was a garish cold light from electric arcs high among steel girders, throwing black shadows on about three acres of cement floor. A long way off was a square opening through which I could see the side of a ship. There were "No Smoking" signs on the concrete walls. Rows of soldiers stood or sat in formation, and uniformed girls with baskets moved between them. We had been there a long time without moving when a woman's voice said, "Why, Horatio; aren't you Horatio Rogers?" It was Virginia Baker in some kind of a uniform. The fel-

13

lows looked enviously and questioningly at me. She said she would go and get some more doughnuts as her basket was empty but before she came back our line began to move. A girl in a gray-green hat was giving out little cloth bags with a red cross sewed on them.

I was approaching a wide door with a sort of ticket window at the left of it. My name was called and as I stepped forward an officer made a checkmark on the list. I went out the door. It was lighter but still drizzling. A long gangplank reached upward to the deck of an ocean liner. As I neared the top of the gangplank I saw a life buoy lashed to the rail with *ADRIATIC* painted on it. It was now or never if I were to decide not to go to France. A moment later and it was too late.

Following the man in front, I stepped on deck, at the same time receiving a card from a sailor's hand. I remember the tang of salt air giving way to a smell of warm oil and rancid grease as I went down flight after flight of iron stairs. Someone must have been leading the way, for six of us found ourselves between rows of bunks in a small enclosure against the ship's side. Someone shut the door so no one else could get in. With admirable presence of mind, for which I often congratulated myself later, I threw my blanket roll into an upper bunk and climbed up after it. The air was bad but I could see no portholes. I tried lying down, and something hard stuck into my back. It was a life belt made of long blocks of cork sewed into a sort of canvas vest.

Sitting up, I looked at the card in my hand. I have it on my desk as I write. It says:

### DAY WATCH
Keep this card with you at all times.
Compartment B    Deck 4    Bunk No. 125
Abandon Ship Station:
Starboard side forward well deck.
Parade or Deck station for muster, same as Abandon Ship Station.
Directions from bunk to Abandon Ship and Parade station:

14

Up ladder thru compartment B-3 to 2nd deck, aft on 2nd deck to ladder to forward well deck, starboard side, and up latter to station.

IMPORTANT:—Upon sounding of bugle call "Assembly" or "Abandon Ship" go at once ON THE DOUBLE to your Parade or Abandon Ship Station as noted above.

KEEP YOUR LIFE PRESERVER AND MESS KIT WITH YOU AT ALL TIMES.

On the reverse side it read:

KEEP THIS CARD WITH YOU AT ALL TIMES.

Troop spaces are lettered and Troop decks are numbered. The letter signifies the space, the number the deck.

Keep your life preserver with you at all times when at sea.

The use of tobacco, either smoking or chewing, is prohibited at all times in berthing spaces.

Matches are not allowed in the ship.

Smoking lamps are provided in messing spaces instead of matches.

Do not throw rubbish of any kind into toilet or wash troughs. All rubbish will be put in the rubbish cans placed about the ship.

Wash your mess gear in troughs provided for that purpose.

Wash your face and hands in Basins in the Wash Rooms.

Troops may use 1st deck and "A" deck on both sides.

Whistling is not permitted.

Troops are forbidden the following places at all times, except when on duty:

"B" or Boat Deck.

Engine and fire rooms.

Steering engine room.

Cargo spaces and hatch trunks.

Inside passageways by staterooms.

IN CASE OF ABANDON SHIP, REMEMBER THERE IS LOTS OF TIME.

None of the forbidden places sounded very attractive. I was beginning to have quite a regard for whoever wrote the card. Across the bottom in large type was printed: "IN CASE OF ABANDON SHIP, REMEMBER THERE IS LOTS OF TIME." A very human sort of fellow, I concluded. He is conscious of having written a disagreeable card for people in our situation and is giving us what friendly reassurance he can to take the bad taste away.

I next examined the red-cross bag which was still hung on my finger. I think it contained about a dozen small articles supposed to be of use to a soldier, but Bull Durham and a cake of soap was all I remember. I thought of the pile of Ivory soap and two boxes of fresh Edgeworth recently committed to the flames at Boxford.

Making sure that my five cabinmates were installed in bunks of their own and no envious eyes seemed to be directed to mine I hopped down, opened the door, and started out with the intention of exploring the rabbit warren described in the card. Apparently troops were still embarking, as there was an incoming tide of close-packed khaki humanity against which I couldn't swim a yard. I went back and hung my legs over the side of Bunk No. 125. As I looked around at my cabinmates I was conscious of the noises of the ship. There seemed to be a donkey engine working a derrick on deck. Faint thumps and distant voices were audible. From the corridor came muffled sounds of many feet, and occasionally something would rub against our door. Above the hum of sounds I heard a plaintive voice asking, "How the hell can anyone find 'Compartment C' in this blank blank madhouse?"

Let's see if I can remember who was in that cabin. There was Gammell, Beck, and myself, and in the lower bunk across the aisle was Jock McSweeney, a big, raw-boned Irishman from West Medford. He was a transfer from the Coast Artillery and was never really happy with us. He was far from neat in his person, smoked an absurdly small pipe for his six-feet-one, discussed in quaint querulous phrases any subject, never stood up if he could sit down, or better lie down, and had very vague ideas of soldiering. I think he had picked the Special Detail because he thought in it he might escape his bête noir, work.

There was Roley Allen, a chap from Brewster, Cape Cod, with narrow eyes and clawlike hands. He was not popular but he had a sweet technical education. The intricacies of firing data were ABC to him. He was very fussy and stubborn, and we all considered him an old woman but we admired his flair for higher mathematics.

Then Stan Curtis; I always suspected him of being underage. He came from Scituate where his father owned a hardware store. He had the efficient quietness that gets things done. He spoke seldom, never raised his voice, and knew horses inside and out. In France he was to share the doubtful honors of scoutship with me and I couldn't have wished a better partner.

I remember noticing that the noises had stopped and by the new vibration of the ship I judged the engines were in motion. A bugle blew mess call. We took our mess kits and were met outside the cabin by a sergeant who sent us back for our life preservers. He admitted it was unlikely the ship would be torpedoed tied up to the dock but apparently it was the principle of the thing with him. We were herded into a dining room where the smell was a meal in itself. There were long tables with seats screwed to the floor. When we were seated with our life preservers between our feet under the table, a Cockney steward distributed plates of oatmeal which he carried in a high pile so that each plate had almost as much oatmeal sticking to its bottom as was in it. The portholes were all painted over but one was open, and through this I could see the shoreline moving. I caught a glimpse of the Statue of Liberty.

After breakfast I tried to go on deck, but found the hatches closed. "A hell of a note," everyone agreed. There was nothing for it but to go back to the cabin and set to work arranging my equipment in my bunk.

It was some time in the afternoon when the hatches were opened and we swarmed up on deck. There was no land in sight.

17

I remember there was a monstrous wooden packing case, perhaps fifteen feet tall, on each side of the deck at the curve of the bow just forward of the deckhouse. These boxes contained machinery of some sort, tanks we always thought but I don't know. The starboard one came to be the rendezvous of the Special Detail. It was possible to climb up onto the flat top of the box where there was room for half a dozen of us. Here we lay in the sun, visible only to the watchers on the captain's bridge. In some way best known to one of us, a board on the side of the packing case came loose so that it was possible for one man to sit inside among the machinery; it was usually a man who was wanted for guard duty, kitchen police, or some other distasteful job.

The part of the deck that I see in my memory is the bow, from the crates forward to the peak. In good weather it was always crowded with soldiers, sitting or lying on the deck or on hatchcovers, or standing in groups, talking. About in the center of this triangular space was the little house which sheltered the head of the first stairs down to our berth space. On each side of the deck, close to the rail, was a strange-looking metal device, like a baby submarine about ten feet long, and a long coiled wire cable. I learned that these were a protection against mines and torpedoes which were supposed to explode against them as they were towed from the bow of the ship. They were made so they would veer off and tow parallel but at some distance from the ship's side. "Otters" I think they were called.

The sea must have been smooth that first day, for I don't remember seeing anyone sick. I do not recall anything about that night.

When we came on deck the next morning, the ship was in the harbor of Halifax. My impression of it is many ships, the roofs of a town on one side, and patches of white tents on the other. No one went ashore. The next day, September twelfth, the *Adriatic* steamed out of Halifax harbor with five other ships. One, some distance off our starboard bow, was a deep-lying Belgian relief ship with a Norwegian name. She got farther and farther away and finally we lost sight of her.

If I should try to describe our voyage day by day I'd have to make it up. Disconnected incidents and pictures are fresh in my memory but the connecting thread is broken. Our convoy was fourteen days at sea. The *Adriatic* was a big boat, and for the most part the sea was smooth, but there were stormy days. I remember one day when the waves were slapping the port bow and the wind carried sheets of water across the deck to splash against the starboard rail. Everyone stayed under cover. The old *Orduna* was wallowing along in her place about a quarter of a mile to the right of the *Adriatic*, and ahead of us the "*Plattsburg Cruiser*," which led the convoy, was plunging so that one minute I saw the flat of her deck and the next her propeller spinning high and dry in the air, while tons of water spilled off her rising bow. Our game was to lurk in the lee of the deckhouse, waiting for a lull in the storm. Then, as the deck lifted we would make a dash for the companionway door. If the time was ill-judged the adventurer would be floored by a ton of green water between his shoulders and would pick himself out of the lee scuppers amid the derisive applause of his friends.

Whenever I think of seasickness the picture rises to my mind of Jock McSweeney during the stormy weather. Full of fresh air and salt spray I blew into the cabin. McSweeney was lying in his lower bunk with his eyes shut, passively sick for the moment.

"Well Jock, cheer up; it's great on deck. What are you doing down here all day?"

His eyes stayed shut but his lips moved. His prayer was to the effect that the blank blank boat might sink to the bottom of the ocean, and do it damn soon. Even this effort made him turn green about the gills.

"Come on, snap out of it, Jock. Get a good meal aboard and you will feel fine."

One corner of his mouth twitched as if in a sardonic smile. He gulped. His eyes opened but they didn't see. With a great effort he said in a whisper, "Get out of here, you bastard. If I'm ever on land again, by Christ, I'll come home by way of Siberia if I have to crawl on my hands and knees!" This effort was too much for his tenderly balanced equilibrium and I got out just in time. How wise I had been in taking an upper berth!

I remember calm days of warm sunshine, lying at full length on the deck half-asleep, my head on my life preserver. The masts swayed gently above the canvas of the navigator's bridge and I could feel the soft lift and fall and hear the water swishing along the side.

I remember being corporal of the guard at night. With overcoat, blankets, life preserver, belt and pistol, I reported amidships on the starboard promenade deck. There were three reliefs of eight men each. The first relief formed up and, with the sergeant and corporal of the guard, marched off to their posts. The rest of us rolled up in our blankets and slept like a row of sardines. Someone shook my shoulder and said,

"Snap out of it, Corporal; I want some sleep."

I got my eight men up, fell them in, and away we went in the dark, with the corporal of the first relief leading the way. . . . There was a crash. Stars danced before my eyes. I picked myself up, feeling for broken bones, and my hand touched a small iron capstan. I begged its pardon and hobbled after the sound of retreating footsteps.

"Relief, halt! Number One!" said the corporal.

"Where are you, buddy?" came a voice from the dark.

"Right here," answered Number One.

"Well, all you gotta do is close this watertight door when the boat starts to sink, and stay here to see nobody opens it. See?"

"Yeh, I see," said Number One weakly.

"Relief, forward, ho," said I, as the old guard fell in at the rear of the column. We wound down stairs and passages deep in the insides of the ship, across decks swept by a cold wind, past doors through which came the oily warmth and grind of engines, everywhere leaving a new guard and pushing on with the old one until we got back to where we had started. The first relief rolled up in the nearest blankets they felt.

"Gee, Corporal," I asked, "How the hell am I gonna *find* all those guys when I post the third relief?"

"Well, you dumbbell, you got nothin' to do for four hours but snoop around and see where you left 'em."

Before I could think of an appropriate form of thanks, he was snoring.

The days passed. Lying smoking in my bunk I read old letters—all of two weeks old—and the armory, Boxford, home, the R.O.T.C. seemed like things in another world. I remember seeing officers lying in steamer chairs on the upper deck, with Red Cross girls in chairs each side of them. Young fellows, my age, who probably knew no more than I did, but they had stayed in some R.O.T.C. and now they were officers. I often wondered if I had done right.

Suddenly there was a blast on the steam whistle. One, two, three, four, five. My gosh! The signal for abandon ship! This is the end. I rushed to the ladder and crowded up to the boat deck. The ship looked like a disturbed anthill. Lined up beside my lifeboat were my boatmates. Two sailors manned the davits. Were we going over the side? Or was this just another damn boat drill? A short blast on the whistle. It was a boat drill. Sheepishly we returned to our favorite spots out of the wind.

We were in the submarine zone. Life belts now must be worn at all times; not just carried about. They were so fat they impeded the motions of our arms. Lying down in them was most uncomfortable. We were kept on deck from dawn to dark now, except during meals. We would file to our places at table and each stand behind his dish of soup. The sergeant would sit down, and at the signal the twenty men along the sides would sit down too. Twenty dishes of soup would upend in twenty laps as the lifebelts struck their over-hanging edges. It couldn't be helped, the space between the table and the seats was so narrow.

On September twentieth I got a new thrill. We were eleven days out of New York, and land apparently as far off as ever. I don't think

I was especially anxious to land, but neither did I want to be torpedoed. It was growing dark and I was leaning over the bow rail watching the porpoises make oily dives along the side of the ship. Far off on the horizon a light flickered and went out. Then another. I watched, fascinated, while out of the dusk rose eight tiny shapes, equally spaced, each winking a light. They seemed to be signalling in the Morse code, but they came so fast! Nearer and nearer, and now I could make out eight narrow bows throwing out white feathers of foam. Our rail was crowded with eager watchers. Nearer and nearer they raced, and now I could see how they rolled in the trough of the waves. The radio masts were like flags being waved from side to side. With a swish they were on us, eight lean subchasers, and as the fluttering Union Jacks flashed by under our rail a great shout went up that the Kaiser must have heard in Berlin. Peace to the submarine that had the bad luck to stumble into our convoy now!

One more picture and the cruise is done. This time we are all getting our equipment ready to disembark. Outside our cabin is a large wooden hatch-grating through which comes a suffocating, rancid smell from below. It is the only space below decks large enough to make a blanket roll, and we are crowding to get on it, our arms full of blankets. I throw down my shelter half and a dozen hands straighten it out; next the blankets on top, and on them spare socks, shirts, a slicker, and the whole is tightly rolled into a long sausage which I consolidate with strings. The sausage is thrust on me with, "Take it, soldier, and get the hell out of the way," and the work goes on. Everything not actually worn is in the blanket roll or barracks bag. They are on my bunk and I am standing beside it, ready to debark.

It is September twenty-third at 8 a.m. Through an open porthole I see masts and the sides of Liverpool docks. A whistle shrills and I throw my blanket roll over my head, grab the neck of my barracks bag, and drag it behind me as the line begins to move.

# CHAPTER IV

## *Landing in England. A train ride.*

"Liverpool, Sept. 23, 1917. Mersey River; floating dock;
barracks bags; 2nd class across England."

MY GENERAL RECOLLECTIONS of this incident are very vague.
There were ships and wharves, and the sun was trying to break
through a gray mist. With a shock I saw the body of a fighting plane
in an openwork crate. It was gray with colored circles painted on the
fuselage and tail. Beyond it was a heap of barbwire rolls about twenty feet high. The realization of my nearness to the war came suddenly at the sight of those things. Everything looked strange and
sinister. It seemed only yesterday that I was at home. Now I had the
feeling of walking in a dream, with a little touch of nightmare. I had
the sensation of moving towards something terrible without being
able to stop or to turn aside.

A long dock stretched back from the wharf, ending in a large
brick building. We were waiting on this dock, sitting on the cinders
and leaning against our barracks bags. I saw trains on sidings but I
don't remember just where they were. A company of Scotch Highlanders went by quite close. They were marching in step, their kilts
flashing out sideways with every swing of their arms. There were
some negro troops around a freight car, with little brown cloth caps
on their heads. We yelled at them, and they answered us in French! I
remember marching past a high board fence that seemed to reach for
miles; then we were in a train, moving through towns and fields. It
was a second-class day coach with upholstered compartments, and I
thought it very luxurious but very new and odd.

It was on this train ride that I first saw the cavalier fashion in which
Nature's calls are disposed of by troops in Europe. The train went

slowly and stopped often for no apparent reason, as if the engine needed frequent rests. As it was several hours since we had left the *Adriatic*, and as there were no toilets on the train, these halts were made use of by the soldiers to get out in crowds and relieve themselves beside the track. Suddenly the train would start with a little shriek from the engine, and there would be a rush for the doors. Someone was always caught in an awkward predicament, and as he hung on the running board of the car, perhaps hopping along with one foot, hundreds of heads would lean out car windows to give him a rousing cheer.

As we passed through towns we threw hardtack from the cars to see the children scramble for it. At the stations people looked at us with curiosity. Our wide-brimmed hats with pointed tops were new to them. I remember no excitement or demonstrations. We were all eyes, crowding to the windows in an effort not to miss anything. I have a vague recollection of neat fields, hedges, trees, and of houses that looked somehow different.

When our train stopped in a big station it was getting dark.

---

## CHAPTER V

### *A night in Southampton. The English Channel.*

"Southampton, Sept. 23. Night; streets; hands in dark; venereal blankets; crowded pyramid tent; low morale."

---

WE WERE HIKING through the dark streets of Southampton between rows of unlighted houses. A fine rain was falling, but there seemed to be many people on the sidewalks. They would hold out their hands to touch us in the dark. I shook several hands but saw no faces. A woman's voice said, "Keep your pecker up, laddie." It was a heartbreaking job carrying the heavy, clumsy barracks bags over our shoulders. We had left our blanket rolls to follow by truck.

The first halt found us still inside the city. Nevertheless, most of us took the opportunity of relieving ourselves in the gutter. The spectators, if the darkness makes this term permissible, took no notice. Many troops had passed through those streets since the beginning of the war.

My impression is that we marched about two miles with frequent halts before reaching our destination.

I remember standing in line in the rain to receive blankets from an English quartermaster store. They had a peculiar odor and were very coarse and heavy. Ten of us were assigned to a wooden-floored tent which might have held six. It was round and had a pole in the center like our tents at Boxford, but there was no vertical wall, the lax white canvas sagging from the top of the pole to the edge of the floor. It was very small. Lying like the spokes of a wheel with our heads outward our legs crossed in a heap at the center. This promised no comfort, but we settled down in our English blankets. I was no sooner asleep than an officer came along and woke us all up. We went out and found the rest of the Battery standing in the rain, their new blankets in their arms. I asked someone what was the big idea.

"Well," he said, "it seems the last bunch through here was a labor battalion of venereal South African niggers and these are the blankets they used."

We turned them in and got our own blanket rolls from a pile in the mud where the truck had left them.

September twenty-fourth was spent in this camp. When we woke up we found ourselves on the edge of a field next to a flat enclosure holding many hundreds of small tents pitched very close together in rows. There was a large wooden shelter containing shower baths at one side. When I saw it there was a melee going on between English and American troops about who should bathe first. Stan Curtis and I made our blanket rolls and walked over to the English canteen, which looked like an airplane hanger. We bought cookies, some "goldflakes" (the cigarette of the British Army), and a can of "Three Nuns" pipe tobacco, which was cut in thin coils and tasted like dead leaves. The sun was out bright so we walked out of the camp and up the street. In one place we saw about a hundred convalescent wounded in dark blue cotton coats and trousers, some in wheelchairs and some walking with canes. We came to a railroad track and asked a grizzled old Tommy what they were unloading from the freight car.

"Coffins," he said without turning around. Then he looked us over without smiling. "For chaps like you," he offered. "Oh, I've had all I want Out There," he went on. "The Jerries have some bloody sort of gas that comes down like snow. Who it touches, dies. Yes, Jerry's a grand gunner, is Jerry. They all goes out like you chaps, but bloody few of them comes back."

This conversation did nothing to reassure me, and I was so green I never suspected him of pulling our leg. We saw more Highlanders marching in columns of fours at route step towards the port. They wore khaki covers over their kilts and carried steel helmets, gas masks, and rifles. Heavy bundles of strange equipment were carried on poles between two men. We thought they were machine guns. Someone told us this was a replacement battalion going back to the trenches from hospital. It seemed ghastly to have to go back after escaping death so closely and getting well.

Stan and I stopped in several soldiers' pubs for a drink on the way down the tree-shaded street to camp. We messed very poorly on English rations and drank acid, black tea without sugar or milk and spent the afternoon in the tent sleeping.

The walk to the harbor loaded with barracks bags was as bad as I thought it would be. The sun made it hotter than the previous night, so we landed on the little Channel steamer in a state of perspiring exhaustion. I noticed how efficient the British embarkation officers were, and how they seemed accustomed to handling men wholesale as if they were cattle.

That night I shall never forget. The Channel was smooth as a mill-pond with a full moon overhead. It got stinging cold later. The little ship was so crowded with troops that I couldn't find a place even to sit down, and spent the night walking over soldiers who lay so close together that it was hard to put my foot down without stepping on them. I found a sort of shelf inside the boat where it was warm, but it was too high to sit on and so narrow that I couldn't lie on it edge-wise without constantly dropping down on the sleepers below. I made my way to the top deck and found every foot of it occupied. A very large smokestack stood in the center, and around it was a metal rail where there seemed to be a place to sit. Sitting space was at such a premium I couldn't understand this vacancy. I sat on the upper bar with my toes hooked around the lower one, and drowsed forward towards the nice warm smokestack. In five minutes the iron piping had made a groove across my anatomy two inches deep, my eyes, ears, nose, and mouth were full of cinders and I had to quit. I won-dered how many thousands of soldiers now in France had tried that railing.

Dawn found me still shivering around like an unlaid ghost; there were a good many others doing the same: squatting here and there for five minutes, but never finding a large enough space to lie down. I saw the moon set and the stars pale, and felt the cold morning breeze spring up. At 6 a.m. the boat entered the harbor of Havre, and we filed off onto another great dock.

# CHAPTER VI

*France. First impressions of the war. A ride in a boxcar.*

"Havre, Sept. 25, 1917. Endless docks, early morning. 'Rest camp'
or 'Cinder City.' Boche prisoners. Wash."

ON LOOKING AROUND, my first impression was of hugeness.
Everything was on a monstrous scale. As far as I could look were
docks, masts, great sheds, and mountains of merchandise. A railroad
station was serving as a hospital. There was a company of German
prisoners going to work. I studied them and tried to realize what
they meant to me. These, or others like them, were what had taken
me away from college and brought me to France, perhaps to wounds
and death. It was they who had made my father suffer when that
truck rolled away and left him standing on a corner in Boston. I
thought of Alan Seeger's poem about

> . . . those farthest rims of hallowed ground
> Where the forlorn, the gallant charge expires,
> Where the slain bugler long has ceased to sound
> And on the tangled wires
> The last wild rally staggers, crumbles, stops. . . .*

Perhaps there walked some of the Germans who had crouched behind those pitiless machine guns. Terrifying pictures flashed before
my mind—of "some disputed barricade," of "some scarred slope of
battered hill"; of "midnight in some flaming town"†—and the pictures were peopled by men like these, trying to kill me. To look at,
they were forlorn enough, walking huddled together, dragging their
feet, and dressed in dirty, ragged gray-green clothes. Each one had

* Alan Seeger (Harvard 1910, killed in action at Belloy-en-Santerre, July 4, 1916), "Ode in
Memory of the American Volunteers Fallen for France."
† Alan Seeger, "I Have a Rendezvous with Death."

P.G.* painted on his back or the seat of his pants in letters about a foot high. There were old men among them and seventeen-year-old boys. Most of the buttons had been cut from their uniforms for souvenirs. I couldn't decide whether to hate them or to be sorry for them.

Nearby stood a French sentry in a steel helmet, the skirts of his horizon-blue overcoat buttoned back, his chest crossed by two broad straps to hold the weight of his ammunition belt, and in his hand a rifle with a tremendously long, rapierlike bayonet. He looked about forty-five. His face was deeply tanned, and he had a long mustache which stuck out sideways. I decided to have a word with him and see if he was as discouraging as the Tommy at Southampton. He smiled brightly as I came up to him.

"Bonjour, Monsieur," I began.

"Bonjour, mon vieux," he answered in a pleasant voice. "Vos camarades sont des Amèricains, n'est-ce-pas?" I was delighted to find that I could understand what he said. I nodded and tried a question of my own.

"Vous n'aimez pas les Boches?" I asked with a glance towards the prisoners.

"Ah, non. Ils sont des mauvaises sujets, les Boches," he replied, with surprising mildness.

"Ça doit être très terrible au front?" I observed, watching his face anxiously.

"Oh, pas mal," he said with a shrug and a laugh. "On s'y habitue."† With cheerful people like this, I thought, the front really wouldn't be so bad.

That day we spent in a large canvas city, built on cinders and labelled "Rest Camp." With the cinders sending up a cloud of dust at every step, the heat, the crowded tents, and the poor food, we all

* P.G.: Prisonnier de Guerre.

† On s'y habitue: You get used to it.

agreed that it was wrongly named, and that "Cinder City" would have been nearer right.

The bath mentioned in my notebook seems to have left no impression on my memory.

Towards evening several hundred of us were marched from the rest camp to the railroad. All I remember about it is that we carried blanket rolls, and our barracks bags had disappeared. This was my first sight of the toy French engines and "side-door Pullmans" that were to carry us many hundreds of miles before the war was over. The latter were small boxcars, about half the size of those on American railroads, with four wheels and a sliding door on each side amidships. They were sometimes called "cheveaux 8, hommes 40" because that was painted on the outside. Into these we tumbled, and hung our overcoats and equipment on nails around the walls. At 9 p.m. there was a faint shriek from the absurd little engine and the train began to move. As long as there was anything to see we crowded the open doors, but as the darkness increased nothing was visible but the railbed and the edges of fields, so in our car we shut the doors and lay on the floor with our overcoats rolled up under our heads for pillows. There was more horse manure on the floor than I would have chosen, but the monotonous rumble of the wheels in the dark was soothing, the drowsy voices died out, and I was soon asleep.

I remember waking up chilled to the bone and aching from the hard floor. The train had stopped. From the low voices outside, I judged we were in a station. I spread my overcoat across my stomach, put my head on Ritchie's unresisting shoulder, and was lulled to sleep by the clacketing of the wheels which had begun again.

# CHAPTER VII

*Training in Brittany. The French 75. Scouting lessons.*
*"Peggotty." Gammell transferred.*

"Coëtquidan.* Sept. 26, 1917. Training; range. St. Malo de Beignon. Coquineville;
stone barrack. Rennes. Peggotty."

MEMORIES OF FOUR MONTHS cluster around this brief note, flashing up in such rapid succession that I almost despair of getting them
on paper. My only hope is to try to describe them in chronological
order, one at a time.

We were in the boxcars thirty hours. This trip merges into my
recollections of the many similar trips that came later, and I can't
pretend to record it just as it happened. I remember sitting around
the floor as the countryside slipped by. A supply of food had been
placed in each car, and this was rationed out three times a day by
Sergeant Catton: "Percy Catton, the Boy Sergeant." He was a conscientious, unimaginative little chap from Medford who had been in
the Battery on the Mexican Border. What he lacked in inspiration he
made up for by knowing his books. He was sent home as an instructor the day before the Château-Thierry drive started. Our food consisted of cheese, hardtack, canned corned beef, and jam. When the
train stopped at a station, a few from each car would pile out and
look for a water faucet to fill the canteens. A few would adventure a
little farther at the risk of being left behind, and at the warning cry of
the engine would come running from a nearby Debit de Vins and
climb aboard with two or three bottles of red wine under their arms.

At a big station named Laigle, of which the one at Salem, Massachusetts, reminds me, we got our mess cups filled with coffee by a

* Coëtquidan, an artillery camp built by Napoleon, thirty miles southwest of Rennes,
the capital of Ille-et-Vilaine in Brittany.

Frenchman. He had several large milk cans of it on a hand truck which he dragged along the station platform. It was unsweetened and contained no milk.

I have often noticed how quickly one settles down in a new environment. In our boxcar everyone had his own little place where he made himself comfortable, and to which he returned after tiring of sitting in the open doorway or playing cards at the other end of the car. Each nail was endowed with as much privacy as the hatrack at home.

Allen had a map of France on which he found the places as we read the names from the station signs. I remember Alençon, Laval, and Rennes as large places. He tried several times to locate "Dubonnet" on the map before we found it was an advertisement of a drink, rivalled in frequency only by "Chocolat Meunier."

The day passed and another night came. It was near midnight that the train stopped. It was a very dark night as I remember, for when we hopped out with our overcoats and blanket rolls nothing was visible. We waited in the dark for several hours. I think I slept most of the time. When I woke up we were climbing into a truck. When the truck stopped we got out and waited until the whole Battery had assembled. Then we marched across rough fields for a time. At last we seemed to be among buildings. I followed Gammell into the nearest one, opened my blanket roll on a cement floor, and fell asleep immediately.

I know what our barrack must have looked like when we woke up next morning, but my clearest recollection of it is as it looked later, after the beds came and the stove. It was a whitewashed room about twenty feet square and perhaps twelve feet high. The door was in the front wall, the rear wall was blank except for a stovepipe hole high up, and on the side walls, their sills at least six feet from the floor, windows were cut in the thick masonry. The head of my narrow spring bed was below a window so I laid claim to its deep sill as a shelf for odds and ends. Gammell's bed was beyond mine, in the left rear corner of the room. He had a habit of waking up in the night to drink water, and I often heard the furtive tinkle of his canteen top followed by a crescendo glug-glug-glug-glug in the dark. On my other side was Jock McSweeney. Opposite the foot of his bed was a little coal stove, standing almost in the center of the room with a long horizontal stovepipe suspended by wires from the ceiling. Beside McSweeney's bed was Willie Saindon's. He was a little French-Kanuck shoemaker from Auburn, Maine, whose front teeth had been worn away by cobblers' nails. At first I could hardly understand a word he said, and I found the French people had the same difficulty, but he had a disarming grin and I never knew his good nature to fail. To his right was Pete Murray from Framingham. He was also a runt. Most of his remarks took the form of "wisecracks," some of which were witty.

Across the room were five other beds occupied by Roley Allen, Stan Curtis, a telephone man named Eykelbosch who insisted on being called Eykel, and Tom Furness—"good old Tom," as everyone called him, universally liked for his extreme modesty, a little slow to catch on, and a safe butt for anyone's jokes because his only repartee was a sheepish smile. Good old Tom was badly gassed and won the Distinguished Service Cross at the capture of Vaux a few months later. The fifth was Southworth Lancaster, appropriately called "Sow." He came from Worcester, was a Harvard man, and was a little too refined for the company in which he found himself.

Against the rear wall were five beds crowded behind the stove. Beck and Ritchie occupied two of them, Ritchie's being directly under the stovepipe. One night McSweeney had a toothache, and someone told him chewing tobacco would be good for it. In his sleep he swallowed the tobacco and woke up on the verge of being violently ill. Stopping for nothing, he made a dash towards the open air. The stove was in his path. There was a crash, followed by earnest cursing. Someone lit a match and I saw the exquisite Ritchie, black with soot, crawling out from under the stovepipe, while McSweeney was being sick in the coal box.

The other beds were occupied by Merriam, Derby, and Peabody. Joe Merriam came from South Framingham. He had graduated from Harvard in 1916 and completed a year at Tufts Medical School. After the war he and I were together at the Harvard Medical School, and he now is a successful general practitioner in Framingham. Then he was excessively bashful and conscientious, and although more intelligent than the average he would worry about things he thought he couldn't excel in. Henry Derby of Somerville was just the opposite. He had been at Tech when war was declared. He was small, snub-nosed, bright-faced, alert, enthusiastic, and confident. Ellery Peabody came from West Newton. He had been in the leather business with his father. He was large, well built, and handsome, with big, brown, sympathetic eyes that reflected an honorable, reliable, lovable disposition. He was light-hearted, gentle, full of play, but I never saw anyone try to take advantage of his good nature. Poor Peabo was killed one moonlight night on a road north of Verdun, trying to guide the Battery out of a storm of shellfire.

The coal for the stove was kept in a wooden box inside the door. By day the room was lighted by the windows, and after dark everyone provided his own light with a candle perched over the head of his bed. How pleasant and snug it was on a winter night in the candlelit warmth of our barrack. I remember coming in late from the range and finding everybody eating. Gammell had a package from home, containing a large round tin box of chocolates "from Mr. Page and Mr. Shaw." But I am losing sight of my chronological order.

The morning after our arrival I walked around to get oriented. There were no guns or horses so our duties were light. I stepped out of our door and found myself on a narrow dirt street lined by trees, sloping downhill, with stone barracks on both sides about fifty feet apart. These were all the same. They were long, one-story structures built of massive masonry. Each had a single rough stone step, and beside it, built against the barrack wall, was an iron hydrant operated by pressing down a knob on top. To prevent wasting water the thrifty French had built it so the knob sprang up as soon as released. "Ne mettez pas pierre dessus"* was cast in the iron face of the hydrant, and supplied the necessary hint for getting a continuous flow of water.

The barrack at the top of the street was the guardhouse and contained a few French prisoners. Ours was the next barrack down. The one below ours was occupied by part of B Battery, and there were perhaps four more below that. I walked across the street and found our guidon, a lance bearing a red flag marked with A 101, standing at the door of the barrack opposite ours. This marked the quarters of the Top Sergeant, Storer, and the office of the Battery clerk. Behind this barrack was another street parallel to mine and also lined by stone barracks. I walked between them to see what was beyond, and saw a wide stretch of rolling country with a dirt road leading into it. This was the beginning of the Range.

In the foreground I saw a curious structure of iron and concrete with an impressive flight of broad steps leading up to it. It suggested a public monument of some sort. At the top of the steps were several iron half-doors, each giving access to a small cubicle. The floor of each cubicle was of cement, with a hole in its center. Walking around this monument, I found a row of large galvanized iron barrels under the cubicles. This explained the elevated position of the cubicles. It was a French latrine. We christened it "Grant's Tomb." Every day the cans were emptied into a great vat on two wheels drawn by a Percheron horse, and this equipage was known to us as the "Honey Cart." When the regimental guard was established, "Grant's Tomb" was one of the regular posts. The chief duty of the man on guard there was to chase "Camp Butterflies," which were windblown bits of toilet paper. One day when Shepley was on guard at "Grant's Tomb," the Officer of the Day found an old French woman using the latrine. Shepley was summoned to the Orderly Room to explain.

* Do not put a rock on it.

His explanation gave him an undying reputation for naivete. It was: "Why the hell shouldn't I let her in? There was a place empty."

Not wishing to explore the Range, I returned to my own barrack and passed to its rear end. Here was a wide dirt road leading down the hill behind the barracks. As I followed it down I met a large group of German prisoners carrying picks and shovels under guard of a Frenchman, who, to my surprise, seemed to be paying no more attention to them than if they were sheep. Later there were several thousand prisoners employed in building new barracks, and we all had a turn at guarding them. The only place any of them tried to escape to was the kitchen swill cans.

Below the barracks on the left of the road was a large stone watering trough. After we got our horses, and the stables were built on the right of the road, we watered here three times a day. The distance was so short that no one rode, and I have often covered it in five jumps, swinging between two galloping horses' heads like the tongue of a bell.

Back from the road behind the trough was a large barn standing in an ocean of mud. This was immediately fitted up as the regimental kitchen, and for the two or three weeks before each battery got its own kitchen built all the food for the Regiment was cooked and served here. The batteries would form in single file in the mud, and they took turns at being first. As there were eight batteries, each one ate first about once a week. I have stood in line in the mud for over an hour when A Battery was eating last, but I soon learned to slip out of line and buy a meal down at St. Malo. This practice was winked at in the early days because the regimental food was exceptionally nauseous, and little secret eating clubs soon sprang up in various houses in the town.

About a quarter of a mile below the camp was a crossroad lined on the lower side by a dozen houses straggling out of sight around the shoulder of the hill. This was the nearest edge of St. Malo de Beignon, called "Coquineville" by the French soldiers. There were two or three soldiers' bazaars where various small articles were displayed for sale. I immediately bought a briquet, which I still have. It was a sort of flint and steel arrangement for striking a spark against the end of a piece of yellow wick of the thickness of a pencil. After lighting one's cigarette on the glowing end of the wick, one pulled it down into a little metal cylinder automatically sealed by a ball, and put the thing in one's pocket. Sometimes it wouldn't set fire to one's pants, sometimes it would.

In the fifth house to the left lived a lady known as "Naa Ploo," from her favorite remark, "Il n'y en a plus."* This was my place for getting omelettes, pommes frits, and de la viande. Continuing down the main road, which still led downhill, I entered the heart of St. Malo. It had perhaps five hundred inhabitants. All the houses were of stone. Most of the streets were crooked, cobbled, narrow, and steep. The moss-covered walls gave an air of great antiquity. It was just such villages we were to see in the battle zone reduced to heaps of rubble.

Beyond St. Malo the road stretched straight to Beignon, whose church tower I could see about two miles away.

I remember hikes the Battery took to get the men into good condition. We would swing along the roads, uphill and down, sometimes between hedgerows growing on ridges of earth that had been built up by centuries of peasants dragging roots and stones to the edges of their fields, sometimes halting near thickets of blackberry bushes loaded with fruit—the largest I have ever seen—neglected since the beginning of the war.

But the walks I remember with the greatest pleasure were the ones Ives Gammell and I used to take on bright Sundays, often being gone from camp all day. We would trudge along in the beautiful October weather, stopping often to eat blackberries or to admire a roadside calvaire or some quaint corner of antiquity that might have been unchanged since the fourteenth century. I used to feel a detachment

* There isn't any more.

from reality, so that if a company of mounted knights in armor had come clattering around a bend in the road I would not have felt the least surprise. Plèlan, Paimpont, Augan, Ploermel, and Campeneac were some of the villages we visited. I remember in Augan we found the church door open and heard music inside. Seated in a rear pew I heard the organ playing. As my eyes became accustomed to the dim light I saw old Gothic arches, groined ceilings, great stone pillars, and on a sort of little balcony which was lighted by a single ray of sunshine from the great south window stood a nun in a blue habit, so lost in meditation that I couldn't tell whether she was a statue or a woman until she moved.

I remember a meal we had in Campeneac. We sat on benches beside a trestle table black with age, in a tiny tavern-room where old Bretagne peasants with long black ribbons on their Sunday hats sat at the two other tables, taking snuff and talking in an incomprehensible dialect. Our food was cooked over the open fire. Through the diamond-paned window I saw the heads of several small boys peering in at us. There was soon a crowd on the sidewalk looking in. The old men at the tables also kept stealing looks at us, and I had the feeling that we were the subject of their talk. When we had paid and stepped out into the street we saw a gendarme on a bicycle. We asked him why we were the cause of so much interest and he said, "You are the first American soldiers to come to Campaneac, and some of the people feel sure you are escaped German prisoners in disguise."

The people in these Brittany towns were a sight to behold on Sundays. The women wore tremendous starched caps, some of them of the most complicated design. The men wore wide-brimmed hats with long black ribbons. The children looked much the same as on weekdays, most of them wearing black smocks and sabots stuffed with straw. On one of our trips I purchased a pair of sabots to wear around the barracks in the evening, especially when I went out in the mud to brush my teeth at the "Mettez pas pierre dessus." It broke my heart to leave them behind when we left Coëtquidan for the front.

I remember one Sunday when Ives and I had rambled as far as Augan and were enjoying a luxurious dinner cooked by the Madame of the local "Hotel de France," who had just told us we were the only Americans in Augan, when Pat Lynch appeared from a back room, wearing felt slippers and looking very much at home. Pat had enlisted in A Battery as an artilleryman, turned bugler at Boxford, and colonel's chauffeur at Coëtquidan. We asked him for an explanation.

"Well, I stopped here for supper a coupla days ago, see, and it seems I reminded the Madame of some Frog that got bumped off, and she gave me to understand the place was mine, so I figured I'd stick around." I admired the Madame's powers of expressing herself, for Pat hadn't a word of French.

"What about the colonel's car, Pat?" I asked.

"In the barn," said Pat. "If anybody at Camp asks you, tell them the ignition's gone back on me, and I'm spoiling my health trying to make it run."

During our excursions Ives and I enjoyed the beauty and romance of Brittany at every step, and we discussed all possible subjects with the greatest success, but if ever I made the mistake of trying to explain *why* I found something beautiful I was told I had "the soul of a cab-man." The soul of an artist is extraordinarily sensitive.

At the end of the first week, our four French "canons de soixante-quinze" arrived. I didn't have much to do with them, being a scout, but I saw the cannoneers at all hours of the day deep in the mysteries of their construction, with French gunners as tutors. At first the new guns were curiosities, but soon each section developed such a parental feeling for its own gun that christenings were held. "Pinard," "Cafard,"* and "Xantippe" were the adopted children of the second, third, and fourth sections. The first section gun was not named.

* Cafard: Fed up.

Pinard and Cafard were to serve their new parents throughout the war, but the first section gun was to perish with its crew under German fire, and Xantippe was to destroy itself and Ralph Farnsworth, its gunner corporal, in a thicket near the Paris-Metz road.

After three weeks of studying the guns, the cannoneers were allowed to tow them out on the Range with motortrucks, for actual firing. I remember the thrill of first hearing the savage bark of the 75 accompanied by the swift recoil, and the click of the opening breech and clang of the empty shell case as the muzzle slid noiselessly back into position. In a moment a cottony puff of smoke would bloom on a distant hillside, and long after would come the muffled crunch of the exploding shell.

What varied emotions I experienced on that Range. It consisted of many square miles of waste land, fields, hills, woods, ravines, deserted villages, ruined mills, and through it all a network of cart roads, some well worn and others scarcely visible. After the horses came we played games of hide-and-seek against the imaginary enemy, sometimes our Battery alone and sometimes the whole brigade; sometimes by daylight, sometimes at night; and often in the rain. My job was to be able always to find my way, and with or without a map to reach the designated point on time. Some of it was fair sailing where the landmarks were easily memorized. But many were the traps lying ready to catch the unwary scout: the road forks that looked almost alike, the mill that wasn't the one I thought it was, the dead tree I had relied on as a landmark that proved to have a dozen identical relatives miles apart.

Any spot on the map could be designated by its coordinates. The map was arbitrarily marked off in squares, each horizontal and vertical line being numbered. To find the coordinates of any point we drew a vertical and a horizontal line from it to the edge of the map, and by interpolation determined the number on which they fell. Thus, an order might read, "The firing battery will take position at 103,692–427,351 and register on target 89,602–113,527. The limbers

_Camp d'Instruction_
_de Coëtquidan_
_Ille et Vilaine_
_Bretagne_
_Nov, 1, 1917_

"The morning after our arrival
I walked around to get oriented."

Taken in November 1917 at Coëtquidan by an itinerant
French photographer. Note the stone barracks in background. The steel helmet is worn over a knitted cap because
of cold weather.

will withdraw to the ravine $\frac{1}{2}$ kilometer to the rear. The spare ammunition caissons will proceed to 369,476–103,601, arriving there at 11.30 a.m. and halting for further orders." My job perhaps would be to lead the caissons to the designated spot, where someone else would be sent to find them. Or else after a night problem, I might be ordered to pick up the third section at coordinate 103,692–427,351, a place I had perhaps never been, and bring them back to camp. How carefully I would study the map and plan my route to the wretched place, and how earnestly I would pray, as I rode along through the darkness, to be allowed to find it. I learned to turn every condition to my purpose: the stars, if any showed, the direction of the wind, the slope of the land, the color of the sky around its edges, the shapes of trees that might be recognized on the way back, and how they looked from both directions. My pocket compass was almost worn out from use. On the return trip I would be as anxious as a mother hen with her chicks.

"Where the hell do you think you're taking us, Horace?" would yell a driver; or the lieutenant would ride alongside and say, "Corporal, are you sure that last turn was right?"

I would set my back teeth in my chaw of tobacco, inwardly damning the treacherous dark and the deceitful Range, and wonder where I would come out if the last turn really had been wrong, and whether to gallop back for another look or push ahead in the hope of seeing a familiar landmark. A conical shape would loom up blacker against the dark sky. Ah, the old mill at last! Now I know where I am. I would breathe with relief. But no. Where is the broken beam that should stick out on its west side near the top? This is some other mill, and I don't know *where* we are! The picture of the warm candlelit barrack would rise like a mirage before my eyes. I guess I'll tell the lieutenant I'm lost and to hell with it, I'd think. But wait! There's that damn beam after all. I never noticed you couldn't see it from this angle. Out on the main road of the Range at last, with familiar landmarks everywhere, I would begin to feel quite proud of myself.

"Gee, Horace, how do you do it?" would yell a friendly voice from behind.

"Oh, it's a gift," I'd say without troubling to turn my head.

"Well, I sure thought you'd lost us back there at the fork, Corporal," murmured the lieutenant at my side.

"I never worried about that, Lieutenant," I lied happily.

After watering Peggotty and tying her up at the stables I would stamp into the barrack, to find everyone lying around reading letters and eating Gammell's candy.

"God, what a job!" I'd say bitterly as I collapsed on my bed.

"Why, you sour-belly, you've got the softest job in the Battery," was all the sympathy I ever got.

Peggotty was a dark brown mare, a little tall in the withers, a little narrow through the shoulders, a little prone to stumble without cause, but with a lovely disposition. In a word, she was well-meaning but ineffectual. It's a wonder she never broke my neck with her silly falls. I never really loved Peggotty, and I finally grew to hate her. When a shell splinter eventually got her through the lungs, I'm afraid I didn't grieve as I should. Her successor, Peanuts, was a real horse. I found him at Rangeval where the First Division had abandoned him because of a sore back. After this was cured he became an ideal horse for my purpose. He was a lightly built chestnut horse, wide between the eyes, short in the barrel, with iron muscles and small feet. He was alert, high-spirited, fearless, and dainty. Instead of a walk, he had a little dancing step. His trot was very rapid, and when he galloped he ran. I believe he was considered the fastest singlemount in the Battery. Stan Curtis had a fast horse too, but he could never catch Peanuts.

Stan and I would often exercise our horses on the Range, either bareback or with blanket and surcingle. We set up jumps and practiced circus tricks, and I must say in justice to Peggotty that she never seemed surprised. I found that walking or galloping, Peggotty and I could stay together but when she trotted her old backbone felt like the ridgepole of a barn, so I would plan to strike it off center, and when each bump would land me farther to the side I would lose my balance and ignominiously roll in the dust. Peggotty would eat grass while I got up and mounted her again. I never received much sympathy from Curtis, whose horse had a plump rounded back.

As time went on new buildings sprang up by hundreds, so that the place we had left the trucks that first night was now the center of a huge camp where one might get lost and wander for hours between wooden barracks, stables, hospitals, recreation huts, officers' quarters, kitchens, gun parks, ammunition dumps, and prison pens for the Germans.

Cold weather came, turning the deep mud to granite. What suffering it was to leave a warm bed, line up shivering beside our barrack, and march down to the stables to feed horses in the dark. The horses were hitched in two long rows separated by a wooden partition about five feet high, with a wooden roof over all. There were two of these sheds parallel, and between them a low harness rack. When the horses heard us coming they would get restless. Each of us would take a filled nose bag from the pile prepared by the stable guard and edge in between the horses' heads. Most of them had the trick of tossing their heads when the nose bags were being put on. This would tear the straps from our frozen fingers, and the oats would go on the ground.

I remember A. Soule (he who was "born on horseback") one day getting into the horses' heads and not daring to come out. He crawled under the halter shanks looking for an empty place, and finally climbed over the partition to get out the other side, where he saw two horses wide apart. Unfortunately for him, one of the two was "Lil," the terror of the seventh section, and out of the corner of her eye she saw A. Soule's maneuver. Out she lashed with both heels, and lifted the equestrian Soule onto the harness rack, whence he was carried to his bed.

The sorriest nag in the Battery was a ewe-necked, spavined, dark-gray bag of bones named "Beautiful Blue Danube." One day the men at the stables saw her being solemnly led around on a long rope by Corporal Lloyd. The sight was so absurd that everyone laughed. Lloyd paid no attention to their jibes, and asked the captain if he could have the horse. The captain thought it was a joke, and said yes. Lloyd then led the Blue Danube everywhere he went, and when the stable sergeant protested, Lloyd appealed to the captain. It was found to be no joke, for Lloyd's mind had become deranged by the constant sound of the guns, and he was sent home insane without ever reaching the front.

One of the stone barracks across the street from us was labelled "Salle des Bains." How we hated that place in the cold weather. On A Battery bath days, a detail of men would be assigned to bath duty. They would build a fire in an old iron range and heat water in an iron kettle about three feet in diameter. There were half a dozen old-fashioned wooden washtubs full of water on the floor. Just enough hot water was ladled in to each to take the chill off, and six men would be commanded to bathe. In spite of the steam in the air, the cold wind would bite into our naked hides and I never saw anyone dawdling over his bath. When the scum got too thick around the sides of a tub, the soapy water was dumped on the floor and ran out under the door. The cement floor got very slippery, and I found my sabots from Campeneac most useful on these disagreeable days. As I recall it, they came around once a week.

I remember getting a pass to Rennes, the nearest big town to our camp. I started out early in the morning with a list of errands for friends that would have taken six men a week to execute. A narrow-gauge train ran to Rennes once a day, returning in the evening. The tracks passed around the foot of our hill near St. Malo de Beignon. It was called a "Decauville" railroad and was a toylike affair, the tracks being in sections attached to iron sleepers like the ones in store windows around Christmas time. The little engine was stoked with coal dust cast into bricks. My travelling companions were mostly peasant women and a few old men. The trip was very slow with interminable stops, but at last we pulled into Rennes. I have a vague picture of walking on streets over canals that reminded me of Providence, and of a business section of stone buildings, none above three stories high. There was an "Arcade" on a corner which monopolized my attention as it contained most of the things I had been commissioned to buy. I don't remember where I had dinner. It was in Rennes that I first saw Russian soldiers in their beautiful high boots, Algerians in fezzes, and munition workers with their skin and hair stained canary-yellow by the fumes of picric acid. I returned to camp laden with maps, compasses, pencils, map cases, and eatables, and spent most of the night adjusting claims and making change. It must have been just after payday.

On paydays, the Battery formed single file at the Battery-clerk's office, in the alphabetical payroll order. At a table sat the regimental pay-officer behind stacks of French money. As each man's name was read off, his thirty-odd dollars were handed over in francs—our pay being about a dollar a day—and his name checked off the list. I carried my money in a belt next my skin. There was an arrangement by which a portion of each month's pay could be allotted home and deducted from the total. Many of us subscribed to Liberty Bonds, and most of us took out Government War Risk Insurance. Mine was for $10,000, to be paid to my father on my death. I think the monthly premium was $6. Joe Zwinge, a driver, was always the last to be paid because his name began with Z. He had been a star schoolboy athlete in Arlington, but he was deaf so had had to bluff through his physical examination in order to enlist. Joe was the first man killed in the Battery, and his deafness was the cause of his death.

I remember one winter day when our Battery took a long road march. The newly fallen snow lay thick under a cold sun. No wheel tracks marred the soft smoothness of the roads. The holly trees with their brilliant leaves and berries looked as if they had been arranged for artistic effect. As the head of the column crested a gentle hill, I saw the fluttering guidon bright red against the snow, and the steaming horses framed by the heavy evergreens that bowed their tops together across the road.

On Christmas we decorated the mess shack with holly and fir trees. The ninth section had built a stone fireplace for the occasion and kept a roaring blaze in it all day. Joe Wilner, the mess-sergeant, was greasy and fat, about forty, with the most hooked nose I have ever seen on a man, but he rose to the occasion and provided a feast out of "extrys" he had bought with the Battery fund at Rennes. In the evening there was an entertainment in the mess shack, mostly imitations and songs which I don't remember, and wouldn't write if I did. But the real Christmas for me was the package from home. It had to conform to certain weight and measurements—14″×4″×4″, as I remember—but it contained a hint of all the things that I had associated with Christmas since I was two years old, and almost broke me up.

Packages and letters from home always had a double effect on me. There was the thrill of getting them and of gloating over them, and there was the accompanying pang of homesickness. Particularly at the front, I had difficulty in answering those brave letters which so pitifully tried to hide the worry of the hearts they sprang from. I have many of them still, and I can't read them even now without a lump in my throat. There is one exception. My correspondence with "Ros," a sentimental attachment of some months' standing before the war, gave no pain, and I think was a source of unalloyed gratification on both sides. In my letters to her I used every subtle trick to make myself out a glamorous hero, and always felt immensely pleased with myself while doing it. I was the soldier-lover at the wars, kind but stern, bearing my lady's scarf into the fiercest of the fight, held high on my plumèd helm. I think I took for my model a mixture of Sir Launcelot and Henry of Navarre. They weren't love letters, but outbursts of beautiful vanity. I don't think Ros ever produced such masterpieces as she received, but she did well. Hers were on the "solemn pride in our soldiers" note, with pages filled with what she had been doing in the rare moments snatched from her Red Cross work. I pictured her working her fingers to the bone so that I and her country might not perish. She enclosed photographs of herself, and looking at them now I'm bound to admit they show no evidences of overwork. I harrowed myself with thoughts of what would become of her if I never returned from "over there." I even wrote Carl Morss to look after her if anything should happen to me. I can remember still how proud I was of that touch. It seemed to round off the picture of unselfish heroism to my complete satisfaction. Ros is now one of the smart, "horsey," young married set, with a hard face and a prominent position on the Society Page. It's a good thing for Carl he never had to carry out my dying request.

The icy going was often a menace during the winter. Gammell had a stupid, yellow horse named "Boris," with a stiff tuft of yellow mane like a pineapple top between his ears. One day the Special Detail were riding in from the Range at a fast trot, and just as we turned the corner by the kitchen there was a thud. We stopped and saw Ives and Boris sprawled on the ground. I thought Ives must as least have cracked his skull, for the place he fell was glare ice. Before I could get to him, he had picked himself up and got to his horse's head. I overheard him saying, "Boris, are you hurt?"!

I don't remember when our little family in the stone barrack was broken up, but I know that towards the end I lived in a new wooden Adrian near the Battery kitchen. The Adrians were wooden sheds made in sections on a dirt floor. They were very long and low, with a door at each end, but their distinguishing characteristic was the outward flare of the walls about four feet from the ground. Along each side was a row of straw bedticks on which we slept in our blankets. On cold nights we borrowed one or two saddle blankets from the stables. My bed was near the farther door, and Gammell's was next to mine. Through the open door we could see the Range and a back road down the hill towards St. Malo. Ives and I kept a supply of bread, jam, and fromage de Brie under our blankets, and we spent many hours conversing as we ate. Everything in Ives' artistic soul revolted at the thought of living at the front, and he always referred to that form of existence as "wallowing." One day he got word that by the unsolicited intervention of some influential relative, he was to receive a commission in the Intelligence Department of G.H.Q.

"So when you go awallowing, Horace," I remember his saying, "think of me in Paris wearing civilian clothes and a long, black beard." A few days later he got his travel orders. I helped him carry his barracks bag down the hill to the toy railroad station beside the narrow-gauge track to Rennes. We said goodbye, and I walked back up the hill alone. Halfway up, I looked around and saw his small figure standing lonesomely beside the huge barracks bag.

Coëtquidan never seemed right to me after Ives left, and I don't remember much about it.

One thing occurs to me that must have happened about this time. Gas masks and steel helmets were issued. The masks* were French and consisted of a pale blue padded cloth facepiece fitted with goggle eyes. It was carried in a cloth pouch by a strap over the shoulder. One day we were put through a poison-gas chamber containing a concentration ten times as great as would be encountered in actual warfare, so we were told. I don't remember taking it very seriously, and for all I know there may not have been any gas in it at all. The steel helmet seemed heavy at first, but it was really comfortable as there was a close-fitting leather band inside, and a chin strap to keep it steady. This strap was adjustable so it could be shortened and worn behind the head. I have never found anything so good as a steel helmet for keeping off heavy rain.

Realizing that I would have no barracks bag at the front, I had written home for a piece of waterproof canvas and had made several small bags with drawstrings to avoid having loose articles in my blanket roll and saddlebags. These proved a great comfort. My last preparation for the front was to sew up a 20-franc gold-piece in can-

* Later we got British "box respirators."

vas and hang it around my neck on a leather thong with my identification discs. I never touched this money, however strong the temptation, but kept it against a real emergency. The identification discs were two aluminum tags the size of silver dollars. In case of death one was to be cut off and forwarded to the War Department while the other was left on the body and buried with it. Everyone had these.

There is one other occurrence worth mentioning before our departure for the front. The Fifty-first Artillery Brigade was inspected by Pershing and his staff. This was preceded by a day and night of polishing harness, grooming horses, cleaning guns, drawing equipment from Elmer Fall, our autocratic supply sergeant, and putting the barracks in apple-pie order. On the day of the inspection we were at the stables long before dawn and had the Battery harnessed and hitched. Every strap was buckled neatly, every saddlebag contained the correct articles, every blanket roll was molded snugly behind the saddle, with its ends fastened tight to the girth rings by 60-inch straps, across every pommel was a neatly rolled slicker and a spare feed of oats in a nose bag. Every gun carriage was above reproach, and every caisson held its hundred rounds of ammunition. Every man was freshly shaved, his trench boots slick with dubbin, his spiral puttees wound so the frayed edges were hidden, his uniform free from spots, and his automatic pistol beautifully clean.

The field inspection took place on the Range, and I remember that the impressiveness of the occasion was marred by an accident to Roley Allen. Just as the general passed our Battery, Roley's horse gave a snort and plunged into the sacred space in front of the Battery where our officers sat on their horses like statues. Roley pulled in his reins, fell onto the horse's neck, and his helmet tumbled off and rolled on the ground. I don't remember much more about the field inspection, but I do remember the bunk inspection that followed it.

Everyone stood at attention at the foot of his bunk as the general walked through the barracks with his glistening staff. The bunks were arranged according to a uniform pattern, and I have before me a tattered sketch of it made at the time. Every aluminum tent peg had its place, and once my layout was complete I never dared take my eyes off it. It was uncanny the way small articles disappeared from one bunk to complete a deficiency on another one if there was a momentary relaxation of vigilance. At last the inspection was over, and the Brigade found fit for action.

A week later, we harnessed and hitched again and left Coëtquidan for the front.

---

## CHAPTER VIII

*The Regiment leaves for the front. A night in Soissons.*

"Soissons, Feb. 3, 1918. Detrained. Abbey with cots; up at 4:30 to scout ahead. Beck, Allen, Curtis; rum."

---

IT WAS FEBRUARY FIRST when we hiked over the road to Guer in heavy marching order with horses, guns, caissons, battery wagon, park wagon, fourgon, soup gun, and all. Some of the Forty-second Division artillerymen had ridden over from camp to watch us pull out. They still wore the old Stetson hats which we had long ago discarded for tight-fitting overseas caps. I remember feeling sorry for them and envying them at the same time.

We found the train waiting: a combination of boxcars and flats. The loading ramp was on a level with the floor of the cars. This was my first experience at loading horses and carriages on a troop train, and I was impressed by the resourcefulness of some of my comrades. As each section drove onto the ramp, the drivers unhitched the horses and led them into a boxcar where they hitched four at each end with their harnesses on. Their heads had to be tied up short so they could not put a leg over the halter shank and get thrown. Some

"We found the train waiting"

This was an easy way if there was only one car to load. We much preferred loading from a long ramp the height of the railroad cars' floor; then all the cars alongside the ramp could be loaded at the same time.

of the horses were frightened and required blindfolds, ropes, prayers, and curses to get them aboard. In the narrow space between their heels was dumped a bale of hay and a bag of oats. One driver had to ride in this space to keep the horses out of trouble. Meanwhile the cannoneers were hauling the carriages onto the flatcars and lashing them fast. Everything was soon in order, the men who could find no room on the flatcars jumped into the boxcars intended for them, the engine whistled, and the train began to move.

We must have been on the train about twenty-four hours. I remember riding part of the time on the high seat of the park wagon whence I could see the flat country for miles. This must have been late the second afternoon, for I saw many old rotting trenches and rusty barbwire entanglements. The ground was scarred by grass-grown holes, some of them as large as a room. With a sickening sensation I realized that these were old shell holes.

During the halts the drivers watered the horses, and everyone else ran to a flatcar in the middle of the train where Joe Wilner and cook Lorenzen presided over the rolling kitchen, full of hot coffee, and handed out hardtack and canned Willie.*

Around sunset the train pulled into the suburbs of a large city which everyone said was Soissons. I saw a queer series of little round white clouds in the sky, and while I was trying to think why they should form such a perfect line, I saw a new one appear, smaller than the others but quickly swelling to the same size. About the same time I heard a faint bark and caught sight of a black speck moving rapidly in front of the smallest cloud. As I watched it, a succession of new little clouds seemed to be forming behind it but never quite catching up. By this time, the clouds on the back end of the line were fading out. A turn of the wind brought me the irregular droning sound of an airplane engine. The train meanwhile had come to a stop in a sort of freight yard. I looked inquiringly at a French sentry who stood near the track. "Avion Boche," he said.

* Canned corned beef.

It was dark while we were unloading the train. I remember how cold it was as we plodded along between towering black houses and high garden walls, the rumbling jingle of the carriages and the staccato roll of the horses hoofs on the hard pavement being the only sounds to break the silence.

By the dim light of a lantern I remember rows of horses tied in a shed on the muddy slope of a hill. I was almost asleep as I rode through the dark to some watering place a long way off. Against the sky I could see the denser shapes of trees and an occasional irregular roof.

Later in the night I was carrying one end of a stretcher along a street lined by very tall trees. Someone had given out—Bowers I think his name was—and he was damnably heavy. Once we rested beside the road on a grassy bank. I don't remember who carried the other end of the stretcher, or who it was that was lugging Bowers' blanket roll and his own. I was dead with sleep when someone yelled from a gateway. I went up some stairs and struck a match.

"Douse that light," barked several voices. It had been enough to show me an empty wire bunk with straw in it, and without bothering to open my blanket roll, I flopped down on the bunk and went to sleep.

Someone was shaking me by the shoulder and yelling something in my ear. Something about getting up and a blanket roll, it was. I felt numb all over with cold. I opened my eyes and found it was still dark.

"Get up quick, Horace, and help me make this roll." I recognized Beck's voice and stumbled to my feet. I had cramps in my stomach as if I hadn't eaten for a week. On the floor there was the sound of moving, and as I waked up I understood that Beck was trying to roll his blankets in the dark.

"What the hell's the idea?" I muttered.

Beck said that he and Allen and I were to start right away and scout ahead up to the lines. I put out my hand to make sure my saddlebags and roll were where I had dropped them, and then helped Beck roll his blankets.

Out in the air it was as cold as Greenland but there was a faint light in the sky. A few men stood shivering around the soup gun* in the corner of a flagged courtyard where Lorenzen had started making coffee. Around us rose the gray walls of an old abbey. Before going to find my horse I got a mess kit full of cold canned tomatoes and a handful of hardtack. I think it was Allen who offered me a drink out of a bottle of rum he had bought in Rennes. All the way to the stables and back I could feel the warmth of that drink spreading over my body.

When we rode into the courtyard the sky was lighter, and most of the men were lining up for mess or sitting around the flagstones with their backs to the wall, eating. Lieutenant Clarke—"Jimmy" to his friends, an easy-going Bostonian and a superb horseman—was already mounted. Allen and I quickly adjusted our saddlebags, fastened our blanket rolls across our cantles, mounted, and joined Jimmy Clarke. Beck was fussing around in the center of the courtyard, to the amusement of his large audience. He was having trouble with his blanket roll which was too fat to strap down properly behind his cantle. It lay like a limp log of wood across his saddle with a shoe threatening to leak out of one end. The horse stood still, apparently indifferent to the whole proceeding. At last Beck gave up the struggle to make the job presentable. He gathered the reins, put his left foot in the stirrup, and swung his right foot off the ground. His foot caught under the end of his blanket roll, his girth began to slip, and while the horse stood motionless, the saddle turned slowly over and Beck landed flat on his back underneath the horse. I could still hear laughter from the courtyard when Allen, Jimmy, and I trotted around the first corner and turned into a long, straight street. We had gone several blocks before Beck joined us, coming like a whirlwind, with spare articles of clothing flying from both ends of his roll.

* Rolling kitchen.

The early morning light increased as we clattered through the deserted streets. Leaving the town, we rode along straight poplar-lined roads between fields and farms and as the sun was rising, entered a village that showed the marks of war. Along the main street had been neatly piled the rubble from the crumbling, roofless houses. Barricades of cobblestones and barbwire had been partially removed to allow free passage. French soldiers in horizon-blue fatigue caps smoked pipes in front of sandbagged doors on which were painted, "abri pour 10," "abri pour 15," or "abris de gaz." We asked them if we were on the road to Chassemy. They nodded, smiled, pointed, and answered, "Toujours tout droit." It was months before I learned whether this meant "Keep going to the right" or "Go straight ahead." We kept straight as there were no other roads in sight, and at last saw a church tower in the distance.

For the last mile I had been conscious of a dull rumbling as from a distant bowling alley, and now as the wind brought it nearer I knew it was the sound of the guns.

---

## CHAPTER IX

*Behind the lines. Our first echelon. Cooties.*

"Chassemy, Feb. 4. Echelon. Mud; work; leaky dugout; air raids.
Braisne; bad morale."

---

THE SUN WAS WARM when we trotted into the village of Chassemy, which was to be the Battery echelon for the next six weeks. There was a squat church with a low steeple standing at a crossroads, surrounded by several stone houses, whose gardens were backed by fields and woods. Many of the roofs showed gaping holes, but the houses were not badly ruined. Several French soldiers in fatigue caps walked about the streets. One of them brought us to a French officer who showed us where our echelon was to be.

This was a muddy place in the woods about half a mile behind the village. These woods contained no trees over eight or nine inches in diameter, and no evergreens. The woods were not straggling, like ours at home, but stopped in straight lines along the edges. A muddy cart road led to a sort of clearing where the underbrush had been cut away, and here two long wooden horse sheds had been built under the trees. A few French soldiers were still at work on them as we rode up.

Lieutenant Clarke told us to take a good look around so we could find the place again, and then to ride back to Soissons and get the Battery.

My recollections of this ride are very pleasant. Beck had fixed his blanket roll to suit him, and we all were in high spirits and feeling very important. I was hungry, but counted on eating when we reached Soissons. Somewhat to my disappointment we met the Battery on the road. It was sometime in the afternoon that we led them into the woods behind Chassemy.

My next recollection is of looking for a place to sleep. We had watered the horses at a brook across the fields and tied them up under the sheds. In the meantime it had started to drizzle. Some of the men had pitched pup tents in the mud, and their blankets were getting wet already. Beck and I found a caved-in hole full of dead leaves not far from the horse sheds. We stole a shovel from the park wagon and worked like beavers to clear it out. The soil was sandy, and before dark we had enlarged the hole to about seven feet square and three feet deep. We found poles in the woods to lay across it, and some old pieces of moldy tar paper for a roof. The woods were full of old junk. I got a start when I thought I saw a body lying in a clump of bushes. It proved to be an old German uniform. I found several rusty German helmets and rifles. We piled a little sand on the tar paper to keep it from blowing away and surveyed our work with satisfaction.

By the time it was dark the rain was coming down hard. We got some supper at the soup gun and on the way back I almost fell over a bale of hay behind the stables. It was easy to carry off an armful of this in the dark and to feather our nest with it. Beck and I spread our shelter halves over the hay, opened our dry blankets, fixed a lighted candle-end on a stick in the wall, and ate our supper reclining in great comfort while the rain beat harmlessly on our solid roof. After supper we smoked, talked, and read old letters for a while before going to sleep.

Sometime during the night I woke up with the feeling that all was not well. I was cold and wet and couldn't remember where I was. Just then Beck struck a match. Our hole had almost six inches of water in it, and the rain was still coming down in torrents. I don't like to think of the rest of that night.

Early in the morning Beck rode up to the gun position with a few others to learn the ground. I was both relieved and disappointed not to go. During the day the sun came out, so I dried my blankets and dug a trench around the hole to carry future rainstorms off. It was a long time before I was to sleep in that hole again, but I didn't know it then.

After getting warmed up I made a disagreeable discovery. I had been itchy all the previous day, and as I had lain awake shivering in the night it sometimes seemed as if things were crawling on me. At breakfast I forgot about it but now, after a strenuous bout of digging with pick and shovel, I again became aware of several itchy spots. I sat down on a bale of hay in the sun and stripped to the skin. On the inside of my undershirt I found several transparent, oblong beasts with many legs and a dark speck in the center. Lice, by Jeeze, and I must have got them in the old abbey at Soissons where French and German soldiers had been using the same straw to sleep on for years. Before dark I was gratified to see most of my friends "reading their shirts" and finding plenty to interest them too.

My recollections of the echelon are vague, as I saw it only those first two days, and on one or two later visits from the gun positions, and then it was changed by the addition of more stables, harness racks, tar paper shacks, a kitchen shed, and several other improvements. Although it continued to be muddy, and was always subject to air raids which did no harm, it was a very comfortable place to live.

Late in the afternoon one of the advance party came back with word to harness and hitch, and after dark the drivers, gun crews, guns, caissons, and special detail and two cooks started up to the gun positions.

I remember a long march in the dark over roads which later became very familiar to me. We crossed a bridge over the Aisne and bore to our right, following the foot of a long ridge. When we came around the end of the ridge the guns sounded much louder and I could see momentary flares of light a long way ahead. Word was passed down the column to put out all cigarettes. We turned a corner sharp to the left and started to climb a steep hill. It was halfway up this hill that I first heard the scream of a shell. It was a terrifying sound. There were four or five of them, and I felt sure they were going to kill us. They crashed in the darkness somewhere to our right. The next day I found they had landed a good quarter of a mile away, but that was no comfort at the time I heard them.

My spirits were very low when we halted near the top of the hill. The lights I had seen before were much nearer now, and I could see that they were very bright things that floated slowly to the ground where they flickered for a minute before going out. Someone led me into a shoulder-high trench on the left of the road, and I followed him around corners over rough ground for perhaps one hundred yards. He showed me an opening in the wall of the trench. There were several wooden steps leading down very sharply, and I remember hitting my steel helmet on beams as I went down. At the bottom I pushed aside a curtain of sacking and found myself in a little room lighted by a candle. Here I dumped my blanket roll, then felt my way back to the road. The gun limbers had gone but the caissons were still there, being unloaded. I joined the line of men in the trench, and as a shell was tossed to me I caught it and tossed it along. They weighed twenty-four pounds so I did my best not to drop one on my toe but it was so dark that I was not always successful. This seemed to last a long time, and every minute that passed I was surprised to hear no German shells. At last it was done and I stumbled back to the dugout, rolled up in my blankets, and went to sleep.

---

## CHAPTER X

*The front. Introduction to shellfire. The Chemin-des-Dames sector. A trench raid. French artilleurs.*

"Chemin des Dames, Feb. 5. Ostel. Vailly. Dugout; telephone, night.
O.P. Avions. 'Take cover.' Wire bunk. Good morale."

---

A VERY SPECIAL AURA surrounds that six weeks in the Chemin-des-Dames sector. The pictures that rise before my eyes are extraordinarily vivid and in them all is an atmosphere of newness, a sort of romance of discovery that in later scenes is fainter or altogether lacking. I suppose my relief at finding the front no worse temporarily turned my head and gave me a sort of beginner's enthusiasm: "He jests at scars, that never felt a wound." I took nothing seriously and accepted each new experience in a spirit of play, as if it were all a game and I a privileged player with a guarantee against losing. I had many occasions later to look back with wonder on this preposterous folly.

The place I saw next morning was an abandoned French artillery position with trenches, gun pits, and dugouts complete. The surrounding country was badly devastated. Here was the "scarred slope of battered hill" mentioned by Alan Seeger. Every foot of ground had been churned by shells, and what had been forests were now impenetrable tangles of splintered, charred stumps with not a tree standing.

Our position was just below the edge of a plateau, and behind us the hill fell away in steep terraces to a level swamp. Beyond the swamp, about three-quarters of a mile away was a high ridge almost at right angles to our hill.

In front of our guns I could see about one hundred yards of rising ground and a thick tangle of barbwire outlined against the sky where four pale-blue German observation balloons hung along the horizon. The road ran past the right of our Battery and disappeared over this rise. With my steel helmet on my head, my gas mask "at the alert" (that is, tied up under my chin where it could be put on my face in a second), and my loaded pistol at my hip, I walked down the road the way we had come the previous night. This road was narrow, straight, and steep. Before I had gone far I met two French soldiers coming leisurely up. They wore fatigue caps, had no gas masks or pistols, and carried a cane in one hand and a bottle of wine in the other. Around their shoulders were slung several odd-shaped canteens or bidons covered with horizon-blue cloth. They looked at my paraphernalia with astonishment and gave me a cheery "Bonjour." We talked awhile and I learned that they belonged to the Ninth French Battery, which was across the road from us and a little farther up the hill. They gave me a cordial invitation to call on them. I couldn't help asking them how they dared go about without masks and helmets. They looked surprised at the question and said this was a "quiet sector," and besides, gas was no danger on a hill, as it always sank to the low ground. They told me there was a French army cooperative store in Ostel, where I could buy wine, cheese, and jam. We parted with polite aurevoirs, and I continued down the road.

To my left I looked off over a wide valley to a ridge about two miles away. It was in this valley that the shells had burst the night before. Ostel proved to be the place where we had made the right-angle turn. At the crossroads one sign said to Vailly, and in the other direction to Chavonne. Ostel itself was a scattered heap of rubble, where the location of a few houses was still marked by crumbling cellar holes. After a long search, I found the cooperative store in a cellar that had been roofed over and covered with sandbags. In this dimly lighted den, I bought a bottle of Médoc and a can of jam, before climbing the hill to the position.

To describe this old position is like talking about home. The main trench led from the road behind the four gun pits, which were protected by sandbag roofs and sides. The muzzles of the guns were draped by nets tufted over with green and brown rafia. These were removed when the guns fired. The first gun pit was about thirty yards from the road and the others were spaced about twenty yards apart to its left. Built into the trench walls were ammunition racks. There was a shallow sandpit behind the guns, in which was the captain's dugout. Farther along the trench, beyond the guns, were other dugouts. One was very deep but most of them were only eight or twelve feet below the surface. The main trench was about shoulder deep, and about forty yards beyond the fourth gun pit it forked, one fork running to the right towards the German lines and the other getting shallower as it bore to the left obliquely across the slope of the hill till it petered out into a surface path. Some of the deepest dugouts were along this path. The kitchen was housed in a sort of arbor with a corrugated iron roof on the surface of the ground a little beyond the fork in the trench. A few large bushes and small trees grew around it. The telephone dugout, in which I lived, was a very good one at about the center of the position a little way off the main trench. A few wooden steps led down to a sacking curtain which was intended to keep lights from showing. Inside the dugout was a table holding the telephone switchboard, and a double row of chicken-wire bunks on which eight men could sleep, their feet towards the door. In a heavy rain the water dripped from the rusty iron rails of the ceiling onto the bunks.

This dugout was occupied by Beck, Ritchie, Saindon, Peabody, myself, and three others who were not always the same ones. At night we took turns sitting up at the switchboard, watching the signal drops by the light of a candle. As I remember, we had lines to Battalion Headquarters, the French Ninth Battery, the forward observation post, the first piece gunpit, the captain's dugout and perhaps a few others. We laid these lines ourselves, two of us carrying a heavy reel of wire on a stick between us. Over open ground we let the wire lie loose on the surface, but in trenches we pinned it against the walls, and in crossing roads we either buried it or looped it over on poles. The line to Battalion was the most important, and it was essential to keep it open at all times. Battalion Headquarters was a huge cave in the hill across the swamp behind our position. Whenever the swamp was being shelled, as it often was, we would put through test calls every few minutes to be sure the line was in.

I remember the first time the Battalion line went out. It was a rainy afternoon a few days after our arrival. We were all sitting on our beds talking, reading, and writing letters. Outside we could hear the dull explosion of shells in the swamp. Beck had been ringing Battalion with growing impatience for several minutes. At last he put down the earphone and announced, "Shit! Battalion's out! Who wants to come and fix it?"

It was really a one-man job, but several of us insisted on going along to see the fun. Beck, Ritchie, Peabo, Saindon, and I went down the hill with a roll of electric tape and a pair of wire cutters. The wire was tagged as it left the dugout, so we followed it easily through the trench and down the hill past the engineers' dugouts, which we always blamed for any shelling that cut our wires. They were our own engineers but they didn't seem to know any better than to hang blankets out to dry in plain sight of the German balloons. Just as we reached the edge of the swamp I heard a faint thump from the German lines and in a few seconds a crescendo whistling scream. We all dropped flat on the ground, and the scream stopped as if it had been suddenly choked just as it reached its climax. Then, "Bow!" as the shell exploded deep below the surface of the swamp, and we saw a great geyser of mud sail high in the air. Out in the center of the swamp was a smoking hole eight feet across which was rapidly filling with water.

We stood up laughing and walked out into the swamp, Beck leading with the wire running over his arm. There was no grass or anything growing in the swamp but the mud was solid enough to bear us up. I found I could easily push a stick several feet into it, however. It was riddled with shell holes filled to the top with water, and zigzagging between them was a duckboard walk. Duckboards were rough, flimsy, ladderlike gratings which were meant to be laid end to end to make a floor in a muddy trench. Here they had been used to make a boardwalk over the swamp, and each shell that landed on the path caused a new detour when the duckboards were replaced around the new hole. We were a little over halfway across the swamp when Beck found the place where a shell had broken the telephone wire. We had located the broken ends and begun to scrape off the insulation to make a splice, when "Bum-bum-bum-bump!" went the German guns in the distance.

"Cheese it!" yellowed Peabo, jumping into a shell hole up to his neck in ice water. I flopped flat on my face in the mud and pulled my helmet over my eyes. WhooooOO came the scream right for us and BOW! as the mud shook with the explosion. There is no way of adequately expressing on paper the sound a shell makes. It begins as a whine, and then, rising to a terrifying crescendo shriek it ends in a shattering crash. Great gobs of mud kept falling around us and on us for a surprisingly long time. At last it stopped, and Peabo crawled out of the water. Beck, Ritchie, and I stood up and looked around for Willie Saindon. He was crawling with his face almost in the mud.

"Willie! For Christ's sake, are you hit?" yelled Beck.

Saindon's toothless grin rose up from the mud, and we all burst out laughing as he said, "No. Willie, he looking for the wire cutters, boss."

Not to make too long a story of it, we were interrupted three times more and all took our turn in the water before the wire was repaired. The shells then were landing between us and the Battery, so we took to our heels and "dragged ass" towards Battalion. Just at the far edge of the swamp came my closest call. I must have been making enough noise running so I didn't hear the shell coming till it was almost on top of me. Just as I dove came a blinding explosion, and I was buried under a ton of mud. Half-stunned, and with acrid fumes choking my breath, I dragged myself up and saw the ugly smoking hole a few yards away. It was only the softness of the ground, which allowed the shells to penetrate so deep before exploding, that prevented our being hit by flying splinters.

There was a road on a terrace beyond the swamp where we all met and kept running till we were half way to Ostel. We all were weak from laughing.

"You're a great soldier," I said to Peabo; "What was the idea of wetting your nice pants in that shell hole?"

"Well, I'd already wet them myself," said Peabo, "and what's more, I bet you did too!" As a matter of fact we had all experienced that interesting sphincteric phenomenon.

Captain Freddy Huntington had original ideas about life at the front. He had been a hockey star at Harvard and had campaigned on the Mexican Border. Physically, he was a sort of stocky Hercules. He was inclined to be tyrannical, at least the enlisted men thought so, and most of us feared him as much as we admired him. He started the day at the front with a formation before breakfast—a sort of stand-to. At five o'clock, or some such hour the bugle blew assembly, and up from the dugouts would crawl everyone who wasn't on rocket guard or switchboard duty, with helmets, gas masks, pistols, and overcoats. We would all line up on a level space behind the guns, and the sergeants would call roll. If anyone was missing he would be dug out like a rabbit from his burrow. Next, Freddy would order us to put on gas masks. He would then take us for a run down the road and back "to accustom us to wearing gas masks." As we passed the Ninth Battery the Frenchmen would stand aghast. "Quelle follie!" they would murmur; "Quel horreur!"

One unlucky morning Freddy discovered an old trench full of moldy sandbags halfway down the road to Ostel. For the next week he had each man carry two sandbags up the hill every morning, wearing gas masks. The Frenchmen confidentially advised us to shoot Freddy. It was a Boche aviator who finally damped Freddy's zeal by swooping low over the position one morning just as we lined up for roll call, and flying straight back to Germany with the good news. A minute later the shells were skimming over our heads and cutting our telephone lines down in the swamp while we broke formation without orders and scattered to the nearest dugouts. By tacit agreement we had no more roll calls at the front.

Another of Freddy's pranks is worth mentioning to illustrate his ingenuity and zeal. One morning we came out of our dugouts to find the ground covered lightly with snow. As we wished the Germans to believe our position deserted—in spite of the Boche aviator we had treated to the roll call formation—we tried very hard to make no paths in the snow. This little deception wasn't enough for Freddy. He lined up all the men that could be spared from the guns and led them in single file down to the empty valley behind the Ninth French Battery. Choosing an open level patch of snow, he then led us around in four little circles which he connected by paths. Anyone watching us must have put us down for mad as March hares. As we looked back to the scene of our frolic from a point high on the hillside we saw what looked like a new battery position in the snow. Sure enough, that afternoon a Boche photographic plane came over and a few hours later Freddy had the satisfaction of seeing his dummy position most thoroughly shelled.

I remember friendly visits at the Ninth Battery when I sat in garlicky dugouts and drank Pinard out of leather bidons. This took a perfect technique, as you were expected to squeeze the bidon and catch the thin stream of wine in your mouth. The Frenchmen were delighted with our cigarettes, and I never knew one to refuse. "Ah, pour un ami qui fume," seemed to be the polite formula for accepting a cigarette which was to be smoked later. The Frenchmen were really most cordial and they told us thrilling stories of the great attack at Verdun when they had helped check the onslaught of the Crown Prince. War had become the normal way of life to them, and they knew every trick of extracting comfort out of their crude surroundings. Not an unnecessary bit of work was done, but everything essential was accomplished with the ease of long practice. I was particularly impressed by the beautiful condition of their officers' uniforms: the coats were cleaned and brushed, the breeches pressed, and the leggings perfectly polished. Some of the officers even used perfume.

There was one Aspirant in particular who took a great shine to us. Later, when we were in the Toul sector, Allen got a letter from him describing the fate of the Ninth Battery in the overwhelming German attack that overran the Chemin-des-Dames a few days after we left. He said the German infantry were on top of them before they could destroy their guns, and he himself had reached Ostel before he even thought of it. He went back up the hill, alone, shot three Germans in the fourth section gun pit, blew up the gun with the incendiary grenade that was kept under the trail for that purpose and got away without a scratch.

A memorable thrill was the first day I went up to "O.P. Reynard," our forward observation post. Freddy and I set out carrying maps, field glasses, and a portable telephone. We crossed the road behind the Ninth Battery and entered the "Boyau Schonikker," an old German communication trench. The walls were lined with a network of old and new telephone wires. In some places the trench was very deep and in others it was so shallow we had to bend over to keep our heads from showing. I did this instinctively, although there was no need of it except for the balloons which always made me nervous, as if they were malignant blue eyes on stalks looking at me. For about a mile we seemed to be going uphill at a very gentle slope and bearing off far to the right. Then we seemed to reach the highest point of the ridge. The soil was chalky here and the walls of the trench still showed the marks of pick and shovel. I climbed up where the wall was low and looked around. I saw a desert of shell holes and rusty wire. There was a streak of lighter dirt along the summit of the ridge, which marked the site of the Ladies' Way from which this sector got its name. It was about here that Freddy found a German cuirass of iron with hinged segments to protect the wearer's abdomen. It was about half an inch thick, and must have weighed sixty pounds. I suppose it was intended for a sniper's use, as no one could have moved actively in it as an infantryman would have to do. Freddy ordered me to put it on and to bring it along for a souvenir. I hoisted it against my chest where it was held by curved flanges over my shoulders, and followed Freddy down the trench. At the first corner I got rid of it and Freddy never missed it until we arrived at the O.P.

We bore to the left and began to go downhill and soon came to a trench running at right angles across the face of the slope. This was part of the infantry second-line system. I could see the mouths of dugouts in the upper wall of the trench, so I judged it had been built by the Germans when this hillside was in their possession. A few yards along the trench, we came to a wide place with a strong sand-bag parapet protecting a square loophole. A horizontal board had been fastened below the loophole to serve as a map table. This was "O.P. Reynard."

No one was in sight as I sat down in the trench and began looking over the wooden tags on the tangle of telephone wires for Battery A's. I soon found it and connected my portable telephone. After the first turn of the crank I heard Beck's voice rasping over the wire. Meanwhile Freddy was spreading his map on the little table and getting out his field glasses. I moved to where I could get my eye to a crack between the sandbags. Before me was a deserted valley with a canal crossed by the ruins of a red iron bridge about five hundred yards away. Across the canal a barren hillside sloped up to a high ridge. Far off to the right I could see the towers of the Laon cathedral. A road ran up the hill straight in front of me. To the left of it was a straggling cemetery full of shell holes and crooked gravestones; to the right was an old stone mill like the ones on the Range at Coët-quidan. Below me at the foot of the slope were our first-line infantry trenches, of which only the barbwire protections were visible from above. With the glasses I could see bits of German trench on the op-posite slope. One spot caught my attention where I thought I saw shovelfuls of earth being thrown out. This was the only sign of life I saw, but I knew the empty scene before me concealed thousands of German troops.

"Have you got the Battery, Corporal?" asked Freddy.

"Yes, sir," I said.

"I'll register on the mill," said Freddy. "First piece as laid, one round, fire." I repeated this to Beck and could hear him yelling it to the gun crew. Through the telephone came the muffled sound of an explosion and then I heard the whistling cry of the shell overhead. A burst of smoke appeared a little to the left and beyond the mill.

"Right 6, down 2, one round, fire," said Freddy. Again I repeated it to Beck, and again came the sound of the gun and the whiz of the shell. This time the burst appeared squarely in front of the mill, and when the dust and smoke cleared away I could see a jagged hole in its side, near the ground.

"Mark basic deflection, lay parallel to first piece," said Freddy. At his invitation I looked over his shoulder at the map, after repeating the message to Beck. He had drawn a line with a ruler from the point on the map representing our Battery position to the Moulin Rouge, and had written "basic deflection" along the line. The range and di-rection of this line would be chalked on the gun shields and would serve as a basis for figuring firing data on any other map target. All at once we saw two German soldiers come over the hill and start walking down the road. Between them they were carrying a bucket, and through the glasses I could see them talking and laughing as they walked.

"Get back to your telephone and we'll give them a surprise," said Freddy. "Basic deflection, left 14, Battery one round, four three hundred, fire." I heard Beck's voice repeating it, and the four muffled reports of the guns. I clapped the glasses to my eyes and found the Germans just as the shells whizzed overhead. Four sudden bursts of smoke appeared on the road, followed by the sound of the explosions. As the smoke rose I could see one figure running back up the road, but the other one lay still. I couldn't see the bucket anywhere.

"That was a pretty good shot, wasn't it?" came Freddy's voice. "Let's call it a day and get back. By the way, Corporal, where's that souvenir of mine?"

I had to confess my fault, but Freddy said we could pick it up on the way back, and we did.

I have vivid memories of unloading ammunition at night. There was a narrow trench running in from the road in front of the guns, which proved more practicable for this purpose than the main trench. One night a line of us stood in this trench "hopping shells" from the caissons to the racks. I was about twenty feet from the second piece muzzle and plumb in front of it. Suddenly someone yelled, "Normal barrage." There was a blinding flash and a terrific concussion, and I found myself gasping for breath at the bottom of the trench with my head ringing like church bells.

I should say a word about barrages. Each battery was assigned a segment of no-man's-land for which it was held responsible in case of sudden attack. It was expected to be ready at any moment of the day or night to drop a curtain of fire across this segment in response to a telephone call or infantry rocket. The infantry sentry lying in a shell hole in front of his first-line trench was provided with rockets of a specified color to shoot off when he heard Germans creeping up in the dark to attack his trench. If it was one of his own working parties he heard and he shot up the rocket, so much the worse for them, but I believe great care was taken to keep the sentries informed of what working parties and patrols were out. Back at the Battery we kept a man on rocket guard all night. His job was to look through a wooden tube which was set on a tripod and pointed at the spot where the barrage rocket would appear above the hill. Anything of the wrong color or in the wrong place was to be ignored, but when a green rocket soared up into the square of sky framed by the wooden tube the guard yelled, "Normal barrage," and pulled the lanyard of the nearest gun. This woke the gun guards sleeping beside the trails in each gun pit, and before the rocket had dropped behind the hill all four guns would be firing in a steady roar and the Battery would be seething with life in a moment.

The one time I was on rocket guard was an unhappy time for me. I stared so long at the black square of sky that I began to think I saw things. Towards morning my eyes would hardly stay open, and I would wake from my stupor with a start, almost sure a green rocket had just disappeared, and in a frenzy of doubt whether to yell "Normal barrage" and perhaps murder an American patrol or to keep quiet while a German raiding party surprised our doughboys in their trench. It was a weird sensation to watch the outlines of the hills appear against the first grayness in the east, to see the intermittent flares pale in the growing light and to hear the hysterical chatter of the machine guns as the favorite hour approached for surprise attacks. Later in the war I grew blasé to most of the familiar sights and sounds but the sudden cry of "Normal barrage" never quite lost its pulse-quickening quality.

I remember the first attack our Division made in this sector. Rumors of it reached us the day before, and I was particularly interested in the plans because, thanks to my trip to O.P. Reynard, I was one of the few artillerymen who had seen the place it would happen. A party of volunteers from the 101st Infantry and 101st Engineers mixed with a few French troops was to throw a light bridge across the canal in no-man's-land, cross over, and surprise a section of German trench. The object was to capture prisoners for questioning. To prevent the Germans from escaping down their communication trenches, we were going to fire a "box-barrage" to cut them off from the rear. The whole thing had been rehearsed, every participant knew his job, and the number of minutes for each phase of the operation had been determined. Watches were synchronized over the telephone a few hours before "Zero hour." It came at two-fifteen o'clock in the morning. Everyone at the Battery was out to see the fireworks. I kept looking at my watch, and as the minute hand crept up to two o'clock I wondered how the raiding party felt down there in the infantry trench. Two-nine; they must be carrying their section of bridge into no-man's-land. Away off to the left I heard machine guns for a minute, and then silence again. Two-fourteen. They must have bridged the canal. I was watching the second hand now.

"Battery ready-y-y-y" came the long-drawn-out command from somewhere back of the guns. The second hand was racing around to two-fifteen. They must be right up to the German wire.

"Tat-tat-tat-tat-tat," sputtered a machine gun in the dark. They were discovered! Three seconds, two seconds, one second, zero.

"Fire!" With a crash that seemed to shake the ground went every gun in the Brigade. In the sudden glare of light I saw the muzzle of the fourth piece darting at each flash like a snake striking again and again. The volume of sound half stunned me. As I saw the vicious flashes of flame bursting from every hill and heard the air over my head filled with the screeching rush of shells it seemed to me that the end of the world could be no more impressive. A few minutes and it was all over. Only the noise of the German machine guns along the front, sounding small after the gigantic din, and a few desultory shells from the German batteries disturbed the night.

A few of us went down the hill to Ostel to see the prisoners go by on their way to Divisional Headquarters at Vailly. There were twenty-two of them, two officers and twenty men. The officers looked haughty and turned their heads away as they passed. One was a little chap with spectacles held on with adhesive tape; his companion was tall. The others trudged along in stolid apathy. Two doughboys with fixed bayonets brought up the rear of the procession.

When I was in medical school after the war I met Jim Faulkner, a lame medical student in the class below me, and he said that it was in this raid that he had been shot through the leg just after getting across the bridge. He had been in the 101st Engineers.

One day I saw a French balloon shot down at Vailly. There was a military shower bath there, and six of us had walked down from Ostel to get a bath. Later, a wooden shower bath was built at Ostel, but it was never popular because shell splinters came through its walls too often. The walk back to Vailly was through battered, deserted country, but I never saw the road shelled beyond Ostel. Just before entering Vailly we passed Division Headquarters, dug into a steep bank beside the road and heavily reinforced with sandbags. Inside were wooden floors, painted walls, regular furniture, and electric lights. Despatch riders and motorcycle messengers lolled about the entrance. The bathhouse was just inside the town, which began abruptly like all French towns with no transition between country fields and thickly built-up streets. A little way beyond the bathhouse, a big observation balloon was moored to its reel truck which was parked in a garden. It swayed at the end of about three hundred yards of steel cable like a great, bloated, pale-blue elephant in the sky. I could see the observer's head above the edge of the basket. Some people have a soft life, I thought. Just then a racket of machine guns broke out from the street. I saw a German plane flying straight for the balloon, and as it got nearer there must have been twenty machine guns firing at it from the ground. The observer was moving around unhappily in his basket, and the Signal Corps men in the truck were frantically trying to pull the balloon down. Suddenly the German plane veered off and turned back towards Germany. The machine guns died down, and most of them had stopped when I noticed something else: a second German plane diving down from the sky straight as a falling stone and firing incendiary bullets as it came. The machine guns went crazy but they were too late. The balloon was less than halfway to the ground when it burst into flames. I was watching the observer and saw him climb onto the edge of his swaying basket and stand uncertain. I don't think he knew the gasbag was afire at first. A little crowd of spectators had gathered in the street and they all were gesticulating and yelling to him to jump. When he jumped I saw him pulling at the rip cord of his parachute, and I held my breath to see him falling. The parachute opened with a jerk, and for a minute he seemed suspended in the air, swinging slowly but not coming down at all. Blazing fragments of the gasbag kept drifting past him, and he must have been very unhappy. Gradually the parachute carried him off sideways just in time to escape the final collapse of the balloon, which undulated down in a fluttering mass of flames and smoke. The observer landed in a clump of thorny bushes, but I never saw what became of the wily German assassin.

The first haircut I had after leaving Coëtquidan was at the Battery position. A little Italian named Frank Tullo, who had been a barber in civil life, came up from the echelon one day and established a shop in the corner of the main trench. We were still fussy in those days and insisted on our rights to a tuft of hair left standing at the front of our heads and some degree of grading. Later in the war we were glad to have the horse clippers run all over our heads.

I don't know how we spent the days, but there always seemed enough to do. I often went out over the telephone lines. Sometimes it was my turn at the switchboard. Several times a week I went over the swamp to Battalion Headquarters with despatches or reports, and I remember a good many trips to O.P. Reynard for observing fire. One day when the Germans were shelling the road above Ostel I saw a shell land on one of the 101st Engineers' dugouts. I didn't go down to look, but I heard some of the fellows telling what they found when they dug the front of the dugout away. I spent many delightful days at the reserve position, but I'm saving the description of that for the last. At night there was telephone duty, unloading ammunition, and sometimes a special occurrence to interfere with my sleep.

One day after the Boche had been shelling around more actively than usual, Freddy got it into his head that we should deepen our main trench. That night I was on the working detail. Where I was, the trench was too deep to throw the dirt out, so two men filled sandbags and passed them up to the surface. I had been on top hauling sandbags up, and had hung my helmet on a bush because it slipped over my eyes every time I leaned forward. Suddenly I heard the gathering scream of a shell. It seemed to be headed my way all right and I decided to hop down into the trench. In the dark, my hand missed the farther edge of the trench and I did a turtle dive on my head. I woke up several hours later in my bunk with a stiff neck, and my back didn't feel just right for several days.

Two nights specially stand out as more disagreeable than the rest. One was when I had a toothache. It started in my right lower jaw, but soon it spread over my whole face. It was an agonizing ache without any letup, so I walked up and down the dugout in a frenzy and thought I would go insane or, failing that, would be forced to shoot myself. Beck called Battalion Headquarters and asked where the Regimental dentist was. We found he was there but had only a pocket kit with him. I started on the run and went blundering down the hill in the dark and splashed out onto the swamp. I couldn't wait to follow the windings of the duckboard, even if it had been visible, but ran straight ahead, falling down and getting up without stopping. At last I was across and climbed the steep hill up to Battalion as if the devil was after me. I found Lieutenant Baker, the dentist, in one of the big caves. He said again that he had only a pocket kit, but I kept repeating, "Pull it out, pull it out," till he agreed to try. He sat me on an empty ammunition box, and a sergeant held a lighted candle in front of my face. The lieutenant got my head under his arm, there was a splintering twist, a sort of electric current of pain right down to my toes, and I tried to stand up. My legs wouldn't hold me, so I sat there for awhile, and then stumbled back to the Battery in a daze. My face was still sore but the unbearable part of the pain was gone. It was only in 1927 that the last of the roots Lieutenant Baker left in my jaw were dug out under novocaine.

The other night I particularly remember was altogether different. Bill Rogers,* from Dedham, and I had been chosen to go on a French working party because we spoke some French. A new O.P. was being built in the infantry lines, and as we would share it with the Ninth Battery it seemed only fair that we should help build it. After dark Bill and I walked down to Ostel to meet the Frenchmen. We wore our slickers as it had started to rain. Mine was a new extra-long one which my father had bought on Atlantic Avenue and sent over by parcel post while we were at Coëtquidan. We found four or five Frenchmen from the Ninth Battery sitting on a pile of building material in Ostel at the side of a Decauville track† that I had never noticed before. They said we were only going to lug the stuff up. Another crowd would come to do the building. We set to work and piled a little handcar with railroad ties and tole iron. I never found out why it was called tole iron. It was heavy corrugated stuff that came in sheets about eight feet by three. There was also a type called elephant iron, which was curved like the arch of a bridge, with very large corrugations running the long way. When the car was loaded we started pushing it up the track. It was all uphill at a gentle grade, and as well as I could see by the flares over the lines, we were skirting the long ridge to the east of Ostel. Occasionally a German shell would come over, but the Frenchmen seemed to know instinctively where it would land and paid no attention.

After a couple of hours we stopped at the top of a ridge where the

* No relation.
† A very-narrow-gauge railroad track.

Decauville track ended. Below stretched a panorama of darkness in which I could trace the direction of the lines by the distant glow of flares and the sound of intermittent machine guns. We each took a load on our shoulders and slipped down into a trench. I had a railroad tie weighing about fifty pounds. In single file we passed under a sort of culvert and began to descend the hill. The trench we were in must have been a very old one for the walls had slid down until they met in a V at the bottom, where duckboards had once made a dry footing. Now the duckboards were covered by a foot of soft mud and some of the sections were tipped on edge and some were missing altogether. We went slowly in single file. I did well enough at first, but soon my feet got balled with mud and my railroad tie began to get heavy. The Frenchman in front of me stepped on a loose duckboard which sprang up and hit me in the shins. I fell heavily. When I tried to push myself up, my hands sank to the elbow in mud. I got the railroad tie onto my shoulder after a struggle, and soon came to a place where there was no duckboard and sank almost to my waist. I couldn't understand how the Frenchmen managed to go so fast. At last I was thoroughly blown and ready to sit down and cry, but still we pushed on, falling, stumbling, scrambling through the mud, the rain soaking down relentlessly and the night as dark as a rat hole. We must have gone a mile before the Frenchmen stopped and we heard them throwing down their loads.

"Ça-y-est!" gasped one. I was too tired even to say "Thank God!" and sank onto the mud with my head on the railroad tie.

After a rest, we started back. Everything seemed quiet and dark, so we climbed out of the trench to see if the going was better on top. At first it was, but at a barbwire entanglement our party got separated, and Bill and I found ourselves in the company of one Frenchman who claimed he knew a shortcut. We skirted the wire, only to strike another trench which we fell into before we knew it was there. We sloshed down the trench a short distance, but it was so bad we got out on top again and struck cross-country. Here the shell holes were very deep and close together, with barbwire every few steps, which tore my slicker in the dark. After about an hour's wandering the Frenchman said he was going back to the trench because he was all turned round. Bill and I didn't think he could find the trench so we let him go.

We groped our way along for another hour, hoping to strike a road or perhaps the Decauville track. The rain petered out and finally stopped, and still we floundered on. Sometimes we would stop and listen for voices, but we heard only the distant grumbling of artillery and the staccato clack of machine guns nearby. There was a ground fog which prevented our seeing the light of the flares so we got no help from our eyes. I would have given a good deal for a look at my compass but my matches were wet and there was no way of getting a light. At one time we considered sitting down to wait for morning, and we did try it, but about ten minutes was all we could stand. A little breeze sprang up which chilled us through our wet clothes and the fog must have begun to clear for suddenly a flare went up directly in front of us and a machine gun broke out almost under our feet. We froze as if we had stepped on a rattlesnake.

"Christ Almighty," whispered Bill, "we were walking right into the Boche front line!" As soon as the flare went down, we backed away and went as fast as we could in the opposite direction. Overhead the clouds were moving in ragged masses; through an opening I saw a few stars and thought I recognized the belt and dagger of Orion.

"Bill," I said, "I believe that's the south over there, and we should strike out about like this."

"Don't let me stop you," said Bill.

In a little while we came to a steep hillside, where the going was almost impossible through wire and splintered tree stumps. We must have fought our way upwards for over an hour. When we were ready to give up there came from just above the unmistakable bang-bang-bang-bang of a battery of 75s, followed by the clanging rattle of empty shellcases, and in five minutes we found ourselves on the road behind the old Ninth Battery and it was only a step to home.

Peabo looked up as I came into the telephone dugout, and at sight of me his jaw fell.

"Jumping Jehosophat," he gasped, "you look as though you'd been through a concrete mixer!"

By the candlelight I looked myself over. All that was left of my new slicker was a neckband from which hung a few long streamers of cloth. My puttees were gone altogether, and I was mud to the waist and mud from hands to shoulders. It didn't take me long to roll up in dry blankets, and the next day I walked back to the echelon to touch Sergeant Fall for a new uniform.

I like to think of the peaceful mornings and afternoons I spent at the reserve position, or "Camp Putter" as we called it. It was an old German artillery position in a ravine about a mile behind Ostel, where we planned to make a stand if the Germans should break through.* There was a certain amount of work to be done on it, but no one took it seriously. If we got bored, someone would say, "Well, it's a nice day. Let's take a walk over to Camp Putter." The ravine was about a quarter of a mile long, heavily wooded, and with steep sides fifty feet high. The dugouts were roomy and dry and needed little to put them in good repair. At the foot of the ravine was an old grave with a wooden cross saying something about "Deutches helden" on it, and surmounted by an aviator's helmet. There were many curiosities and souvenirs lying around. Once we found a box of German grenades and amused ourselves for an hour throwing them at targets. I remember finding a German gas mask which looked just like a dog's muzzle. There was an ingenious wire cable on pulleys across the ravine, and no end of interesting discoveries to tempt us to explore.

One sunny afternoon that I walked over alone was particularly pleasant. The first buds were showing on the trees, and the birds

* As they did a few days after our departure.

were singing as I strolled along a woodland path towards the ravine. There was an airplane battle going on far up among the clouds, and I remember lying on the grass and watching it as I smoked a cigarette. I suppose its sense of peacefulness and security was the real secret of Camp Putter's attractiveness.

I haven't said enough about the Boche planes. They came over our position often, and we were afraid of them because we thought they would spot us and bring down artillery fire on us. I'm sure I don't know why they never did. We hung up an empty shell case near the rocket station, and when this gong sounded everyone was supposed to stand still without looking up. An upturned human face was supposed to be easily visible from a plane. I don't recall ever having seen anyone fail to look up when a Boche flew over. They even came over at night on bombing flights, and the echelon at Chassemy was bombed several times. We could hear their irregular drone overhead as they passed unseen through the darkness.

It was the night of March nineteenth that the limbers came up the hill from Ostel and pulled the four guns out onto the road. We said goodbye to our French friends of the Ninth Battery, who stood beside the road to see us go. Back we went over the familiar way through Vailly, over the bridge, and across the flat country beyond the Aisne to Chassemy. The echelon was an empty shell with everything packed up and the horses standing ready harnessed. I just had time to have a last look at the old hole where Beck and I spent our first night, before saddling Peggotty and taking my place in the column which was slowly moving out of the woods to the Soissons Road.

# CHAPTER XI

*Over the road to rest billets. The first town, Radonvilliers.*

"March 21, 1918. Radonvilliers. Bien reçu. Supper with farmer's daughter.
Muddy horse line; pottery; barn floor."

AT SOISSONS the Battery again entrained with guns and horses but I don't remember anything about it. Nor do I remember the ride or where we left the train. I have a picture of the column winding along a straight road under a double line of trees in the last rays of the setting sun.

My next recollection is of entering a village street by moonlight. To anyone who has heard a battery of field artillery on the march the sound is unforgettable. The constant drumming of the hoofs, the drivers' sharp words of encouragement to their tired horses, the jingle of the toggle chains, and the hollow rumbling of the ironshod wheels all blend into a monotonous, continuous harmony of sound. I saw a stone fountain in a square and the irregular outline of roofs against the sky. Half the square was in black shadow and half in moonlight. I remember stumbling into a dark barn and falling asleep the minute my back touched the fragrant hay.

By daylight the village of Radonvilliers appeared as a collection of old stone façades lining a paved street. There was a stone bridge with low balustrades over a meadow stream. A dirt road ran out of the square, past a rambling pottery works on the left, and lost itself in the level fields. To the right of this road, in a swampy place outside the town, our rolling stock had been drawn up in rows with picket lines for the horses stretched between the limber wheels.

The kitchen was in a stone-paved barnyard entered through a wide gate on the main street of the town. Each morning as we ate our breakfast a monstrous Percheron horse, driven by a bare-legged girl sitting sideways on his back, pulled an enormous two-wheeled wain down the street. I always wondered what made her wooden shoes stay on. The old farmer who appeared to own the barnyard seemed fascinated by everything we did. He craved razor blades for a safety razor some soldier had given him, and he must have got enough from us to last the rest of his life.

All the people of Radonvilliers were cordial and inquisitive, asking us innumerable questions, following us when we went to groom horses at the picket line, and inviting some of us to meals.

Allen, Peabo, and I went to supper at a farmer's house where we met the rider of the Percheron horse, who proved a fascinating hostess. She seemed sorry to learn that America was not at present overrun by "bisons" and "peaux-rouges," as Fenimore Cooper had led her to believe. She filled us with omelettes and urged us to sweeten our coffee with the few precious lumps of sugar which represented the family's allowance for a month. The next day we stole a bag of sugar from under Joe Wilner's nose and overwhelmed her with the gift of it.

Just when we were beginning to feel at home in Radonvilliers word came to harness and hitch, and again the stone-flagged street echoed to the drumming of field artillery on the march. I could hear the rising hum of it as I galloped ahead to find the road towards La Chaise.

# CHAPTER XII

## *The second town, La Chaise.*
"La Chaise, March 23, 1918. Model farm, broad sunny acres.
Band concert. Hayloft; stallions."

THESE WERE HAPPY DAYS for our Battery, and the reason I think was twofold. We had found the front not at all the bad place we expected, and we knew we were headed for comfortable rest billets far in the rear.

The weather during these days on the road was like the first weeks of May at home, with warm, sunny days and cool, soft nights. The column wound along at an easy pace with frequent halts to ease the harness and to water the horses. It was pleasant to discard helmets and to be able to travel by day without fear of observation. The only unhappy man in the Battery was Henry Derby, who brought up the rear with the spare horses, and I must say they were a choice lot of crowbait. They hung back and dragged their heads and stopped to have the heaves, and it was a wonder they didn't all die on the road. Poor Henry got no benefit from the halts because he had to use them to catch his miserable charges up to the tail of the column.

We reached La Chaise by daylight. The whole Battery found room in the hayloft of an enormous barn built around three sides of a courtyard. The wide hay door of each wing was reached by an iron ladder. The stables were part of a model farm belonging to the château where the officers were quartered. As far as the eye could see were broad, green meadows divided from each other by low hedgerows. In the enclosure across the road were two spirited stallions with flowing manes and tails. It was a joy to watch them frisk and gallop and roll in the luscious grass.

The other batteries of the Regiment were quartered nearby, and

after supper the band gave a concert on the sloping lawn of the château. All the people of the village turned out to dance in the streets,
and they were quickly joined by enthusiastic Americans who made
up in energy what they lacked in skill. Ritchie and I strolled along the
street in the dusk for a final quiet smoke before turning in for a long
sleep in the sweet-smelling hay.

---

## CHAPTER XIII

### *The third town, Thil.*

"Thil, March 25, 1918. Huge barn with plenty of straw."

---

THE NEXT DAY saw another easy stage of our journey towards
Signville, the town reputed to be our resting place. Of Thil, I remember nothing except that there was a brook down a lane where I
took a shivering cold bath.

---

## CHAPTER XIV

### *The fourth town, Brachay.*

"Brachay, March 26, 1918. Doulevant. Pancakes drunk.
Billet in empty house with fireplace."

---

BRACHAY WAS A LITTLE TOWN in a valley. It was early afternoon when the Battery came down a hill into the main square of the
town. I remember there was a brook flowing in a paved bed beside
the street, and we halted near a sort of turnout for driving carts into
the water. Across the street was a public building with a wide flight
of stone steps.

Many of the houses were unoccupied, and the Special Detail was assigned to one of these. It stood on a corner with a door on each street, the slanting one being reached by an outside staircase. Behind the house was a high cemetery wall over which I could see the elaborate beaded wreaths on the monuments. Our house was a very small one, with three or four rooms on the ground floor. There was no furniture in it. The bare walls, tiled floors, and empty stone fireplace were all very clean but not cheery. Our scheme for starting a fire failed when we couldn't find anything to burn.

There must have been a store in Brachay because about bedtime Ritchie came home full of cognac and kept us all awake, talking about how he was going to parade down Michigan Boulevard all alone after the war was over. We kept putting him out, but he always came in the other door, still talking. Finally he quieted down and let us go to sleep. The next morning he was very apologetic, but Beck and I had no mercy on him and teased him about it for a long time afterwards.

---

## CHAPTER XV

*We arrive at Signville. The "rest." News of a big German attack. March orders.*

"Signville, March 27, 1918. 'Permanent' billets. Rimaucourt. Empty house with fireplace."

---

THE MARCH FROM BRACHAY to our final destination was an unusually long one. Late in the afternoon we met Allen waiting for us in a large town called Rimaucourt. We knew he had been sent ahead to arrange for our billets, and we all thought this must be the place. Allen said it was a few miles farther, and not much of a town.

The rain began to fall as darkness came, and the familiar cry of

"When do we eat?" became more and more frequent. After a heart-breaking, long hill we halted in a bleak little town of scattered houses. I was disappointed in our permanent billets but glad to be there. Again we drew an empty house, but before turning in Curtis and I called at several farms to buy straw for beds. We couldn't get any nor were there any eggs for sale, so I suspected that other American troops had been before us. We had to steal what straw we could from the battery wagon and we determined to get more in the morning.

It was still raining when I woke up, and Signville looked as miserable to me by daylight as I had feared it would. The weather had turned suddenly cold, so that when the drivers went to an orchard where the horses had been tied for the night they found them trembling and bedraggled. Our first duty was to untie the whole lot and lead them a mile down the road and back in the rain to warm them up.

When I returned from doing that I found all our barracks bags dumped in the street. I soon located mine in spite of the crowd that was swarming over them. I dragged mine into the stone house where I lived and discovered that a truckload of mail had arrived. Of course this took precedence over everything else, so I joined the line outside the Battery clerk's house and was rewarded with several large packages full of food and a bundle of letters. I just had time to put them in my billet before being called away to groom horses.

All that afternoon I looked forward to an evening of opening mail and making myself comfortable with the treasures in my barracks bag, which I hadn't seen since leaving Coëtquidan. Just after supper, however, I was ordered to report to Regimental Headquarters, so my good time had to be postponed.

As I walked down the hill to a château in a ravine where headquarters was billeted I felt that this long-heralded rest in Signville was not starting out very pleasantly. I found the château easily by its lighted windows and reported to an officer who led me up a stone staircase and along a corridor. He told me to wait and disappeared through a door on the left.

84

I drowsed on a bench at the end of the corridor for hours, getting more and more impatient and wondering what it was all about. Later I was joined by runners from some of the other batteries. When a mud-splattered despatch rider came along the corridor we stopped him at the door and asked him what was up.

"Don't you guys know?" he asked in surprise. "Where have you been for the last week?!"

"Well, spit it out, Buddy; we don't hear no news like you dog robbers," said someone from the bench.

"Why, the goddamned Boches have broke through on a front of fifty miles and we've got to drag ass back into the lines. How do you like them news?"

"The dirty son-of-a-bitches" seemed to be the unanimous opinion. We were still discussing this unexpected calamity when the door opened and an officer came out.

"You will all return to your batteries," he announced, "and say the Regiment is returning to the front. The batteries must be prepared to move at a minute's notice. Battery A will lead the column."

As I climbed the hill in the dark I kept wondering if we would be able to stop the Germans, and I felt a dread in the stomach.

"A hell of a rest this is," I muttered to the falling rain.

---

## CHAPTER XVI

*To the front by forced marches. A night in Neufchâteau.*

"Neufchâteau, March 30, 1918. Rain, no sleep, no food 24 hrs.
Mauvais morale. Hay shed."

---

BEFORE DAWN the Battery was on the road again, and the rain showed no signs of letting up. With nothing to look forward to but the trenches the ride seemed interminable, and we must have covered a considerable distance for we hit a hard pace and drove the horses unmercifully. I don't remember getting anything to eat all day.

At dusk we pulled through the suburbs of Neufchâteau, which looked very bleak in the rain. When we halted in a field Roley Allen, who was riding at my side, burst out in a hysterical tirade of some sort, and I saw his nerve was broken by fatigue. I was perfectly stolid and didn't seem to care what happened. All that was left of Ritchie's customary enthusiasm was a wry smile. Wet to the skin and stiff from hours in the saddle and from cold, we dismounted, fed our horses, rubbed their legs down with hay, and tied them to the picket line. Then, shouldering our saddlebags and rolls, we straggled off down the street in an irregular, demoralized column.

It was dark when we reached a building like a railroad terminus set in a large fenced enclosure. By the light of a few lanterns I could see that it was full of soldiers sleeping on the dirt floor and on bales of hay that were piled almost to the roof in places. There must have been thousands of tons of baled hay in that store-shed. Ritchie and I, who had clung together, climbed up over the rickety footing, narrowly escaping crevasses forty feet deep, until we were at the very top and against the wall at the angle of the roof. We didn't dare unroll our blankets for fear of losing them between the bales, so we lay down in our wet overcoats with our equipment on, and used our blanket rolls for pillows. I put my arm through the strap of my helmet to keep from losing it. I was just dozing off when a whistle shrilled down on the floor, and a harsh voice began yelling, "Everybody up. All out to get the horses under cover."

I could see the shadows shifting across the roof as someone moved about with a lantern, waking people up. I looked at Ritchie. He was asleep, or pretending to be, so I followed his example. Whoever it was must have got all the men he needed without climbing up to our shadowy retreat for the commotion soon died down and I went to sleep in earnest.

# CHAPTER XVII

## *Allain. Dining out.*

"Allain, March 31, 1918. Colombey. Attic of straw loft. Supper with paralytic. Barrage; eggs; rain; bon mor."*

ALTHOUGH RITCHIE AND I had slept cold, we were repaid in the morning by seeing the confusion of those who had opened their blanket rolls and lost their equipment down the cracks of the hay bales. While they were looking for pistols and shoes and puttees in the dark we had only to put on our steel helmets and we were dressed.

After a sketchy breakfast of canned corned beef and hardtack the Regiment took the road. It was still raining, but the heavy showers of the day before had given place to a steady gray drizzle. Again we pushed the horses hard all day, and after passing through the town of Colombey in the late afternoon we followed a wide, level tree-lined road into the main street of Allain about dusk. The horses were picketed and fed and then billets were assigned. The Special Detail drew a comfortable loft full of dry, clean straw.

Ritchie, Peabo, and I went to the rolling kitchen for supper, but on seeing that the rain had stopped and that Allain seemed to be a considerable town we decided to try for something better. We walked along the right-hand side of the street looking for a likely place, and at the second corner we met a woman with a basket of eggs. I asked her if they were for sale, and she said they were, but how could we cook them. Not being satisfied with our answer, she insisted on our coming home with her and she would cook them for us. It was only a few doors away, and when we went in I saw a sad-faced man sitting in an armchair.

"Mon mari est paralyzé depuis mille neufcent quatorze," said the woman by way of introduction, and to him she rattled something off

* Bon morale.

87

so fast that all I understood were the words "amis américains." While she bustled about preparing a meal, we sat down and talked to the paralytic. He seemed to welcome the chance of talking with us and asked many questions about the American troops. As we described our training camps at home, and the two million men already under arms, his face lighted up in hope as he murmured, "On les aura, enfin on les aura!"

During our hearty supper of omelettes, bread, and wine we talked with the greatest friendliness and when the time came for us to leave, our hosts refused to let us pay.

We walked back through the dark streets and climbed into our loft in a greatly improved frame of mind and settled down for a luxurious warm sleep in our blankets with our shoes off and our shirts well searched for cooties. Before I fell asleep I thought I heard the distant sound of a barrage, but it might have been thunder.

When we woke up it was raining again. We were surprised to see the forenoon wearing away without any sign of harnessing. We took advantage of the opportunity to groom our horses, overhaul our equipment, read our shirts, and get up to date on our sleep. Late in the afternoon I was arranging my blankets on the straw and gloating over the idea of another comfortable night when I heard Storer's whistle blowing outside in the rain.

"All out, A Battery; harness and hitch," he yelled, and I heard the whistle grow fainter as he passed on to the next billet.

"Did you ever notice what a disagreeable voice Storer has?" asked Ritchie, who was yawning and pulling on his wet boots. Beck glared at him through his spectacles and cackled bitterly.

"I guess *this* isn't your night for parading down Michigan Boulevard, is it?" he said, and ducked under the straw just in time to escape the boot that Ritchie tossed at his head.

As our column turned the corner out of Allain's main street our hostess called, "Bonne chance" from her doorstep and I saw her husband smiling through the windowpane at us and nodding his head.

# CHAPTER XVIII
## *A night march in the rain.*

"Bois l'Evêque, April 1, 1918. Night march; black; steady rain. Blunders of Plattsburgers. 'April fool.' No sleep. Low morale."

WHAT A MARCH that was! The rain came down in vertical sheets; the night was so black we couldn't tell whether we were riding in a forest or a desert, and the road was heavy with mud. The cannoneers, slogging along on foot, had to keep a hand on the nearest stirrup leather to avoid walking off the road into the ditch. Hour after hour we toiled along with the steady patter of the rain against our steel helmets. Often I dismounted and stumbled along half-asleep to bring back the circulation in my legs. Once when the Battery halted to breathe the horses at the foot of a hill I flopped down on a pile of crushed stone beside the road and was sound asleep in a minute. Peggotty woke me by stepping on my stomach as the column started and dragged me to my feet by the bridle, through which I had put my arm.

Our army slickers, of some waterproofed material, were soon wet through and the rain quickly penetrated to the skin. As I sat on my horse I could feel drops of water running down the middle of my back, and from each side of my slicker a little stream emptied into my boots.

Once, after many hours the column halted and I thought we had arrived. It was past midnight so the date was April first. As the order came to resume the march and the weary men kicked their horses into life, some wit yelled, "April fool."

On a long hill many of the horses fell and lay in their harness, too spent to respond to any effort of ours to get them on their feet. There was nothing to do but cut them free, drag them into the ditch and end their suffering with a bullet through the head.

89

Towards 2 a.m. the column again halted, and this time the order was passed back to pull off to the side of the road and unhitch. I threw my saddle, saddlebags, and blanket roll down in the dark and led Peggotty towards the head of the column where there was a gate on the left, with drivers leading their horses in. I followed them and came to a watering trough from which Peggotty drank. Then I led her into a large cavalry stable lighted by a lantern, and found a vacant place to hitch her. There was a sort of pungent warmth in the stables from the steaming horses, and I looked for a place to sleep but every inch was occupied by horses. Curtis said he knew where we were supposed to sleep, and together we went out into the rain.

"What kind of a place is this, Stan?" I asked, and he said, "A frog camp of some kind, Camp l'Evêque, or Camp Beck, or something like that. The goddamned Plattsburgers were supposed to ride ahead and get us billeted, but they've fudged everything up and don't even know where to sleep themselves."

I haven't said much about these synthetic officers who were assigned to our Regiment from the Officers' Training Camp at Plattsburg, New York, because I never came into contact with them. They were not held in great respect by the troops in France, and it was a standing joke at the front to ask, "What supplies came up on the caissons tonight?" The answer was to the effect "A case of jam, two bags of flour, and an issue of Plattsburgers!" Of course, some of them were all right.

Curtis and I reached a wooden shed open at both ends, where a few men were sleeping on the floor. As someone walked by with a lantern I could see Ritchie asleep with a puddle of water spreading from his clothes. Curtis and I lay down beside him. I lay on my back with my steel helmet for a pillow, and at first the comfort of lying down was so great that I fell asleep. I soon woke up though, when the cold air had chilled my wet clothes, and lay shivering with my eyes shut, half-asleep and half-awake.

At 4 o'clock the whistles blew and I saw lanterns moving about outside. With chattering teeth Ritchie and I got up and, seeing a lighted doorway, stumbled through the mud to a shed where Wilner and Lorenzen were making coffee. We got some coffee and hardtack, and as we thawed by the warm fire several more bedraggled men came in. One of them was Storer who took Ritchie and me aside.

"We're headed for a town called Brulez," he said; "and you fellows saddle right up and start ahead. Find the way through Toul and be ready to take the column through. For God's sake, don't pull any boners." I was too wretched even to cuss.

We somehow found our way out to the road and walked along beside the line of carriages* to where we had left our saddles. Although it was still raining, the darkness was less intense out on the road and I could see the black shapes of things against the sky. I felt around with my feet for the saddle and suddenly slipped into a ditch up to my knees in running water. In the ditch was my saddle where I had thrown it two hours before, and Ritchie's was a few feet upstream.

"You get the horses," I said, "while I dredge our stuff out of the river." We were soon saddled and moving down the road in the growing light.

---

## CHAPTER XIX

*A morning ride. Adventure with chasseurs. Brulez.*

"Brulez, Apr. 2. Toul. Pancakes and I advance scouts. Rain, cold, mud;
billet with French; sleep."

---

BEFORE RITCHIE AND I got to the bottom of the long hill it was light enough to see a few huddled shapes of dead horses in the ditch beside the road and an occasional wagon which had been abandoned in the mud. Then we struck a level stretch, clattered through a clump

* Carriage: the generic name for any horse-drawn thing on wheels.

of phantom houses and over a wooden bridge. From the surface of a weedy stream at the right of the road small brown clouds of mist were rolling up.

The light grew as we cantered up a hill, and when we reached the top we stood in a slanting ray of sunlight. How our spirits rose with the warmth of exercise and the sun! We trotted along talking and laughing with the sun growing warmer on our backs, and when we saw an estaminet on the left we pulled up and dismounted.

"Do you think we can spare the time?" I said. "The Battery may have started."

"To hell with the Battery," said Pancakes, and we went in and had a drink of cognac. Once more on the road our spirits were lighter than ever and we even agreed that it was a pleasant war.

We soon entered the outskirts of Toul where we found a large crossroad beside a canal. We asked a Frenchman the way to Brulez, and he said, "À gauche." This took us to the business section of the city, and we agreed that a back road would be better for the Battery. After an hour of inquiring and riding about, we satisfied ourselves of the best route and galloped back to meet the head of the column.

We hadn't long to wait—just long enough for a drink apiece at an estaminet while the other held the horses and watched up the road. The sun was out warm and bright by now and the column clanked through the streets of Toul and out onto the dirt road on the other side, with the men calling greetings to the bystanders and the horses steaming as their wet skins dried in the sun.

Mile after mile rolled by, and about sunset we sighted Brulez. It was built on the side of a steep hill, and all the houses faced crosswise so that we could see no gables but only the sides of red roofs rising one above another, themselves like big red shingles on a gigantic slanting roof. A little way outside the town was a level field on the right of the road. Here we parked the guns and wagons and established the picket line. The field was boggy in places with tufts of coarse marsh grass growing in scattered patches.

On entering Brulez I saw that the main street was built up the side of the hill and was lined by red-roofed houses close together. I was surprised to hear a strange bugle call, much faster and somewhat different from any of ours. Farther on I saw a lance bearing a blue pennon leaning against a housefront and several French cavalrymen sitting about in the sun. One was polishing a sabre. He told me his troop had been quartered in the town for three days and expected to go up to the lines at any time.

I found our billet on the right of the street in a long narrow room up a flight of wooden stairs. The left side of the room had been partitioned off into bunk spaces by nailing boards on edge about two feet apart and parallel to each other, the space between being filled with macerated straw. I knew from experience that such straw was full of lice, and I was right this time but could do nothing about it.

After supper Peabo and I walked down to the picket line to see that our horses were comfortable for the night, and then we strolled up the hill exchanging greetings with the French cavalrymen we met. Towards the upper end of the street we stopped to listen to sounds coming from a low-doored café on the left. There was singing and the clink of glasses.

"That's us," said Peabo, and walked through the doorway. We went along a dark corridor, and on opening the door at the end of it I saw a scene that I have always remembered. It was a low-ceiled, smoky room, the corners in dark shadow, and seated about a long table lighted by candles were a dozen French chasseurs very much at their ease. At the head of the table, facing us, sat a man with a black beard and very white teeth, a wine cup in his hand, with which he seemed to be beating time to a song he was singing. It reminded me of the lines from "A Dutch Picture":*

> They sit there in the shadow and shine
> Of the flickering fire of the winter night;
> Figures in color and design

* Longfellow's "Birds of Passage, Flight the Fifth," second poem, "A Dutch Picture."

Like those of Rembrandt of the Rhine,
Half darkness, and half light.

As Peabo and I hesitated on the threshold they all rose to their feet and, holding their cups towards us, they swung into the refrain of the song their leader had been singing, some stirring march of the French Army. At the same time, the two nearest pulled up chairs from the shadows and made places for us at the table, and someone filled us each a glass from the bottles which were passed around from hand to hand. As the song ended I raised my glass and said, "Vive la France!"

Peabo and I found the rollicking cordial atmosphere entirely to our taste, and we spent the whole evening with our new friends. I remember that later, after much talk and laughing, the bearded man stood up as if to make a speech, but instead he began singing "Madelon," and I was surprised to find that he was making up the words to fit us. He sang about the "caporals américains sont dans la guerre," each verse being part of our imaginary adventures in France; and at the end of each stanza the whole table, with smiling faces turned in our direction and glasses raised, roared out the chorus.

Peabo and I reluctantly took our leave after much cordial hand-shaking, to a chorus of "Bonne chance, mes vieux" from the open door. Lying on my straw that night, the rollicking refrain of "Madelon" persisted in running through my head until I fell asleep.

# CHAPTER XX

*Our second echelon. The regulars at Rangeval.*
*The Toul sector.*

"Rangeval, April 4, 1918. Echelon; regulars; brickyard. Carneyville."

IN THE MORNING we found the street running with water after an all-night rain and the picket line turned into a quagmire. Several of the horses had become bogged in the mud and were so exhausted that we had to shoot them. They all were in such dreadful shape that it would take hours with a currycomb to find out if they were horses or crocodiles. Nevertheless, the drivers succeeded in hauling most of them out of the mud and the Battery resumed its march towards the front. I remember nothing about it except that the sky was overcast all day with a fine drizzle of misty rain.

The next clear recollection I have is Rangeval. Looking along a level road with flat, bare country on both sides, I saw a group of spreading low buildings with what looked like a factory chimney towering above them. The chimney proved to belong to a brickyard with a large court beside it. Beyond was a gray stone monastery, and there were a few straggling sheds and houses between. In the court-yard of the brick factory were a number of artillery hitches driven by men from the First Division. They drew aside to let us pass, and our Battery halted in the courtyard. The ground floor of the factory had been used as a stable, with picket lines stretched the long way from pillar to pillar. We tied our horses here, and the men found quarters on the floor above. The Seventh Field Artillery were moving out and they were leaving several sick horses behind. Among them was Peanuts, who became my singlemount when his saddle sore healed.

We were in such a hustle caring for the horses and getting settled that it was dark before I really had a chance to look around and then it was too late. While I was looking for a place to sleep I was ordered to get my blanket roll and accompany the first platoon guns to the front. I found the cannoneers in the courtyard talking with two sections of drivers from the First Division. It seemed that they were going to take our two guns up and bring two of their own back on the return trip. As I had no idea of where we were going or how long I might stay I decided to go dismounted, so I entrusted my horse and saddle bags to Curtis, put on my overcoat, helmet, pistol belt, and mask and returned to the courtyard just as the little column was turning to the left onto the road.

## CHAPTER XXI

*At the front again. Shellfire and gas in Rambucourt.*
*The swamp position.*

"Rambucourt (3721387)* April 4. Front; night; mud. Xivray. Marvoisin.
Beaumont. Mandres. Narrow-gauge."

THE MIST must have cleared, for I remember seeing flares low in the sky on the right as I walked along with the cannoneers behind the two gun carriages. Soon the road curved to the right and entered some dark woods. We followed the sound of the horses ahead and hoped the drivers knew where they were going. After a long time we emerged from the woods and started across a sort of open plain where the going was very rough. The road, if it was one, was full of holes and soft muddy ruts. I could see flares straight ahead. Soon the road took us up a gentle rise, at the top of which I saw the silhouette

---

* The numbers refer to the locations of two battery positions designated by their map coordinates.

of houses against the light of the flares. The drivers halted at the top of the rise and dismounted.

Several men came out of the darkness at our right, among them Roley Allen and one of our officers who had gone up the night before to reconnoiter. While the others were engaged in pulling the two First Division guns from their gun pits and substituting ours I had a chance to ask Allen where we were.

"This is Rambucourt," he said. "All the country around is nothing but mud, and the town is the only solid place with protection for artillery. It's a sweet place, too. It's only two hundred meters from the infantry, and the Boches bang hell out of it all the time. We had a sweet time last night getting caught on the street in a gas attack. Come on and I'll show you a dugout." He led the way into a trench at the right of the road, and by the sounds I could tell the cannoneers were at work in the gun pits somewhere ahead. We passed a battery of French 90s and just beyond them came to a curtain hanging over a doorway in the left wall of the trench. At the bottom of a steep flight of steps Allen pushed aside another curtain and led the way into a small dugout lighted by a candle stuck on top of a switchboard, where a telephone man sat on an empty shell box.

"Well, Buddy," he said, "this sure is a hell of a place for a redleg,* and I wish you guys joy of it."

While I was admiring the solid construction of the dugout, and especially the ceiling formed of I-beams laid side by side, I heard the most infernal racket of Klaxons and horns. The din seemed to start far off and get louder and louder till I could hardly hear the telephone man when he explained: "It's those dizzy bastards down Beaumont way starting a gas alarm. Every time they hear a gas shell come over they start worrying, and the noise spreads all up the line. Just stick your nose outside and see if you smell anything."

I climbed up to the outer curtain, but I smelled no gas. There

* Redleg: artilleryman in the regular army. Their dress uniform had a red stripe down the leg.

seemed to be some shelling going on far to the right, which probably explained the alarm. The racket had ceased in Rambucourt and, as I heard the Klaxons growing fainter to the left, I wondered how far the warning would travel before it died out. Apparently, the drivers had departed with the First Division guns as there was no sound from the road. As I turned to reenter the dugout, I heard a sudden whine and "plunk," followed by several more in quick succession.

"I guess they're shelling around here now," I reported to the telephone man, "but they sound like all duds."

"Them ain't duds, Buddy; them's gas shells," was his answer, but the rest of it was drowned out by the sudden clamor of the Klaxons just over our heads. I wanted to ask him more about gas attacks, but he had started testing his lines so I backed up the stairs and cautiously put my head out of the curtain. This time I was rewarded by a stinging sensation in my nose and throat and a faint odor of chocolate. Except for the sound of desultory gas shells, Rambucourt had lapsed into silence but the alarm had been taken up by the neighboring towns and I could hear it dying away far to the right and left. There were bursts of machine gun fire just in front of us, and the flares that went up were so close that I judged they came from our own infantry lines and that the doughboys were afraid the gas might be the forerunner of a night raid on our trenches. I felt very uncomfortable and was relieved to see Allen and the telephone man sitting peacefully in the dugout when I went in.

"There's gas out there all right," I said carelessly. "Shouldn't we put on our masks?"

"What do you think them gas curtains is for?" grunted the telephone man. "You're all right as long as you stay in here. Nobody goes out when they're gassing the place."

"But suppose a feller was to get taken short," I objected, remembering the usual physical manifestations of nervousness such as I was beginning to feel.

"Piss in one of them empty shell cases in the corner, Buddy," said

98

the imperturbable telephone man, "and chuck it out the door after you're through."

There was nothing for Allen and me to do that night so we made ourselves comfortable in a couple of wire bunks in the dugout and went to sleep.

Once I was wakened by a crash immediately above my head and a jarring of the whole dugout. I could hear stones and dirt sliding down the steps, and I judged there had been a direct hit on the roof. The telephone man was sitting at his switchboard as if nothing had happened.

"More gas shells, Buddy?" I asked sleepily.

"Naw, high explosive," he said, and I rolled over and went to sleep again. If anything else happened in Rambucourt that night, I never knew it.

In the morning I came up out of the stuffy dugout into the trench, and stood breathing the fresh air as I looked around. I could see that we were about sixty yards from the road, and every few feet there was a dugout entrance guarded by a gas curtain. All of them were extremely strong, having eight or ten feet of iron rails, concrete slabs, and sandbags on their roofs. The shell that had waked me up had only blown away some sandbags and scattered dirt into the trench. It was probably a light caliber, perhaps a '77. I walked along the trench and found the gun pits almost as strongly built as the dugouts. The first two were occupied by our first and second sections, and the others by strangers from the Seventh Field. Beyond was another battery of 90s and I examined it curiously as I had never seen these antiquated guns before. They had no recoil mechanism like the 75, but rolled back on their wheels at every shot, and had to be aimed anew each time. They fired a 90-millimeter projectile which was put into the breech first, and a little silk bag of powder was put in after it. After talking to the French gunners for a few minutes, I walked back past the Battery and out onto the road.

Behind me I could see the road over which we had come until it entered a distant patch of woods. In front, about fifty yards from where I stood, was the first battered house of Rambucourt, and most of the other houses were farther to the right, disappearing over the crest of a low ridge. To get a better view I walked up the road to the top and turned to the right down what looked like the principal street. It was lined by ruined houses, and on the left was a church with the belfry shot away. The street was deserted except for a few doughboys lounging near the entrances of cellars where gas curtains had been hung. Outside one of these entrances I saw an empty shell case hanging by a wire, with a short length of iron pipe to hit it with as a gas warning. This must have been part of the infernal din I had heard during the night. Beyond the edge of Rambucourt the road ran parallel with the front to the next town of Beaumont, about a mile away, and beyond that I could see the square steeple of the church in Mandres. As I walked farther down the street one of the doughboys yelled at me not to go past the corner. I went over and sat down beside him and asked him why not.

"Because that's in sight of the Boche balloons," he said. "Look between those two houses and you'll see them."

I crossed the street and got a new outlook towards the front, where I counted nine German observation balloons, the one just before Rambucourt so close that I could plainly see the observer's basket. Turning back, I noticed several places where high camouflage nets had been stretched between the houses on the side of the road towards the balloons.

"This way, Buddy," yelled the doughboy from across the street, as he and his companions suddenly ducked out of sight down some cellar stairs. At the same moment, I heard the approaching whine of a shell. It was too far to cross the street, so I flattened myself against the building at the corner, partly sheltered by a doorway. "Crash!" went the shell, as a cloud of smoke and rubbish blossomed among the buildings a few doors down and a house wall fell forward into the street. While I was making up my mind for a dash in the direction of the cellar, three more shells exploded in about the same place. I cowered in my doorway, afraid to move, and watched black smoke slowly spreading over the roofs. Now's my chance, I thought, and made a break from my doorway, when again came the terrifying whine. I dropped flat where I was and held my breath. "Crash," came the explosion, but this time behind me. I knew I couldn't stay in the open street, so I jumped up and ran blindly back towards the end of town where the Battery was as fast as I could step. One more shell burst, but I didn't stop or look around till I got to the end of the street. There I saw a crowd of men looking around the corner of a ruined wall, and I made for them.

"Well," said someone, "you must be in a hurry for a doughnut. There they are." And he pointed to a gas curtain hung over a cellar door. I went in and found myself in a dimly lighted vault about twenty feet square, with a rough counter across one end, where several men were being served with doughnuts and coffee by a Salvation Army man and his wife. I ate two doughnuts and drank a cup of hot coffee, and then reached in my pocket to pay for them.

"We don't take money from the soldiers," the woman said with a smile.

"This ain't the Y.M.C.A., Buddy," growled a doughboy next to me. "They're all in Paris, and this here's the front."

That night the remaining two guns of our Battery came up and we saw the last of the First Division artillery.

All I remember about the next day was the uncertainty of meals. Our kitchen was some distance back on the other side of the road, and there was no protected place to sit and eat there so as soon as we got our mess kits and cups filled we would start back to our dugouts, balancing them carefully as we picked our way over the rough road. At the first whine of a shell everyone would slide for the ditch and our mess kits would clatter in all directions.

I think it was late that afternoon that Storer took me across the fields behind Rambucourt and showed me a new position the Battery would occupy that night. He pointed out that the ground was very soft, and asked me if I could find a route across it for the guns before it got dark. I thought I could, so he went back to Rangeval to get the horses and limbers, while I began a critical inspection of the possibilities.

The new position was in an empty field about half a mile behind Rambucourt and slightly to the right. The intervening country consisted of perfectly flat fields, with clumps of bushes, thickets, and large puddles or shallow ponds scattered over it. The only road was the one by which we had reached Rambucourt, which, after leaving the town, swung to the right and ran parallel to the front through Beaumont to Mandres. I could see Mandres about two miles to the right front, but the ground behind it looked even more marshy than that behind Rambucourt. I at once rejected the possibility of taking this long route through Mandres, and considered the chance of pulling back on the road behind Rambucourt and cutting straight across country from there. I found a way of doing this that was feasible, but it offered no advantages over the direct cross-country route from Rambucourt and was much longer. So I began working my way towards Rambucourt, testing the ground for solid spots and marking them with sticks which I cut from the bushes. For part of the way I found I could use a Decauville track which ran up from the rear through dense woods and, passing close to the new position, crossed a field and entered a smaller clump of woods in front. The guns could never have negotiated these woods, so I swung off to the left and skirted along their edge. From the corner of the woods, the fields ran flat to the back of Rambucourt, so I worked along, planting my sticks on the patches of solid ground till I reached the town.

Here I got an old newspaper from the Salvation Army dugout, and retraced my steps, tying a piece of paper to the top of each stick and planting more sticks between till I thought they were close enough together to be visible at night. In some places I was able to straighten out a very crooked stretch by shifting the sticks to another patch of fairly solid ground, but when I was done the route looked crooked enough.

By the time I got back to Rambucourt the last light had faded, so all I could do was wait for Storer to come up with the limbers. I had some very unpleasant thoughts during this wait. What if the night got so dark that I couldn't see my sticks? Suppose the guns bogged in some place that I had thought safe? They would have to be abandoned and would be in plain sight of the German balloons when morning came. At last I heard the jingle of harness coming up the road, and as the four limbers swung past the end of the trench and turned to the right towards the gun pits, Storer dismounted beside me.

"Well, what's the dope?" he asked.

"I've got a way marked," I answered, "but it's awful twisty, and there's plenty of soft spots in it. I think they can be crossed at a gallop, but if a gun should stop in the wrong place, we're licked."

"What are you going to do about it then?"

"Well, I've got to be on foot to find my sticks," I said, "and I could post men along the easy part, and keep far enough in front to tell the drivers when to gallop. How soon are you starting?"

"As soon as the Lord'll let us," said Storer. "Take Curtis and who you need and go ahead."

As we started across the shell holes back of Rambucourt, I was relieved to find that I could see two sticks ahead in spite of the darkness. The ground, however, looked solid black. I ran along, leaving two men at intervals, until I came to the first patch of really solid ground, where I stopped and waited. I soon heard the horses coming, and when the first team loomed up in front of me, I yelled, "Whoa!" They stopped and the three others closed up behind. Storer was riding at the head of the first hitch.

"Here's where you have to gallop," I told him. "Give me a little start, and then keep going as long as I'm ahead of you." With that, I began to run along the line of sticks, falling and scrambling up whenever my foot sank in the boggy mud, and behind me I could hear the horses panting and the drivers urging them on as they gained on me. My lungs were bursting when I reached the next piece of dry ground, and I hardly had breath to yell at the drivers to stop and rest their horses. I was rewarded when Storer rode up and told me all four guns had got safely across. After repeating this performance two or three times more, we arrived at the corner of the woods, and from there to the Decauville track and down it to the position was a simple matter.

My responsibility was now ended, and while the guns were being put into the gun pits and Curtis was leading the limbers back to Rambucourt, I looked around for a place to sleep. By daylight I had noticed that the position was covered by a huge wire camouflage net stretched tight about six feet above the ground and pegged down around the edges, but I had not wasted any time exploring it. I now crawled under the edge of the net and entered a shallow trench which grew deeper as it approached the other end of the net. I was soon up to my knees in water, so I turned back and discovered a dugout entrance with what looked like a fire hose coming out of it. I went down three or four steps and lighted a match and was soon joined by Beck and Peabo who started to fix it up for a telephone central. The water on the floor was about two feet deep but around the sides were wire bunks, one above another, and only the lower bunks were flooded. In the middle of the floor was a big pump with the handle sticking out of the water. While I threw my blankets into a top bunk Beck began attaching wires to his portable switchboard, selecting them from a bunch of tagged ends that entered the dugout along the ceiling. Before he had finished I was asleep.

The next morning I heard a clanking sound and found two men working the pump. They had lowered the level of the water to about a foot so I got down from my bunk and waded outside. The trench ran the length of the position, and at the farther end it contained about six feet of water. Two dugouts at this end appeared to be flooded level with the tops of the doors. In front of the trench the four shallow gun pits were equally spaced and the net almost touched their shields. There was a removable panel in the net in front of each muzzle. After looking the layout over I was perplexed to understand how anyone could live there. The telephone dugout was the only possible place for anyone to sleep, and four or five men were all it could hold.

I was enlightened when I crawled out from under the net and followed the Decauville track about two hundred yards back into the woods. Just inside the edge of the woods was a cluster of crude tar-paper shacks built on the mud on both sides of the track, and here I found most of the Battery eating breakfast. After breakfast I went exploring around and followed the edge of the woods about a mile till I came to the Rambucourt Road. There I turned and followed the Decauville track deeper into the woods. Here I ran into some engineer outfit building concrete emplacements for heavy guns. They told me that if I followed the track far enough I would come out on a road leading to Corneyville and Rangeval. Dinner time was approaching, so I took their word for it.

We stayed in this position, 387 as it was called, for a week, waiting for the Germans to start an attack, in which case their infantry would have overrun Rambucourt at the first rush and it would have been up to us to stop them. But nothing happened. We drank the water in the deep part of the trench, at first using it only in coffee, but later drinking it freely. It was brackish but seemed to contain no taint of gas. I continued to sleep in the telephone dugout and so made myself morally responsible for a certain amount of telephone work. Some of the infantry wires had been going dead without any obvious reason and it was suspected that Germans were coming over at night and cutting them, as they easily could do because our infantry lines were very lightly held by a chain of patrol posts instead of in the usual manner. For this reason orders had been issued to shoot anyone seen tampering with the wires unless he wore a red brassard on his arm.

I remember one solitary expedition I made to Mandres—"Mandrees" we called it—to find a break in the telephone line. It was a clear, warm afternoon, with beautiful visibility, so the seven menacing balloons appeared to be growing in our very dooryard, and every detail of the ruined houses in Rambucourt stood out in sharp light and shadow. As I followed the wire behind Beaumont I was walking in deep green grass dotted with buttercups. In the most marshy places the wire was held a foot or so above the ground by short stakes, but the rest of the way it lay in the grass. There were no trenches and very little barbwire in these fields. Beyond a clump of small woods I got a clear view of Beaumont, standing on a little elevation, and to the right of the last house I could see the road running towards Mandres.

Mandres had been in sight all the time, a squatty square belfry surrounded by red roofs clustered in a hollow. About now I found the break in the wire and repaired it, but instead of turning back I decided to keep on and have a look at the town. Skirting a large marsh behind the woods and crossing about a half mile of fields, I came to the road back of Mandres. The first thing I saw was a wrecked ration cart and a dead horse lying in the road. I turned to the left and around the next bend found an ambulance lying on its side with the rear end shot away. When I was about a hundred yards from the town shells began exploding among the houses. Two infantrymen came running up the road and stopped for breath when they got to where I was standing.

"Got a cigarette, Buddy?" one of them asked.

"Sure," I said. "Where you from?"

"Seicheprey," he replied, "and it's one nasty little place. Nothing but water and rats. Why? Ya going down there?"

"No, I guess this is good enough for me," I said. "They seem to have their eye on this piece of road here."

"Hell, that's nothing," remarked the doughboy. "You oughta see the windy place the other side of Mandres. Dead Man's Curve,

they call it. Believe me, they's not much gets by there in daytime."
With that, they resumed their way and left me undecided what to
do. The shells were still falling in Mandres with monotonous regularity, and finally discretion got the better of curiosity and I turned
back through the fields and reached the Battery in time for supper.

Not much work was accomplished at 387, although there was
plenty to be done and the men always seemed to keep busy. Pump-
ing out the water was certainly a losing game for it seeped into the
trenches and dugouts almost as fast as it was removed. However, the
position remained undiscovered by the Germans and no shells came
near enough to bother us. It seemed a miracle that no one was hit,
living in tar paper shacks on the surface of the ground without protection of any kind, but so it was, and moving day found us all
intact.

It was the evening of April 12th when the limbers came up just
after dusk. To avoid going all the way up to Rambucourt and then
back across the fields, the way the guns had come, they had followed
the edge of the woods around from the Rambucourt Road* and
halted the other side of the Decauville track from the position. We
had pulled the guns out of the position by hand and were all ready
for them. The gun trails were no sooner hitched to the limbers than
I heard shells whine and explode about fifty yards away with the
dull plunk characteristic of gas. Immediately I began to smell the
prickly chocolate odor, and as more shells dropped, it kept getting
stronger. A man leading the horses pushed his way up to where I stood
near the woods adjusting my gas mask, and started yelling my name.
I went to meet him and found it was Curtis with my horse, Peanuts.

"Here, take him," he yelled, "I've got troubles enough of my
own." I couldn't say anything with my mask on, so I grabbed the
bridle and felt under Peanut's neck where his gas mask should be. I
found it, and mostly by feeling I managed to pull the baglike mask

* I.e., the route I had considered for bringing the guns from Rambucourt to 387. The
ground was drier now than when I had first explored it.

out of its case and fasten it over Peanut's nose in spite of his struggles. He apparently thought I was trying to murder him. By the time I was mounted, the guns were in motion and I didn't wait to say goodbye to the old position.

With the gas shells bursting closer, we urged the horses to a trot and the guns went lumbering over the uneven ground with the cannoneers hanging on behind to keep up. After a few hundred yards we were glad to stop and take off our masks for a real breath of air, and the horses seemed to appreciate getting rid of theirs too.

A horse in a gas mask looks like pictures I have seen of sea elephants, with a floppy proboscis hanging down in front.

A few days of sun had dried out the ground enough so that we got the guns onto the road without much trouble. Turning to the left, we pushed through the woods and, passing through Rangeval, kept on going towards the west.

---

## CHAPTER XXII

### "Peanuts." The echelon at Boncourt.

"Boncourt, April 13, 1918. Echelon. Forced march. No food.
No sleep. 30 minutes' notice."

---

THE WHOLE NIGHT was spent in a forced march during which I had my first chance to test Peanuts. He delighted me with his sudden bursts of speed when I wanted to ride to the head of the column with a message, and his inexhaustible energy. When we pulled into the town of Boncourt at seven o'clock in the morning, he still danced along with a jaunty little single-foot step as if he had just left the stables.

Boncourt was built on the side of a hill with an upper and a lower road. We came in over the cobblestones of the lower road and along between rows of houses until we came to an angle at the far end of town, where an acute left turn brought us onto the upper road. A hundred yards along this we halted and parked the carriages in a sloping field above the road. A row of wooden sheds at the upper end of the field served as stables. I rode Peanuts bareback down to a watering trough in the center of the town and, after giving him a feed of oats, was very glad to find the rolling kitchen doing business in the courtyard of an empty house.

The soup gun, chow wagon, or rolling kitchen, as it was variously called, deserves a word of description. The main part of it was a two-wheeled cart containing a firebox and grate in the center, surrounded by metal containers for hot food and covered with a flat iron top on which broiling or frying could be done. A three-foot stovepipe gave it a far-fetched resemblance to a gun, which was increased by the fact that it had a sort of two-wheeled limber on which the cook sat to drive the horses. The hind part was attached to the limber by lunettes and pintle just as the guns were attached to their limbers. The great advantage of the soup gun was that hot food could be prepared in it while on the march so as to be ready for the men as soon as they arrived at their destination. The cooks did not shine in horsemanship, however, and the unwieldy thing was forever breaking down or getting stuck in the mud or taking a wrong turn, so that usually someone had to go back and look for it when it was most needed.

There were a good many troops of other outfits in the town, and from them I was surprised to learn that although Boncourt was in range of the German guns, most of the townspeople were still living there. I had very little chance to look around, for before I had even taken my blanket roll off my saddle I was ordered to ride up to the front with one of the officers to learn the way by daylight.

# CHAPTER XXIII

## On high ground. A new kind of shellfire.
## Our first man killed.

"Louiville 284, April 13, 1918. Front. St. Miheil Saliant.
Joe Zwinge killed. Rafales. Nerve-trying."

PEANUTS WAS far more enthusiastic than I was, for all I wanted to do was get a little sleep. Leaving Boncourt at the opposite end from which we had entered, we trotted along a sandy road which led us across a bare ridge and then swung to the right around the shoulder of a hill. The general conformation of the ground suggested smooth, round-topped waves on the ocean. There were a few patches of woods, but they consisted of bushes rather than trees. When the road reached a place where it followed the crest of a ridge straight towards the sound of the guns I caught sight of several German balloons, and again had the disagreeable sensation of being watched.

Just before we reached a patch of scrub-pine woods the road forked and we took the right fork, descending into a basinlike hollow. Riding through this we entered a wide ravine between two steep, bare-faced hills. The officer, I forget who he was, said he thought Battalion Headquarters would be near the top of the left-hand hill and our position would be on the right-hand one. As we followed the road up the ravine I saw that the two hills were connected by a curve of higher ground, closing us up in a sort of sandy cul-de-sac. The road bore a little to the right and then began climbing the slope in a series of hairpin turns. We negotiated them easily enough, but I couldn't help wondering how the guns would be able to do it. At the summit of the hill the road ran along level ground behind the edge of more scrub-pine woods, passed a French battery of 90s, and then, after crossing about five hundred yards of

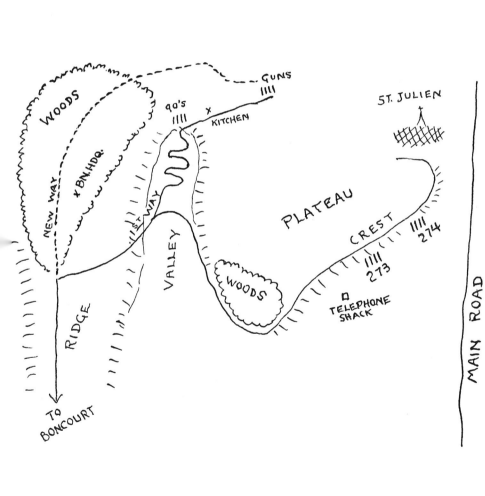

BOCHE BALLOONS

INFANTRY FRONT LINE

WOODS

NEW WAY

x BN. HDQ.

ST. WAY

90's
||||

GUNS
||||

x
KITCHEN

RIDGE

VALLEY

WOODS

PLATEAU

CREST

||||
273

||||
274

ST. JULIEN

TELEPHONE
SHACK

TO
BONCOURT

MAIN ROAD

open hilltop, reached an empty battery position. It was slightly below the crest of the hill but I could see the Boche balloons, so I suppose it was in sight of them. The officer left me to get acquainted with the place, and rode back to Boncourt for the guns.

The position was of the usual pattern, with four gun pits connected by a trench running behind them. This trench was dug in hard, chalky soil, reminding me of the Chemin-des-Dames. Opening off the trench were several beautiful dry dugouts, not very deep, but strongly protected by alternate layers of iron and crushed stone several feet thick above the roof. I recognized the telephone dugout by the wires entering it and left my blankets there; then I rode Peanuts back to the woods and tied him to a tree. Those woods looked so much like the woods I had seen just before we took the right fork of the road that I wondered if they might not really be the same, and I determined to find out the first chance I got.

Walking back to the position I was impressed by the great number of recent shell holes, and by the fact that they were all shallow, as if the ground were too hard for the shells to penetrate before they exploded. The view in front of the position was just a field curving out of sight. To the rear, another range of hills was visible across a narrow valley. Satisfied that I had the lay of the land, I arranged my blankets in the best bunk in the telephone dugout and, after stopping to talk to the Frenchmen at the 90 position, mounted Peanuts and started slowly back down the road to meet the guns.

A heavy mist had settled during the afternoon, so I heard them coming before I could see them. As the first hitch came up to me I turned and rode along beside them. Storer was in charge, as I remember, and the officer who had come up with me was showing them the way. The guns were far apart on the road to minimize the danger in case of heavy shelling, but when the leading gun stuck at the first hairpin turn the others all closed up. Storer told me to ride back to Boncourt and bring up the eight caissons full of ammunition after dark, so I left him at that point and, following out a scheme of my own since there was no hurry, I rode on up to the position.

Looking back from the top of the hill I saw all four guns stuck at the hairpin turns with the horses straining and the cannoneers heaving on the wheels. If the Germans had started shelling then they would have got the whole lot.

I rode Peanuts across the field in front of the position and found another road running parallel with the front. I turned to the left on it and soon entered scrub-pine woods. After about a mile of riding through the woods I began to be afraid I was lost but around the next curve I saw where the trees ended and, on coming out into the open, I was delighted to recognize the fork where the lieutenant and I had turned to the right. If we had kept straight we would have reached the position without the necessity of climbing around the hairpin turns at the head of the ravine. I determined to bring the caissons up by this new route and felt quite pleased with myself all the way back to Boncourt.

After supper the caissons were loaded with shells, the horses hitched in, and we started out. There was no trace of mist in the air, and the road looked white in the glow of a full moon. I had left Peanuts at Boncourt as there was no shelter for him near the position, so I sat on a caisson trail and enjoyed the beauty of the night. When we arrived at the fork there were shells bursting in the ravine to the right, and this would have determined me on the new route if there had been any question in my mind. We kept straight ahead into the woods where it was so dark that we could keep on the road only by following the open space where the stars showed between the trees overhead. On emerging from the woods into the moonlight, we crossed the open ground to the field in front of the position and, swinging to the right, drove right up to the muzzles of the guns.

Apparently all four had successfully been extricated from the sandy hill where I had last seen them and they were now in the gun pits. Every available man turned out to unload ammunition so that the horses could be gotten out of danger as soon as possible, and as soon as that was done I went down to the telephone dugout and enjoyed the sleep I had been wanting for a long time.

In my sleep I seemed to hear loud noises, but I was too tired to wake up. The next morning I learned that there had been six direct hits on our dugouts, but they were light shells and no damage had been done.

Going to breakfast gave me an idea of what a "fast league" we had gotten into. The kitchen was set up in the woods near the 90 battery, about five hundred yards of open road away, with no protection except shell holes, most of which were too shallow to be any good. Three times I had to drop everything and jump for one of them before I reached the kitchen. The Germans were firing "rafales" on the road, of which they had the range very accurately. From the high velocity of the shells I judged they were 88s. This was a new experience for us, as at the Chemin-des-Dames we had got used to the heavier calibers which gave ample warning of their approach. The 88s, on the other hand, came so fast that it was necessary to be always on the alert for the first whisper of a distant whine, as the explosion followed immediately and you couldn't dive for the ground too soon.

Rafale fire was a sudden scatter of shells, usually directed against a road or trench, and intended to catch the enemy unawares. The rafales were purposely fired at irregular intervals. Sometimes they would come every ten minutes all day, and the next day they would come at alternate intervals of ten and twelve minutes, with occasional rests of an hour thrown in to tempt us out of our dugouts. A favorite way was to send over a second rafale about two minutes after the first, to catch the stretcher bearers or whoever might have run out to the help of the wounded men.

While I was at the kitchen a driver named Joe Zwinge was killed in the road. He came up leading a horse for the captain, and didn't hear*

* He couldn't hear it because he was deaf. Lt. Dick Miller, the Battalion Surgeon, to be a "good fellow" passed him through his physical exam anyway.

114

the warning whine of the shells which exploded near him in the road. A splinter struck him between the eyes, and when the Frenchmen from the 90 battery saw him lying in the road with the horse eating grass nearby, they ran out and carried him into one of their dugouts to wait for an ambulance. He died on the way back to Boncourt.

I got my cup of coffee and my mess kit full of stew and started to carry them back to the telephone dugout. I was more than halfway and was breaking into a shuffling trot, with one eye on the coffee and the other on the nearest decent shell hole, when I heard the dreaded whine and dove headfirst, the mess kit flying from my hand. After the shells had burst and the splinters had whistled over my head I got up and went back to the kitchen for more. This time I succeeded in getting my breakfast back to the dugout.

It was just this way all the time for the four days that we were in this position and yet, by an odd series of chances, no one else got hurt, not even the horses when they brought ammunition up at night and stood in the open space in front of the guns while it was being unloaded.

My only other recollection of these four days is of being scared and jumpy all the time. On the nineteenth we got word that we were going to pull back to another position that night.

# CHAPTER XXIV

*Changing positions. A gun crew wiped out.
I get gassed. The quiet life.*

" '273+274' April 19, 1918. Moonlight night. Rain. Risky. Ist piece blown up;
killed Lawrence, Sawyer, Rigby. Sickening. Rest. Bon morale."

I THINK the moonlight night refers to the one already described on which I brought the caissons up. It was dark and raining on the night of the nineteenth when the limbers halted in front of the position and we dragged the guns out of the pits and limbered up. The prayers of the drivers to hurry were not needed to make us work fast, for everyone had an ear cocked for the expected rafale which would have caught us at its mercy. It was only a few minutes but it seemed an hour before everything was ready and the drivers set spurs to their horses. At a fast trot, with the dismounted men running alongside, the carriages lumbered across the field and swung into the road. Just as we entered the woods we heard a vicious rafale drop on the empty position behind us.

This time, instead of keeping straight towards Boncourt, we turned down the left fork into the hollow as if we were going back to the position by the other way, but we passed the road leading up the ravine and followed a cart track through a marshy bottom and over the shoulder of a hill beside some woods. We then turned to the left and went across about half a mile of rough fields along the crest of a ridge until we came to a gap in a straggling hedge. Through this we drove, and found an empty battery position just behind the crest. Two guns were placed in this position, and the other two were placed in another empty position a couple of hundred yards farther on. The drivers then took the limbers back to Boncourt.

This time the telephone dugout was in a tar paper shack half-dug

116

into the side of a steep bank, and here I threw my blankets into one of the eight low wire bunks built around the sides. Before I went to sleep I noticed by the light of a candle that the walls were covered with pictures from "La Vie Parisienne."

We stayed in this position almost a month, and except for the catastrophe of the next day it was one of the pleasantest times of the war.

By daylight I saw that we were just behind the crest of a very steep ridge which sloped away behind us to a wide road where trucks and motorcycle riders were passing most of the time. This road was often shelled by heavy guns, and to hit it the shells had to graze our hill. Sometimes they burst on the sloping plateau in front of us, but those did us no harm. The back slope of our hill was covered with vineyards, and I was astonished to see two or three French peasants working in them.* One was a woman. From the position I could see the top of a square church tower above the trees in St. Julien, about a mile to our right front.

About noon on April twentieth the whole first section gun crew were firing a problem from position #274, the farther one of the two the Battery occupied. Ordinarily two men were enough to keep a gun firing, but on this day everything seemed so peaceful and quiet that the captain ordered a little formal gun drill for the sake of discipline. Dave Lawrence was acting gunner corporal, with Clif Sawyer and Rigby at numbers 2 and 3 in the gun pit. Ben James stood in the doorway checking firing data, and Ted Storer stood behind him as executive officer. He had received his commission in France.

I was about two hundred yards away at the telephone shack when the thing happened. There was a heavy explosion followed by cries of "Stretcher-bearer," and when I looked across I saw the first

* On many clear days we saw a civilian ploughing a field behind the road. We suspected he might be a spy because he sometimes used a black, sometimes a white horse, and the areas he ploughed were of irregular shapes. He could have been giving messages to the German aviators.

section gun pit enveloped in smoke. I joined several men who were running towards the place, and when I got there the sight made me sick to my stomach. A German 150-millimeter shell had exploded between the wheels of the gun, reducing it to junk and turning the gun pit into a shambles. Storer* and Ben James lay on the ground a little way down the hill. The remains of the other three were in the gun pit. Rigby was still alive and conscious, but died on the stretcher before he could be put in an ambulance at the foot of the hill. There was a wire camouflage net above the pit, and from its meshes hung bits of bloody flesh and rags.

I took one look inside and turned away. After the ambulance had left with Ben James and Rigby's body, we all tried to go about our work, but no one could find spirit for anything. That night a new gun crew came up with another gun and cleaned out the gun pit. The drivers took several sacksful of material back to Boncourt for burial. The following night E Battery, the original owners of position 274, returned and we gladly moved our first and second guns over to 273 where the third and fourth had been put when we arrived.

For the rest of our stay we had beautiful spring weather. After supper we would sit outside our shack enjoying the long evenings until it got too dark to see, and then we would put a lighted candle on the table in the shack and play cards or read until we got sleepy. In our little dooryard stood a tree with a branch like a horizontal bar which was just out of reach above a steep sandbank. Our game was to jump for the branch and swing on it or, if we missed, go head over heels down the bank out of sight. Peabo always missed, and he was so stubborn that he would keep trying again and again until the rest of us were weak laughing at him.

There was a little French canteen in St. Julien where we could buy canned butter, jam, and wine. I got a package of solid alcohol from home about this time, so we made a toaster out of wire and, as long as the alcohol lasted we ate buttered toast before going to bed every

* Storer was stunned but not wounded.

night, and whoever came in late or had to sit up at the switchboard found that it went to the right spot.

Most of the days were spent in digging trenches and dugouts to complete the position and in shoring them with heavy timbers which came up at night on the limbers from Boncourt. I often was sent with messages to Battalion Headquarters and, although I usually enjoyed these solitary rambles, I occasionally had terrifying moments. Sometimes I would get caught in the open plateau in front of the position by scattered shelling, and I got to know each hole and gully from long use. But the place was so exposed and the sense of protection afforded by these shallow holes was so slight that I often avoided the place by going a different way. This was to follow the vineyards along the back side of the ridge for about a mile and then, turning to the left around the shoulder of the hill, to pass through St. Julien and reach the ravine below Battalion Headquarters.

One day I had delivered my message and was strolling back at my leisure, admiring the early spring foliage and listening to the birds sing from every thicket. About halfway through the vineyard I heard a shell coming and jumped down into a trench that ran along the side of the hill. The shell exploded with a dull plunk just above me, and I was enveloped in a suffocating vapor of gas. Not stopping to put on my mask, I began to run along the trench to get away from the place before more shells landed. But I must have inhaled several full breaths of the poison, for after a few steps my head began to swim and I was seized with violent nausea. I crawled up to the position feeling very weak and reported to the captain, who sent me back to Boncourt that night on the empty caissons, and Curtis took my place at the front.

At Boncourt I slept, ate, groomed Peanuts, lay in the sun, and quietly recovered from my gassing. After three or four days I returned to the position and resumed my former life with only the addition of a cough. I found the new first section gun crew well established, and they had named their gun "Lil."

About this time I was given the additional job of acting ammunition sergeant. That meant that I was responsible for all the ammunition at the position. It amounted to keeping it sorted into lots and seeing that the correct lots were used and submitting a list every day accounting for all that had been fired by each gun, both shells and fuses, and what was on hand in the racks. It was not an arduous job but the paperwork was a nuisance, and I often had to steal a few fuses of the right kind from a neighboring battery to make my figures tally.

Firing short was one of the artillery's unpardonable sins, as there was nothing that destroyed the infantryman's morale quicker than being shot up by his own guns. It was at this position that Jimmie Clarke fired short through an error in figuring. The shells landed harmlessly in an empty field, but by bad luck a brigadier-general happened to be passing that field in his car, and the next day Jimmie was relieved of his command and attached to the 101st Infantry as liaison officer.*

I see by an old record that we fired 3494 rounds from this position. The Germans continued to shell the road behind us and the fields in front, but we suffered no further damage.

One day I was walking along the hedge at the top of the crest on my way to Battalion when I saw an American plane flying very low. It was soon apparent that the pilot intended to make a landing on the field in front of the Battery. He came lower and lower and, as the plane skimmed along about two feet from the ground, the wheels caught in a barbwire entanglement and the plane turned a somersault and lay on its back. I ran up to it in time to see the pilot crawling out of the wreck unhurt. He said his fuel had given out and he had no idea where he was but saw a perfect field for a forced landing. I took him

---

* Where he was kept throughout the Château-Thierry drive. He was the last man out of Epieds when the Fourth Prussian Guards took it in a counterattack. We all were astonished that he returned to Battery A unscathed. The reason he had figured the firing data himself was to avoid waking Roley Allen.

to the telephone dugout where he was able to get in touch with his airdrome, and then he went back to try to protect his machine from souvenir hunters until help came.

I don't recall anything else of particular interest until the night of May tenth, when the limbers came up to take the guns back to Boncourt, ending our easy life at the St. Julien position.

---

## CHAPTER XXV

### *A battle against mud. Another swamp position.*

"388. May 11, 1918. Guns stuck in mud 2 nights. Narrow-gauge; echelon at Rangeval. Peanuts. Quiet, damp, hot."

---

THERE WAS a night march which took us out of the hilly country into a region of low, flat fields with level roads, and here we halted in sight of the flares along the front.

The first section gun team pulled off the road to the left and started across marshy ground with the gun sinking to the hubs and all six horses straining as the drivers shouted and spurred to keep them moving. After a short struggle they lost momentum and, floundering in the mud, they gave up pulling on what became an immovable load as soon as the guns were given a chance to sink to the breech. At first a crowd of cannoneers took hold of the wheels and tried to get it started while the drivers threw their horses forward, but it was soon apparent that nothing could be accomplished in that way. The mud was too deep for the men to get a foothold and, as soon as the gun settled lower the frightened horses refused to bruise their necks against the unyielding collars. Storer was leading the way, and he now came back to see what was the matter. Captain Huntington had been sent back to Coëtquidan as a teacher a few days earlier, so the command of the Battery fell on Lieutenant Mac-

Namee. He and Storer looked over the situation which to me seemed fairly hopeless.

While they were talking I left Peanuts in the road and walked on past the bogged gun for about three hundred yards to what I took to be an empty artillery position under some trees. Everywhere the ground was swampy. As well as I could in the dark, I circled around looking for more solid footing, but it seemed all the same.

When I got back to the road I saw that seven teams of horses had been hitched together for a new attempt to pull the first piece out. When everything was ready, the drivers started the horses with a shout, but they only floundered and got tangled in the traces. The next move was to get shovels off the limbers and dig the mud from in front of the wheels. While some of the cannoneers worked at this, the rest of us found planks and sections of duckboard in the position to throw down in the mud for the wheels to run on. When a sort of a track had been made with these, the two strongest wheel horses in the Battery, Pete and Shrimp, were hitched to the gun by Dan Charleton, their driver, and with everyone pulling on ropes, the guns began to move. By superb driving Dan kept the traces taut, and Shrimp and Pete dragged through until the gun rested behind the first piece gun pit.

One by one the other guns followed in the same track, and one by one they sank in the soft mud, the second piece getting about three-quarters of the way, and the fourth settling fifty yards from the road. We worked on them all night but never succeeded in moving them another inch. By the early morning light I saw Lieutenant Mac-Namee standing up to his knees in mud, using a dapper little bamboo cane to direct the men in camouflaging the three derelicts with bushes. The drivers started back with the horses and limbers so as not to be caught by daylight on the road, and the men of the firing battery walked over to the new position.

As the light improved I saw that it was in a place less swampy than the surrounding ground, but there was a great deal of semifluid surface mud in all the trenches and, in fact, everywhere. A high hedge of bushes ran past the right end of the position, and I found close to the hedge the ground was fairly solid. By going farther along the road and crossing to the hedge it looked possible to get the guns in at the next attempt. A few tall trees shadowed the position, and irregular clumps of smaller trees and bushes straggled back into the edge of a considerable wood.

I followed a muddy path behind the position into the woods. Beside the path were several piles of ammunition held out of the mud on duckboards. There were some tar paper shacks just in the edge of the woods and much deeper in was a large shack which was being used for a kitchen. There was no ground vegetation under the trees but only bare mud, on the surface of which I noticed a great number of orange-colored slugs.

My particular friends, Beck, Peabo, Ritchie, Allen, Saindon, and a few others had settled in the shack nearest the position, so I got my blankets and joined them. The hut contained six wire bunks. There were no windows, and the floor was several inches deep with soft mud.

At the position there wasn't much to be done until the other guns could be brought in, but there was nothing to prevent getting the telephone established. There were no dugouts, and we found that the only place for the switchboard was in a sort of wigwam which had been built by leaning posts against a tree and piling sandbags around them in a conical shape. There was just room for one man to stand or sit inside.

During the day we saw German balloons watching, but no shells landed near enough to make us think our camouflaged guns had been discovered. A few hours after dark the horses and limbers came back, and before morning we had succeeded in digging the guns out of the mud and pulling them to the position by way of the hedge. The drivers said the echelon was now at Rangeval again, with everything the same as before we went away.

The next day I found that our position was just off the road be-behind Mandres, and our old swamp position was only two miles or so to the left, with Rambucourt in front of it.

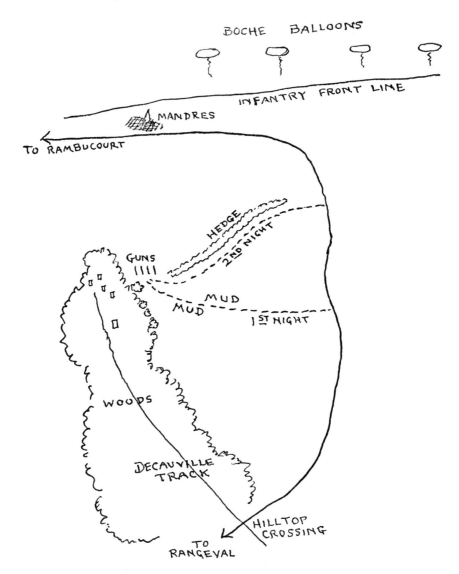

The nine days we now spent were very lazy but disagreeable be-cause of the heat and dampness. The drivers had brought us rubber boots, which were luxurious at first but when they got wet inside

124

there was no way of drying them so our feet were always wet. After about a week I found that the skin was coming off between my toes, and it looked as if one little toe might come off altogether. We kept our feet covered with oil and tallow but I never saw that it did much good. The skin was always waterlogged and pulled off just the same.

Going to meals was no pleasure in this place because there was nothing to sit down on, and we stood around in the mud eating our meals like a lot of cranes. The only asset was that we were never shelled.

By the night of May nineteenth the ground had become sufficiently steamed out by days of sun so that when the horses came up after dark they were able to drag the guns back to the road with no great difficulty. We started up the road towards Rangeval, but after about half a mile we halted at a place called Hilltop Crossing* where there was an engineers' supply dump beside a Decauville track. All of us who were afoot were ordered to wait here, while the drivers swung to the left and disappeared in the darkness.

Before long two big auto trucks pulled up and turned around. No sooner had we climbed into them with our blanket rolls and sat on the floor then off they went at about thirty miles an hour with not a light showing.

* After the first two nights the drivers never came all the way up the road, but stopped at Hilltop Crossing. From here the supplies and ammunition were pushed by hand up to the guns on Decauville cars over a track through the woods.

# CHAPTER XXVI

## *The Battery goes raiding. Impressions of the French Senegalese.*

"Guizoncourt, May 20, 1918, by truck. Arr. 1.30 a.m. Town,
good sleep; eggs, wine, sunshine; swim in brook;
sunbath. Lazy; slept in billet."

AT FIRST I tried to keep track of the turns we took but I soon found that we were in unfamiliar country and the roads meant nothing to me. By an occasional glimpse of flares over the front I judged that we were going about southeast. I must have slept on the floor of the truck the rest of the way, for the next thing I remember is piling out in the dark and carrying my blanket roll across a street and up a flight of stairs to a room full of sleeping soldiers, where I lay down on the wooden floor and was myself asleep in no time.

It was broad day when I woke up feeling very fit and went out into the sunshine. Guizoncourt was not entirely deserted, for Ritchie and I found a house right off where we bought eggs and wine. It appeared that we had the whole day to rest so we walked around to look the place over.

The next thing we found was the drivers watering their horses at a sizable brook. There was a crowd on a little wooden bridge watching the rest in swimming. A driver named Jack Dunn was furnishing a lot of entertainment by riding his horse into the water while he sat naked on its back. The fellows on the bridge were throwing stones to make the horse dump Jack into the brook. It was so hot that Ritchie and I took off our clothes and had a swim before walking back to the town. As we stood talking to a woman in a doorway we heard shouts and laughter down the street, and saw a naked man on a galloping horse come tearing around a corner and ride the length of the town. It was Jack Dunn, and I judge that he had also found a place to buy wine. The woman was greatly amused and asked us if that was customary in America.

She told us there was a camp of Senegal negro troops near the town and, following her directions, we started off to find them. After about a mile of hot road, we saw several wooden barracks on the left with negroes sitting around the doors. When we got closer I found that they were like no negroes I had ever seen before. They were all big men of powerful physique, and not one of them was wearing a full uniform. What they had was the mustard-yellow of the French Colonial Army, but one man wore only a hat and a breech-cloth, another only a pair of pants, another a shirt and a pair of shoes. Several of them were crouching in a circle on the ground playing a sort of crap game with tiny conch shells. As we watched them at close quarters, I noticed that they all had patterns tattooed or scarred on their faces, and most of them had their front teeth filed to points. Many of them had holes through the septum of their noses for ornaments, and they all carried long knives in sheaths around their waists. Among themselves they spoke some kind of savage West African language, but to a white French officer I heard one of them speaking French.

We made friends with this officer who invited us to walk over the camp with him. He told us he had just locked one of the Senegalese up for cutting his horse's throat. The horse was pulling a manure cart, and because he wouldn't back up quickly enough, the soldier had cut his throat. The Frenchman said our artillery had been brought up for a raid in which the Senegalese were going over the top, and that they were splendid for raids as the Germans feared them. He said that when they got excited they forgot everything they had been told, threw their guns away, and used their knives exclusively. They were no good for holding the line as they hated shellfire and would never leave their dugouts, but in a spirited trench raid they were right at home. Ritchie noticed that they all wore shell amulets and asked the officer to get one for him as a souvenir, but it seemed the Senegalese were superstitious about their amulets and relied on them for protection. We compromised by each getting a knife.* For mine I gave a great black savage a pipe and five francs.

We spent most of the morning there and returned to town just in time for mess. After mess Ritchie bought a bottle of what purported to be champagne, but it didn't taste like it to me. Coming back through the town square we met a big Senegalese who had apparently come to look our outfit over. He walked up to Ritchie and held out his hand for a drink from the bottle. Ritchie probably thought it was good policy to humor him, so he handed it over. The big negro put the bottle to his lips, tipped back his head, and to Ritchie's dismay drank the wine to the last drop. As he handed back the empty bottle Ritchie looked at me and said, "My God, what a man!"

We spent the afternoon dozing in the sun until, at about five o'clock the whistle blew and we found four trucks in the square. The drivers were bringing the guns up to the trucks, and the cannoneers were loading them in on inclined tracks from the ground to the back of each truck. When each of the four guns was in a truck the tailboards were put up. We all piled in where we could find room and the trucks started off down the road away from Guizoncourt.

---

* Lost with blanket roll second morning of Château-Thierry drive.

# CHAPTER XXVII

## The raid at Mamey. Days of rest.

"Mamey, May 21, 1918, by truck, late afternoon. Beautiful;
hot; coup-de-main. Slept in wine vault."

I REMEMBER that ride through the slanting rays of the afternoon
sun, and how I could see the ribbon of dust still hanging between
the rows of trees for half a mile behind us on the road. The sun had
set behind the low horizon, but it was still daylight when our trucks
rolled into the street of the deserted town of Mamey. The town was
deserted by its usual inhabitants, but we saw a good many Chasseurs
Alpins with their dark blue berets, and a few brown-clad Algerian
colonials.

Our food had been brought up in the trucks, and our first concern
was to eat a cold supper served from a makeshift kitchen in the angle
of a high wall. Afterwards Ritchie and I walked up the street and
found a recreation room that the French soldiers had fixed up for
themselves. A little chasseur about five feet tall with powerful-
looking shoulders and a tunic decorated with the ribbons of the Legion of Honor, the Croix de Guerre with five palms, and several
other orders I had never even heard of invited us inside. We each
wrote a letter home on French army paper, and then strolled back
to our end of town.

We found the boys playing "duck on the rock," but whenever a
rat ran across the street they all stopped the game and threw stones
at it. I saw a cannoneer named Doc Gleason make a remarkably
pretty shot at an old gray rat that stopped in the middle of the road
to clean his whiskers. The rock hit him fair and killed him instantly.
Doc was so surprised and pleased that he offered to treat everyone to
a drink. We all accepted, but it appeared Doc had nothing with
which to make good his offer.

At dusk four limbers came into Mamey driven by French artil-lerymen. They limbered up to our guns where the trucks had left them, and led the way along a dirt road out of the town with our men following on foot. At the first rise I saw where the front line was by the flares, and about a mile farther along we turned into a very rough field full of shell holes and stopped behind a row of grass-grown mounds which proved to be old gun pits. Neatly piled between them I counted 170 new diphosgene shells, 449 high explosive shells, and a box of fuses. The Frenchmen must have brought them up just before we arrived. The limbers dropped our guns and disappeared, and it was only the work of an hour for us to get the guns into the pits and to distribute the ammunition. Then when we had covered everything carefully with bushes we walked back to Mamey and went to bed.

Ritchie and I found a little wine cellar with a stone arched roof, where we made ourselves snug in two wire bunks and had a smoke by candlelight before turning in.

After a luxurious all-night sleep we woke to another beautiful sunny morning. It seemed the coup-de-main was scheduled for that night so there was nothing to do all day. A few of the men and an officer went up to register the guns with a couple of shots, but most of us lolled around Mamey fraternizing with the Frenchmen and playing games in the part of the street that was not in view of the Boche balloons.

We found we could get any amount of "pinard" from the Frenchmen in exchange for Bull Durham and cigarettes. During the day the irrepressible Doc Gleason made the discovery that a mixture of pinard, lemon extract, and sugar produced a very pleasing drink, and he took the precaution of stealing all Wilner's lemon extract before making his discovery public. The result was that he spent a busy day selling his discovery to converts for cigarettes with which to buy more pinard, and the consumption of this devilish mixture was taking on alarming proportions when darkness came and we got orders to go up to the guns.

This raid was a mild affair compared to the one I had seen at Ostel. We lay in the dark watching the flares and listening to the distant chatter of machine guns and the nearby chirp of crickets until we got the word to fire. Then everything was drowned out by the roar and flash of our guns as we rapidly sent over the six hundred shells which were our contribution to the raid. Meanwhile I could see several other batteries firing from unexpected places near us. Our part was over in less than an hour and, as soon as the guns were concealed again by bushes, we all went back to Mamey and went to bed.

The next morning we heard from the Frenchmen that the raid had been a great success. The infantry had entered a place called the Goose-Neck Salient, killed a great number of Germans, and taken many prisoners. After another pleasant day of loafing we saw the French drivers bringing our guns into Mamey just after dark, and a little later five trucks entered the town to take us away.

One gun and its section loaded into each of the first four, the kitchen and special detail into the fifth, and a minute later we had seen the last of Mamey. Everyone regretted the end of this most enjoyable picnic.

## CHAPTER XXVIII

### We relieve the French at Bernècourt. A lively sector.
### More losses. "On s'y habitue."

"Bernècourt.525. 10 p.m., May 25, 1918. Relieved French. Lively. Rotten chocolate gas.
Newell Ripley killed 1st night. Norman McCann wounded. No sleep for 1st 5 days.
Echelon at Andilly. 119th FA in 2nd platoon position. Relieved by French 9.30 p.m. 6/27."

IT IS HARD for me to write my recollections of Bernècourt in chronological order because in the month that I was there I got so familiar with the place that everything about it is blended in my memory.

As nearly as I can recall, it was a clear night and uncomfortably cold when the trucks stopped beside the wall of a house on the right of a broad street and we tumbled out. As soon as the guns were unloaded the trucks drove away.

I was sitting on a pile of blanket rolls, feeling like a cat in a strange garret when a French noncom asked me where to find the ammunition sergeant. I said I was the man he was after and followed him around a corner and into a splendid dry dugout protected by a gas curtain and smelling of garlic. He was a portly, black-bearded man with a fussy, polite manner. I felt like a child as he brought out his elaborate ammunition report written in a beautiful copperplate hand for my inspection and then led me around to verify the items at various ammunition racks which I wondered if I could ever locate by myself. Some were in trenches, some in dark houses, and some in shallow dugouts. He could have shown me the same one two or three times and I never would have known the difference. After we had acted out our sober farce to an end I asked him what kind of a place Bernècourt was and got only the noncommittal "Pas mal."

"How about gas?" I ventured.

"Oh, il-y-en-a," he said with a shrug, and looked at me with a pitying smile as if to say, "What do you expect?" Thanking him for his polite attentions in respect to the ammunition I went out into the street and found the French battery already mounted and limbered up, waiting under a row of trees.

I noticed how heavily loaded all the gun carriages looked, with stuff tied on in bulging bundles, and that no one had to walk. They certainly knew how to do things comfortably. One thing only suggested that their army regulations might still be somewhat of a nuisance and that was that each mounted man carried a sabre on the off side of his horse. Perhaps they found some use even for the sabres. Their officers came out of a dugout where they had been conferring with Storer and MacNamee and, as soon as they mounted their horses, the French battery rumbled off down the street. I was always impressed by the easy, offhand way the French got things done.

I had noticed the wires in the dugout where the ammunition sergeant had taken me, so I got my blanket roll and put it into a bunk down there, as I always slept in the telephone dugout to be in touch with what was going on. In my capacity as scout corporal I was theoretically responsible only to the captain, and was supposed to be ready to carry out his orders at a moment's notice. Consequently I was either loaded with responsibility or had none at all, and in either case I was entirely on my own, which had its advantages. Just at present my only concern was to see that the guns were supplied with ammunition, so I began exploring around to find them.

As near as I could tell, we were on a street corner among houses, and I could see no houses on the other three corners. Across the street in one direction were tall trees, with the dark shapes of roofs some distance beyond. Going around the corner, I passed the pile of blanket rolls and got a vista of flat ground with the road disappearing into it and a skyline lighted by distant flares. To my right was a large brick building of which I could see only the doorway with Decauville tracks running out of it, by which I judged it was a carbarn or supply dump of some kind. Going around behind it I fell over trenches and shell holes and following my ears I located the two gun crews of the first platoon establishing their guns in covered pits behind which ran a deep, narrow trench. They appeared to be all right for ammunition, so I followed the trench to the left behind them and after about one hundred yards came out on the road again.

On the other side of the road was an empty house where the Frenchman had showed me some fuses in a lower room, and I went across to have another feel of them. When I got there I found the second platoon guns in a field at the side of the house. They were just getting their aiming sticks up and trying to make the little electric bulbs on them work.

Perhaps I should explain what aiming sticks are. If the guns never moved while firing there would be no need of correcting them between shots once they were laid on a target, but because of the recoil they did move to a certain extent. Usually in the daytime and always at night the actual target was invisible, so there had to be something visible to sight at in order to return the gun to the same position for each shot. Any prominent point in the landscape would have served, but it was found more convenient to use stakes driven into the ground about sixty yards in front of the guns, and for use at night these were equipped with a little electric bulb run by a dry-cell battery. Each gun determined its own deflection from its aiming stick to the various targets, so that with the proper deflection laid off on the sights, and the aiming stick as a fixed point to sight on, the gun could continue to drop shells on any target as long as its aiming stick was visible.

That night our guns were laid on the French aiming sticks, and the range and deflection for normal barrage had been given to our officers by the French when they turned the position over to us.

When I yelled to Ripley, the third section gunner sergeant, and asked him if he had ammunition, he said he'd let me know later; he hadn't finished getting his gun in yet.

I had located all the gun pits, the captain's dugout, which was near the telephone dugout, and most of the ammunition, and was just getting my blankets arranged and talking with Beck and Ritchie while they connected the switchboard, when "Crash, crash, crash," came a flock of shells outside. Among the jarring detonations of high explosives I could distinguish another sound—the plunk of gas shells, and soon I began to get the chocolate odor. Beck had the switchboard working by this time, and there was a long buzz on the telephone. A second later Beck jumped for the dugout stairs yelling, "Normal barrage!" As he pushed the curtain aside a reek of gas came down the dugout stairs and the candle almost flickered out.

"Christ, it's rotten with gas out there," he said as he sat down again at the switchboard. I could now hear our guns barking and the clang of empty shell cases.

"How are they fixed for ammunition in the pits?" asked Ritchie. That reminded me that I didn't know about the second platoon, so I got down from my bunk, picked up my helmet and mask, and started out.

"Don't get hurt, will you," japed Peabo as I reached the top of the stairs.

"Well, I'm damn sure you won't, you Dugout Hound," I yelled back, and then I got a big breath of gas so strong that the tears came to my eyes. I knocked off my helmet with my left hand, according to drill regulations, and with my right pulled the facepiece of my mask out of its case and put it on, with the hose in my mouth and the noseclips pinched on my nostrils. Then I fumbled round on the ground till I found my helmet and put it on again.

The air was full of the whine and crash of shells, most of them going over my head into the houses down the street, but I heard plenty landing near the guns, especially gas shells. I crouched beside the wall and got my bearings through the partly opaque isinglass eyepieces in my mask. There was a whine and a shattering crash somewhere in the dark in front of me, and I made a dash for the empty house near the second platoon. As I went through the doorway my foot touched something soft. Just then two or three men came from inside the house, and one of them struck a match. By its brief flicker of light I saw Ripley's body lying face up across the threshold. I stepped over it, found a tray of fuses, and ran out to the third piece gun pit with them. Both guns were firing steadily. Someone grabbed me by the arm and put his head close to mine.

"Where's Ripley?" came the muffled words through his mask. I took a long breath, pulled the rubber tube out of my mouth, and yelled, "Bumped off. Do you need any more fuses?" The grotesque head shook "No," so I went back and got another load and took them to the fourth piece gun pit. Then, my bit being done for the moment, I made my way back to the telephone dugout. I was almost suffocated, and my eyepieces were so misted up that I was completely blind with the mask on. When I took it off in the dugout I was relieved to find that none of the others were wearing masks, as the curtain had kept most of the gas out.

"Well, where've you been all this time?" was the greeting I got.

"Over to the second platoon," I said. "Ripley's killed."

"Did you see what McCann is doing at the fourth piece?" asked Beck from the switchboard.

"How the hell could I see anything with this damn thing on!" I retorted. "What is he doing?"

"He's squatting out in front of the guns holding up a cigarette butt for an aiming stick light. Storer was just in and told us. Their light was hit by a shell."

"Well, the goddamned fool" was all I could say. I might now add that McCann was wounded by a shell fragment but stuck to his dangerous task until the attack was over, and was cited for the D.S.C. "for conspicuous gallantry in action above and beyond the call of duty."

The first few days and nights in Bernècourt make a confused nightmare in my memory. By daylight I took the earliest opportu-

136

nity to see what kind of place it was. Our battery was in the extreme front edge of the town, at a crossroads formed by the principal street of Bernècourt and the Flirey-Royaumieux Road, a *route nationale*. The corner where the telephone dugout was located had a few ruins on it that had once been houses. The other three corners were vacant lots. Diagonally across the street was an engineers' dump full of Decauville tracks, piles of rock and iron, and old flatcars. The Royaumieux Road was lined by tall trees, and ran out of sight past the dump. On clear days the tower of the church at Royaumieux was visible. Towards the front a dirt road made a straight line across about three-quarters of a mile of open plain, and was lost in a strip of woods called the Bois Juré, where our infantry had their front line trench. Two or three German balloons floated in the sky above the treetops. To the right of this road, about fifty yards from the corner, was the big barnlike building I had noticed the first night, and across the road from it was the empty stone house where I had found Ripley. The second platoon lived in the cellar, as it was the nearest shelter to their guns, which were in a field beside the house. These were the last two houses in the town. Towards the rear the main street was thickly built up on both sides and sloped down hill a little to the center of the town, where there was a public washing pool in a large stone pergola.

In addition to a number of French civilians, the town was occupied by several infantry companies in reserve and some engineers. There was a house where a girl sold bottled beer across the window-sill to the soldiers in the street, and sometimes she had eggs which her father brought up in his cart at night with the beer. We got little chance to buy her wares, as that part of town was full of infantry from the 101st Regiment, and they usually got ahead of us. As a matter of fact her business must have been poor about the time we arrived in Bernècourt because of the shelling day and night.

I remember one night when a load of ammunition came up to us on a Decauville freight car drawn by an engine. The shells were in

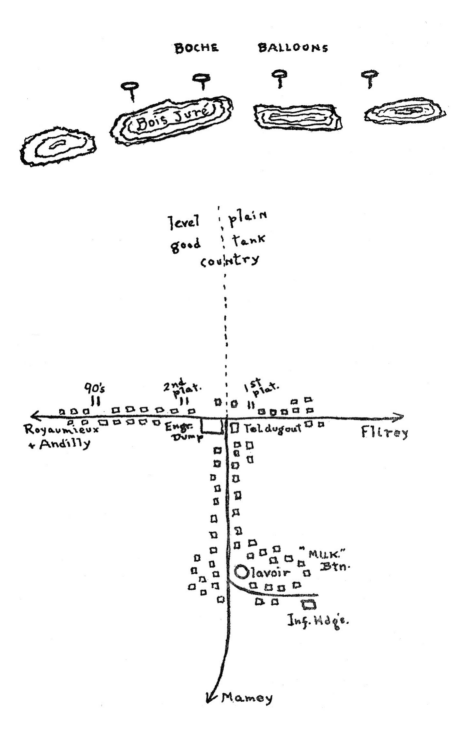

wooden boxes, nine to a box, and the car was piled high. About a dozen of us were unloading when the Germans began to shell. As usual there were gas shells mixed with the H.E. so we had to put on our masks. I was perched on top of the load trying to pry the covers off the boxes with a screwdriver, hampered by the darkness and the gas mask, and feeling very exposed as the shells whined over my head and crashed into the houses where the infantry was quartered. The engine driver was dancing around on the road motioning to us to hurry up, but no one paid any attention to him. It seemed a lifetime before the last box was fumbled open and the last shell piled against the wall. The way that engine backed out of Bernècourt was a caution, and we lost no time in diving down our dugout stairs.

The next day we heard that the infantry had lost a lot of men, as several shells had come through the roofs of houses where they were sleeping. They all happened to belong to companies I, K, L, and M, and the survivors were anxious to retaliate on the Boche. The "Milk Battalion," as it was called, was mostly South Boston Irish and had a reputation for being hard-boiled.

The next night the Germans took advantage of a favorable wind to send over an enormous concentration of gas from projectors in their first-line trench. This hit our infantry very hard, and when the Milk Battalion saw the victims carried into Bernècourt next day, they swore vengeance. About this time orders came down for a raid on the German trenches, and there was grim rejoicing around the infantry kitchens.

That night a party of volunteers from the Milk Battalion went over in a surprise attack. They carried clubs with barbwire wrapped around the heavy end, and they agreed to take no prisoners. Those who got back to Bernècourt alive reported that the score was now even.

In retaliation for this raid the Germans shelled our end of town all the next day and tore down most of our telephone wires where they crossed the road on trees.

After the first week, however, there came a lull, and we all felt free to walk around outdoors. At first we avoided open spaces and parts of the street in sight of German balloons, but as time went on and nothing happened we grew bolder. It became the custom to play ball in the vacant lot behind the second platoon every evening after supper until it got too dark to see. This was finally forbidden, after several games had been broken up by the sudden whine of German shells.

I don't mean to say that Bernècourt was a rest cure at any time. One day a shell tore the side out of the colonel's office at the other end of town, and several times I got caught over at the engineer dump and had to crouch beside a rock pile or under a flatcar till the flurry of shells was over.

The gas menace was so great that Peabo was appointed gas non-com, and was supplied with a lot of gas-proof coats, hats, pants, and mittens which I never saw anyone use. They were intended for mustard gas, which ate right through cloth and caused terrible burns. Peabo's friends took his new office as a great joke, and whenever a gas shell plunked they would invite him to step out and sample the gas as an expert.

Another source of amusement was a battery of old French 90s that was put in our charge. They were in a position a couple of hundred yards down the Royaumieux Road, and the spare men from our Battery moved over there to man them. The rest of us named it "The Chinese Battery" because the guns were so antiquated. Whenever they had a problem to fire we would go over to cheer and hoot. We made fun of the powder in silk bags, the projectiles like candle-pins, the inclined wooden runways for the guns to recoil against, and everything about the place. Our "Chinese gunners" took it in good part and were amused themselves at the extraordinary antics of the old guns. Whereas our 75s could be fired with smoothness and precision as fast as forty rounds a minute, the lumbering old 90s made hard work of firing once in two minutes. After the guns were elaborately loaded everyone would stand clear, the gunner would pull the lanyard, there would be a crash, down would bang the muzzle against the ground, the whole gun would slam backwards up the inclined runway for about fifteen feet and then would come rattling back on its rickety wheels and jolt into place in its gun pit to the cheers of the appreciative audience. As a matter of fact, the old 90s, in spite of their disadvantages, were extraordinarily accurate and had a longer range than the 75s.

For a while, life in Bernècourt was fairly pleasant. After things got settled down and we learned the ropes there was very little work to do during the day and only the ammunition to get in at night, with occasional calls for barrages to the gunners, or wire-mending trips for the telephone men. Our kitchen was in the brick warehouse (or whatever it was), close at hand, the weather was good, the dug-outs were dry, there was no mud, and we all felt we were better off than the drivers grooming horses and doing chores at the echelon in Andilly.

One day there was great excitement because an inquisitive youth named Apollonio found a hand grenade and threw it down the latrine, with far-reaching results when it exploded. He was banished to the echelon for this exploit.

Sometimes staff officers or aviators would come up to Bernècourt in automobiles to "see the front." American aviators were just beginning to make their appearance in France, and I must say they looked snappy in their new uniforms. There was a story that two of them who had been visiting our position when a few gas shells dropped in the field were awarded citations for "gallantry during a gas attack," but that may have been pure malice.

During the first week in June the aviators caused us a bad scare by reporting forty troop trains behind the German lines across from us. This could only mean a big attack, and we were ordered to make all preparations for the following night when it would probably be launched. Of course it was expected that our division would be sacrificed, but we were supposed to resist long enough to enable the staff generals to bring their brains to bear on the situation and to move reserve troops from other areas. That was mighty poor consolation for us. We worked like crazy things all day, putting up barbwire in front of the guns, building barricades in the streets, digging a tank emplacement for the third piece, stocking the gun pits with hand grenades and incendiary bombs to defend the guns till the last minute before destroying them, cleaning ammunition, and making sure our automatic pistols were in working order.

It was thought the Germans would come across the level plain behind tanks, as it was a perfect place for them, so we provided for this contingency. The tanks would have to come through the woods by one of three gaps, so we made a platform out in the open to mount the third piece, and figured the deflection for each of the three gaps. At dusk a man was sent to lie in the grass at each gap, with instructions to fire up a rocket when he saw the tanks coming. What would become of him when we opened fire on the gap was not specified, but we thought he would have a hot time. The unlucky three were Bird, Joyce, and Pete Murray, and no one envied them at all.

When it was dark, the drivers brought the limbers up from Andilly and stood by their horses' heads in the woods behind Bernècourt. They were to gallop in and pull the guns out, if possible, when the German assault wave had almost reached the pits. They showed no relish for their job either.

Well, we stood around all night with our hearts in our throats waiting for the opening bombardment to start, but nothing happened. In the morning Bird, Murray, and Joyce came crawling in to Bernècourt, the drivers went back to Andilly, and we spent the day improving our preparations and arguing the possibility of the forty troop trains being a mistake. That night the whole thing was repeated, and again the next night, but the German attack never came. I don't know yet what it was all about.

Towards the end of the month a battery of green Indiana troops, a battery of the 119th Regiment, moved into our second platoon position to learn from us. They had never before been at the front, so we swelled around and tried to impress them with our superior knowledge. It was very pleasant.

During this time we began the practice of taking one gun a mile or so away during the night and firing a hundred rounds to make the Germans think a new battery had moved in. This "roving gun" went to a different place each night and came back to its gun pit in time to let the horses make the trip to Andilly before dawn.

Towards the end, I knew every corner of Bernècourt and the surrounding fields, and could judge where a shell would land by the sound it made coming through the air. It seemed like leaving home when the horses came up on the night of June 27th and took us away.

---

## CHAPTER XXIX

### *We leave the Toul sector. Andilly.*

"Andilly 12 midnight, June 27th, 1918. Spent day packing. Left 9.30 p.m. 6/28, acting as Battalion Agent."

---

IN THE DARKNESS of an Adrian barrack I found an empty bunk near Curtis and slept till morning. Then I had my first sight of Andilly, where our drivers had lived all the time we were at Bernècourt. It was so far behind the lines that it looked more like a peacetime camp than an echelon.

The picket lines of the whole Regiment were in a large sunny field on a hillside, and across the road were the kitchens and Adrian barracks for the men. The officers lived in the town at the foot of the hill. There were hundreds of Annamite labor troops repairing the roads and building barracks, little yellow men in wide straw hats.

I found that Eykel had been taking care of Peanuts, and he hated to have me claim the horse. I took Peanuts for a canter around the field. His coat was glossy, his feet were sound, and he was more full of life than ever. I was very happy to have him back.

By nightfall everything had been packed up and the Regiment was ready to leave for parts unknown. I reported on Peanuts to the head of the long column, when I was told to ride near the Major with the scouts from B and C Batteries.

---

## CHAPTER XXX

### *A night march and a quiet day.*

"Troussey, 3 a.m. June 29, 1918. Swim; haymaking; ball game; band. Left 6 p.m. 6/30. Curtis and I rode ahead of Battery. Went thru Pagny-sur-Meuse, St. Germaine-sur-Meuse. Vigny. No map; easy."

---

A STREAM about thirty feet wide flowed between stone banks through the town, separated from the street by an iron railing and overhung by tall trees. One of the scouts said he was sick of the artillery and had applied for a transfer to the Tank Corps which was just being formed. It didn't appeal to me. We talked and smoked as the horses walked side by side.

By the time we were clear of the town it was dark. There appeared to be someone ahead who knew the road, for we were not called on for anything except occasionally to ride back to our own batteries with a message to close up. The column moved at an easy pace with frequent halts, and nothing happened until 3 a.m. when we pulled through a dark village and halted just beyond.

This seemed to be our destination, as word was given to picket the horses and find billets for the men. Our Battery pulled into a field beside the road, where I tied Peanuts after rubbing down his legs and then, with some others from the Special Detail, walked back to the town and went to sleep in an empty house.

The next day was sunny and hot. Troussey was a sleepy little town on the banks of the Meuse surrounded by hayfields, where all the inhabitants seemed to be at work getting in their crop. They were mostly women and old men, but enough of them were young girls so that the soldiers felt inspired to offer their services, and a great deal of French hay was made by Americans in the course of the day. This was hot work, so we rewarded ourselves with a cool swim in the stream and basked in the sun while we read our shirts.

In the late afternoon there was a band concert and ballgame in a freshly mowed field near the town, with the French people as interested spectators.

At 6 p.m. Lieutenant MacNamee told Curtis and me to ride ahead to a place called Vaucouleurs where we were to entrain. He didn't have a map, but he said we could ask the way, and for one of us to hold up at any doubtful corners until the Battery came in sight. We saddled our horses and galloped down the road while the rest of the Battery was getting packed and harnessed.

We had no difficulty finding the place and guiding the Battery to it by 10:30 p.m. It was only about ten kilometers from Troussey.

---

# CHAPTER XXXI

## *We almost go to Paris.*

"Vaucouleurs 10.30 p.m., June 30, 1918. Entrained. Left July 1, 1 a.m. Passed through edge of Paris on train."

---

THERE WAS a tedious wait beside a railroad track before our troop train came along, and when it did we had our work cut out to load guns, wagons, and horses aboard in the dark. Orders were to show no lights as the German bombing planes were active in this region. It was not until one o'clock in the morning that everything was loaded and the train pulled out. I was too sleepy to wonder about where we were going, but some of the men had the idea we were going to parade in Paris on the Fourth of July. The last thing I remember was the familiar, lulling rumble of the wheels as I went to sleep on the boxcar floor.

The next day our troop train rolled along through towns and open country until, late in the afternoon, we were astonished to see the Eiffel Tower and the great Ferris Wheel of Paris. Those who had talked about a Fourth of July parade now made themselves unbearable saying, "I told you so." Their triumph didn't last long, however, for the train only passed through the outskirts of Paris and, curving northward, came again into open country. The prophets in our car hadn't a word to say. The skeptics only smiled a sour smile.

---

## CHAPTER XXXII

### Moving up for the Aisne-Marne offensive.
### Route marking at night.

"St. Mard, 9.30 p.m. July 2, 1918, detrained. Curtis and I rode ahead as scouts. Dick Harding pulled bone. Dark. Villages like deserted. Went through Juilly, Iverny, Meaux, Nanteuil les Meaux. No map; hard work."

---

IT WAS DARK at 9:30 when our train stopped beside the little suburban station of St. Mard. Storer came to our boxcar and said the Major wanted me inside the station. When I got inside I saw a group of men studying maps on a table by the light of a heavily shaded kerosene lamp. I reported to the major and told him who I was.

Without wasting words he showed me where we were on the map. Then he said the Regiment was going to march to a town called Boutigny, and told me I had ten minutes to memorize the map. Then I was to take six mounted men and mark the route. I would have about twenty minutes' start on the first battery, and it would be an all-night march. I saluted as he walked away.

All the time the major had been talking I had kept my eye glued on the point where his finger had touched the map. Now I leaned over it eagerly and began tracing the lines of the road northward through Juilly and Iverny, which looked like small places, to a tangle of lines that was Meaux. I'd have to trust to luck to find my way through there when we got to it, so I picked up the road the other side of Meaux, traced it eastward through Nanteuil, and finally found Boutigny not far from the Marne River. It looked like a long distance, and it came over me that a mistake would be a serious calamity. For ten minutes I studied the roads, their directions and forks, and what landmarks were indicated on the map, as if nothing else in the world existed, and when someone touched my shoulder and said, "Time's up, Corporal," it brought me to life with a start.

When I stepped out into the dark I could still see the map inside my head. I found Peanuts, saddled up, and quickly collected six singlemounted men who were already saddled, and turned into the road at a trot. From a group of figures near the track a motorcycle rider detached himself and drew alongside our cavalcade.

"Are you guys the route markers?" drawled a voice which I recognized above the noise of the engine as Dick Harding's. He belonged to our outfit and had recently got a job as motorcycle rider. "If you are, I'm supposed to go with you."

I told him to shoot ahead to Meaux, spend all his time learning the way through to the Nanteuil Road, and to wait for us this side of the city. As he roared away in the dark I blessed him, for getting through Meaux was my greatest worry.

Once out on the road we struck into a gallop. At the first fork I thought we should take the right, and was glad to be confirmed by a small metal signpost. Leaving one man to wait for the head of the column, the rest of us pushed along. After a few miles we entered a town where there were several streets to choose from. All the houses were dark, and there was no one on the street to ask. I found a signpost, but it was just the name of a street. My companions were bunched together lighting cigarettes. I rode up to the nearest house and pounded on the door. Pretty soon a second-story window opened, and I heard a woman's voice answering.

"Comment s'appelle cette ville-ci?" I yelled.

"Juilly," she said. "Qu'est-ce qu'il-y-a, donc?"

"C'est pour trouver le chemin d'ici a Iverny, Madame," I explained. "Voulez-vous m'aider?" Having by this time concluded we were not highwaymen, she gave me a lot of complicated directions for which I thanked her and pushed on. Before we had gone far I had left all but one of my men at corners. Suddenly I was horrified to see the road end in a large group of buildings. Ringing the bell of the nearest one I found it was a French military hospital. The orderly who answered my ring told me where I had got off the road, so I went back several hundred yards and took the other fork. A little way along this road I found a milestone with Iverny on it, and it certainly looked good. I sent my last man back to wait at the fork and put Peanuts to his best gallop down the road in the other direction.

At Iverny I found more deserted streets and dark houses, but this time I had better luck with the signposts and found the way through to the Meaux highway. I was afraid I had wasted so much time that the column might be catching up to me, but when I got back to the edge of Iverny the road was empty and silent. There was nothing to do now but wait for the first route marker to come up, so I dismounted and, while Peanuts ate grass at the side of the road, I got out a small can of chicken that had been in my saddlebag since I got it in a package from home. I was wondering at the sight of a swarm of fireflies a long way off when I began to hear distant explosions, and I realized that a German air squadron was bombing Meaux. A few minutes later I heard the drone of the planes far overhead.

148

I was relieved to have the nearest route marker gallop up and say that everything was all right; the column was coming, and he had just been relieved by the man behind him. I showed him the way through Iverny and, leaving him to show the next man, I galloped towards Meaux.

Meaux was a big city but it, too, seemed deserted and dark. I found Dick Harding on his motorcycle waiting for me at a stone bridge and asked him if he had the streets straight in his head. He said he had, and here is where I made my mistake. Instead of going ahead with him to make sure, I took his word for it and sat down beside him to smoke a cigarette. Pretty soon the route markers began to come up one after another, and a few minutes after the last one had dismounted I heard the distant rumble of the column growing nearer. When the first horsemen appeared, Dick Harding led them across the bridge and into the business section of the city, and the rest of us rode beside the column. In a few minutes Dick came whizzing back on his motorcycle and gasped out the bad news. He was lost. The streets all looked alike to him and he couldn't tell what turns to take. I never saw anyone so completely demoralized.

While the column halted, we galloped ahead into the city and after half an hour got the maze untangled and led them through, but it spoiled a good job, and I have never forgiven myself for trusting Harding, or him for being such a bonehead.

Once out of Meaux in the faint light of dawn our difficulties were over. We followed a good road through Nanteuil, and at 6:45 a.m. halted in the woods beyond Boutigny.

# CHAPTER XXXIII

## *A day of grace. Boutigny.*

"Boutigny 6.45 a.m., July 3, 1918. Good billets. All in.
In sound of guns. Left 9 p.m., July 4."

I WAS TOO EXHAUSTED to care what happened next, and it was all I could do to keep my eyes open long enough to water Peanuts at a brook and give him a feed of oats. Then I lay down in a barn and slept for a long time.

When I woke up the sun was high, and I could hear the steady grumble of artillery in the distance. I got up, had some dinner, attended to Peanuts, and then went back to sleep till supper time. After supper a big crap game started among the drivers, and I watched around the edge for a while but bed exerted a stronger call and I went back to the barn and turned in.

The next day was July 4th. Some of the boys rode back to Meaux for athletic sports with the 101st Infantry. I spent the day grooming Peanuts and lying around in the sun. There were beautiful hayfields just beyond the woods where our horse lines were stretched, and the air was full of the warm smell of hay.

Late in the afternoon came orders to harness and hitch. As we got ready to pull out, we envied the athletes who were still in Meaux because when they found us gone they could turn in and have a peaceful night's sleep. We waited beside the horses about three hours for the order to march, but instead were ordered to unharness and return to our billets for the night. This was a very pleasant surprise and the order was joyfully carried out. While I was spreading my blankets in the barn the boys began to arrive from Meaux. They were dog-tired, but said they had had a glorious day. They got a bite to eat from the rolling kitchen and turned in almost immediately.

Just as it was getting dark we were disgusted to hear a whistle outside and yells of "A Battery harness and hitch. Snap to, we leave in ten minutes. All out A Battery." There was a scramble to make blanket rolls again, then a rush for the picket lines where the horses were quickly harnessed and saddled, and section by section the Battery reported ready. We moved out near the road and formed column, but there was a long wait before anything more happened.

At about nine o'clock we heard the jingle of a battery coming up the road, and after they had passed we turned out behind them and started another night march.

## CHAPTER XXXIV

### *Marching in the dark. Jouarre.*

"Jouarre 3.45 a.m. July 5, 1918. Asleep on horse.
March as regiment. Left July 5, 6 a.m."

I REMEMBER THIS MARCH because the night was so extraordinarily dark. Living outdoors and moving about at night as we did all the time we found that usually it was possible to see pretty well even without moon or stars, except, of course, in the thick woods or in a storm. But during this march the sky was so black that I couldn't see the man in front of me at all, and once our Battery was saved from getting lost in a town only by following the occasional hot coals which had dropped from the soup gun of the battery ahead.

This was the first time I had the experience of falling asleep on horseback. The column moved so slowly on account of the darkness that there was nothing to do but let the horses follow the horse or gun in front of them with the reins slack, and after midnight I began to nod. I tried various things to keep me awake: chewing tobacco, talking, whistling, and even pinching myself, but it was no use. The gentle motion, the absolute darkness, and the rhythmic sound of hoofs and wheels put me to sleep in spite of myself. Once I woke up with a start to find my arms around Peanuts' neck and my legs dragging in the road.

At quarter of four in the morning we went down a long hill on the paved street of a town and halted in a field. Across the street was a watering trough in a walled yard where I gave Peanuts a drink and, after taking off his saddle and hitching him to a caisson wheel, I crawled under a wagon and went to sleep.

Two hours later someone woke me up and said the captain wanted me. I was still half-asleep, but I heard something about saddling up at once for reconnaissance, and by the time I was really awake I found myself riding out of Jouarre in company with half a dozen horsemen.

## CHAPTER XXXV

### *A reconnaissance. Montreuil-aux-Lions.*

"Montreuil-aux-Lions, 9.30 a.m., July 5, 1918. Echelon of 17th F.A. La Ferté-sous-Jouarre. Château-Thierry. Heat; dust; no food; beaucoup cooties. Left 10 p.m."

BY THE GROWING LIGHT we clattered northward out of Jouarre and almost immediately came in sight of the Marne. A short ride along a wide tree-lined street brought us to La Ferté where we crossed the river on a stone bridge. As we bore to the northeast on a straight, dusty road the sound of the guns came to us very clearly. Someone pointed out a clump of light-colored houses on a hill far to the right as part of Château-Thierry, but I don't know if it really was.

After two hours of riding the heat became intense, and the sweat burned into the chafed skin where the weight of my equipment came on my shoulders. The guns sounded very close now, but the country through which we were riding seemed peaceful. It was mostly patches of woods interspersed with wheat fields and an occasional small town.

At 9:30 a.m., after about a three-hour ride, we walked our horses up a hill and stopped to water them at a stone trough in a village square. This village was deserted. The houses were all empty and there were no civilians on the street. We rode around and found a good place for horse lines on a heavily wooded hillside to the left of the road. Here we spent most of the day. I assumed that we were waiting for the Battery. In the afternoon I found a kitchen belonging to the 17th F.A. and bummed a meal. The cook said his outfit was in the lines somewhere to the east. This town, he said, was Montreuil-aux-Lions.

I went back to the square and found the rest of my party sitting on a flight of stone steps. No one seemed to know what to do, so we tried to get some sleep. I was tired enough but I couldn't get to sleep on account of the itching of my cootie bites which I had been scratching all day. It was a long time since I had had a bath and I was fairly crawling with lice. The poison from the bites made some people sick.

At 10 p.m. Jimmy Clarke appeared with news that a German breakthrough was expected during the night and all plans were off. Our artillery was to take up defensive positions commanding the Marne Valley, and he wanted one man to go with him to a place called Cocherel to head off the Second Battalion, which had started before the change of orders. I saddled Peanuts and went with him.

# CHAPTER XXXVI

## *Detached service. A lost regiment.*

"Cocherel 11.30 p.m., July 5, 1918. Jimmy Clarke. Dark. Billeting.
All in. Fever; cramps. Left 4 a.m., July 6."

THIS WAS ANOTHER dark night and my memory of it is all mixed up. I never saw any town, but Jimmy said we were there when we entered some woods. We found a French billeting officer sitting at a desk in a barn and, after telling him we wanted billets for the night for a battalion of artillery and convincing him that it was not impossible, we followed him around through the woods while he flashed an electric torch in the doors of several ramshackle barns and sheds. This took time, and when we got back to the road to wait for the Battalion we were afraid that it might have already passed.

After waiting on the deserted road for a long time, with Jimmy getting more and more restless, we returned to the French officer and told him our fears. I remember riding in the dark in a motorcycle sidecar, but I haven't the least idea who was driving or where we went. After that there was another long wait on the road, during which I felt sick with chills, cramps, and fever.

At 4 a.m. Jimmy and I gave it up as a bad job, and we rode back to Montreuil.

# CHAPTER XXXVII

## *I find the Battery.*

"Limon, 11.30 a.m., July 6, 1918. Through Bèzu. Vin Murphy and I alone. Slept in ambulance. No food till 8 a.m. July 7. Left 10 a.m. July 7, with Medical Corps. Left afoot with equipment, July 7, 9 a.m."

AT MONTREUIL we found Captain Ticknor, the Regimental Adjutant, in an empty house. He had no idea where any of the batteries were and hadn't seen the Colonel since he went off in a sidecar to look for the scattered Regiment. He thought some of the First Battalion might be at a place called Limon, several miles to the southeast, and he told me to ride over and find out.

My last meal had been the afternoon before, so I felt very empty by this time, and sleepy. Peanuts was better off as he could eat grass, but even he wasn't as lively as usual when we rode eastward out of Montreuil. I had an emergency feed of oats on the saddle, but I was saving it till it should be needed worse.

Outside the town I saw a man riding in my direction. When he got nearer I recognized Vin Murphy, the Colonel's orderly, looking about the way I felt.

"Where's the outfit, Vin?" I yelled.

"God knows," he said. "I'm looking for Ticknor now."

"He's in Montreuil, but he doesn't know where anything is," I told him. "Come with me and we'll find the First Battalion." Vin didn't care where he went, so he turned his horse and we rode on together. We were both too tired to talk. The sun beat down on the dusty road, and the horses plodded along with their heads between their knees.

After passing through a little town called Bèzu-le-Guery we swung south and near noon came in sight of some artillery parked in

155

a clearing in the woods. I was overjoyed to find that it was part of A Battery, and I found Storer and told him all I knew. I must have had a little sunstroke or something for I felt feverish and dizzy and all my bones ached. Storer said there was a Medical Corps ambulance down the road and advised me to go find it. I left Peanuts with the drivers and half an hour later was asleep on a canvas stretcher in the ambulance.

From here on everything is very hazy in my memory. I remember carrying a saddle and blanket roll down a road, and I remember crossing a bridge over a river between steep hills. I don't know whether I was alone or not. I also remember finding an infantry kitchen and getting some canned salmon and a piece of bread. Then there was more heat and more road, and I remember climbing a steep hill and finding a place where there were familiar faces. I didn't wake up for several hours.

---

## CHAPTER XXXVIII

### On the defensive. The Marne Valley.

"Le Moncel, July 7, 1.30 p.m. Secondary platoon.
Swim in Marne. Left July 7, 9 p.m."

---

I FOUND MYSELF lying in the grass at the edge of a path. Someone had covered me with an overcoat. When I stood up my first thought was for food. About fifty yards down the path I found Lorensen with the buzzycot set up and a fire under it. He gave me some hot coffee and stew, which made me feel like new.

The two guns of the second platoon were in position beside the path commanding a long sweep of the Marne Valley, up which the Germans were expected to come. The cannoneers said they had been here all night waiting for the attack. At the top of the steep hill be-

156

hind the guns was a big château called Le Moncel. Most of the hillside was covered with vineyards. The boys said there were some ripe cherries in the château park, but I didn't go up.

Before supper some of us walked down the hill and had a glorious swim in the river. We lay on the grassy bank till we were dry before putting on our clothes. My shirt now got the attention that it had been demanding for over a week. After a good supper and a smoke I was ready for anything.

At 9 p.m. two limbers appeared from somewhere and took the guns down the hill to the main road where the rest of the Battery was waiting. Once more mounted on the faithful Peanuts, I rode beside the column as we left the Marne behind in the growing dusk and headed northeast.

## CHAPTER XXXIX

### *Paris Farm. The front again. A wild ride.*

"Le Petite Boulloye, July 8, 1.20 a.m. (N.E. of Montreuil) Paris Farm. Relieved Btry A, 12th F.A. Pos. in edge of woods. Ralph Farnsworth killed July 13. Montreuil July 14. Echelon for rest. Left 2 p.m. July 18."

THE COLUMN MOVED SLOWLY because the road was crowded with troops, and it was midnight before we entered the familiar square of Montreuil-aux-Lions. It seemed years since I had seen it last, although it was only two days. The heavy wagons turned off the road to the left where we had found the wooded slope for the echelon, but the guns and men of the firing battery continued up the hill to the northeast, where the road ran straight over a sort of barren plateau.

I couldn't get much idea of our surroundings in the dark, but I knew when we turned off the road to the left and followed a cart track through some fields and into the woods. There were 75s firing somewhere near us, and I could hear a steady muttering of artillery to the east. There was also the occasional whine and crash of a German shell, but I couldn't see where they were landing. We passed behind a battery of 155s in a hedge, making a sudden roar and flash each time they fired. Across a clearing and around the corner of a neck of woods we came on a place where men were pulling guns out of gun pits, and limbers were picking them up. They were from the Twelfth Field Artillery, whom we were to relieve.

While our cannoneers were getting our guns into the vacant pits, Ritchie and I found a good hole in the woods and put our blankets into it. I gave Peanuts a feed of oats which I found strapped to his saddle, but before I could get back to the hole there was a call for me, and I was sent on a wild-goose chase to find Battalion Headquarters at some farm half a mile away. When I found it there was nothing to do but wait around in the dark, and after an hour or two I got sick of it and went back to the Battery. Ritchie was out somewhere stringing telephone wire, so I rolled up in my blankets and went to sleep.

We stayed in the Paris Farm position for ten days, so I remember the place quite well. It took its name from a big ruined farmhouse on the Paris-Metz Road about a quarter of a mile away. The Germans evidently thought we had a headquarters there, for they shelled it constantly. As a matter of fact, no one went near it except Woody, who drove the water cart for our Battery, and he dashed in every day, filled his tank at the big trough in the barnyard, and galloped out as if the devil were after him. He was a good-natured, bashful youth from somewhere in the corn belt, who was sent to us as a replacement. I never heard him called anything but Woody.

The Paris Farm stood on a crossroads from which one road ran north to Torcy and Belleau. Two of our guns were in the woods beside this road and the other two were about five hundred yards behind them in the edge of another clump of woods. Between were wheat fields scarred by a few large shell holes. To the east we could see the line of the Paris–Metz Road marked by a row of trees, and beyond it several German balloons.

The forward position was being saved for the German attack, which was daily expected, so only a few men lived there to look after the guns, while all the firing was done from the rear position. These two guns fired about four hundred rounds a night. The men slept in holes in the woods a few yards behind the guns. Ritchie and I thought ours was the neatest. It had been lined with shell boxes full of dirt, so we had wooden walls, and there was room to sit up inside without touching the shelter half which protected us from the rain. The kitchen was fifty yards back in the woods. There were no trenches or dugouts anywhere.

We found the ground all around the position covered with human excreta, and one of our first concerns was to clean up the woods and dig a regular latrine.

"If that's the way an outfit from the United States Regular Army leaves a position," said Ritchie, "I'm glad we don't have to follow our friends the Senegalese." There was all kinds of junk in these woods. I found a Marine Corps overcoat that just fitted me, and I wore it on cool nights until it got lost.

It wasn't long before we got the position fixed to suit us, and the days fell into a regular routine, as much as days could at the front. The worst job was carrying shells from the caissons to the gun pits. Every night the drivers brought five or six hundred shells up from some ammunition dump in the rear. The horses could get no nearer than the edge of the woods, so the shells all had to be carried the rest of the way by hand. Four shells weighed about a hundred pounds, and that was all a man could carry, holding two under each arm. Then the projectile end was so much heavier than the shell case that they were very awkward to hold and kept slipping and falling to the ground. We tried using empty sandbags to carry them in, and this was the most satisfactory way. Some of the boys rigged up hand-barrows, but the wood paths were so rough that they found it impossible for two men to carry anything between them. One man alone had trouble enough to keep from falling into the bushes or walking into a hole full of sleeping friends. Someone found a wicker baby carriage which worked pretty well for carrying shells until it collapsed under the weight.

For the first week we seemed to have lost touch with our Quartermaster Department, for all the rations we got were French. The hard black bread wasn't so bad, but there was a sort of semiliquid canned beef—"monkey meat" we called it—that was awful. We felt they should have given us the French issue of wine to offset it but they didn't. One day someone saw a wild pig over near the first platoon position, and we all scoured the woods, pistol in hand and mouths watering, but we never saw the pig again.

In spite of all our firing the position remained undiscovered. A few 210-millimeter shells made deep holes in the field between the platoons, and there was heavy shelling at Paris Farm and in the woods to our rear, but our position was never struck. It was strange because all this time the Germans had command of the air, and their aviators flew around at will. One day a Boche plane came flying low over the treetops and dove towards the guns. I stepped behind the trunk of a tree and heard several of his machine gun bullets whack into it. No one was hurt, not even Peanuts and the water cart horses who were hitched to trees near the kitchen.

On the night of July 13th the third section gun, Xantippe, blew up. The guns had been firing all night, and I was asleep in my hole when I was suddenly wakened by an unusual sound. As I scrambled out of the hole I heard cries for help. The third section gun pit was only about forty yards away, and I was soon there. Someone was already in the gun pit, and by the light of an electric torch I saw Ralph Farnsworth's body lying across the trail of the gun. I had known him at college and I used to play with his cousin Claude on the beach when I was about four years old. His glasses were in the mud close to his head. I picked them up and found they weren't

broken, but when I saw that Ralph was dead, I threw them away.*
A little chap from Pennsylvania, named Dyer, had been firing the
gun with Farnsworth, and we found him running through the woods
screaming that he was blind. The whole back end of the gun had
blown out. As soon as Dyer was caught and started towards Montreuil with two men, we put a blanket over Ralph's body and went
back to bed. I felt sick.

In the morning as we gathered around the kitchen everyone was
very silent. I was glad when MacNamee sent me back to the echelon
for a week's rest.

I found there were really two echelons. Montreuil was so far from
the guns that it made too long a circuit for the drivers on their night-
ly trips to the ammunition dump and from there to the position, so
only the heavy wagons and spare men and horses were at Montreuil
while the drivers and caisson teams had made a forward echelon in
the woods to the right of the Paris-Metz Road.

Jack Kunhardt was acting top sergeant at Montreuil, and one of
the Plattsburg lieutenants was in charge. There were a few drivers
who were not needed at the forward echelon, and the rest were
mechanics, farriers, and cooks. They all lived high and loafed
around in the woods with nothing to do but look after about forty
horses. I entered into the spirit of Montreuil from the first day. All I
had to do was take care of Peanuts. The rest of the time I slept, ate,
walked around, and gossiped with Jack Kunhardt.

One warm night Jack and I had been sitting around his shack
talking and finishing up a bottle of Benedictine he had, when the
spirit moved us to walk up to the picket line in the woods and say
goodnight to our horses. When we had done this Jack remarked,
"There's some open fields on top of the hill. What do you say we
take a ride up there and cool off?" That suited me, so we mounted
our horses bareback and rode them up through the woods without

* The breechblock, weighing about seventy pounds, hit him in the small of the back,
presumably crushing his spine.

even bridles. I shall never forget the next half hour. As the horses raced around the fields high above the treetops, I seemed to be flying between the earth and the stars. If it hadn't been for the Benedictine we would surely have broken our necks.

On the night of July 18th I went to sleep as usual in a comfortable pup tent full of hay and saddle blankets just above the picket line. About one o'clock in the morning I was startled out of a sound sleep by Kunhardt's whistle and somebody yelling, "Everybody up. Harness and stand to horse." At the same time I became aware of a tremendous volume of sound, as if all the artillery in the sector were firing at once. I was among the first to reach the picket line, where sleepy drivers were throwing harness on the horses in the dark. As I saddled Peanuts, Kunhardt came along and I heard someone yell, "Hey, what the hell's the idea!"

"The drive is on, you sap, can't you hear the guns?"

"Yeh, but what of it. They can get along without us, can't they?"

"That's all right. You get those horses harnessed and don't talk so damn much," and Kunhardt's voice lost itself in the direction of the kitchen. Above the jingle of harness I heard scraps of comment, "Thinks he's God Almighty, waking everybody up for nothing."

"Yah, the goddamned fool," and a good deal more, but I had Peanuts saddled and bridled, so I led him back to my pup tent, tied him to a tree, and crawled into my blankets for another nap.

When I woke up in the morning the noise of the barrage had died down to a steady growl. All the horses were standing harnessed at the picket line where we had left them. I fed Peanuts and had some breakfast. Kunhardt was still waiting for orders to move. I strolled out to the road and saw groups of wounded doughboys walking back through Montreuil. They stood aside to let one or two ambulances lurch by, going in the same direction. When I returned to the kitchen everyone was busy packing up and loading wagons, so I made my blanket roll and lay around in the sun waiting for something to happen.

Just after lunch Stan Curtis rode in and found me.

"MacNamee wants a lot of gas stuff," he said. "The Boches are sending over mustard." I was smoking a cigar and hated to be interrupted, but I jumped up and found two bunches of gas-proof hats and mittens in the battery wagon, and a minute later Stan and I were on the road, each with a bundle in front of us on the saddle. We walked our horses up the long hill out of Montreuil, and when we reached the top we stopped. A 155 shell had just burst about two hundred yards in front, right in the center of the road.

"Come in back of this house," said Stan, "and we'll look things over." It was the last house in Montreuil, standing alone at the right of the road. From its shelter we saw the deserted tree-lined road stretched out under the hot sun. Another shell crashed, this time nearer to us, but in the ditch. A tall poplar slowly leaned farther and farther over and fell across the road like a railroad-crossing gate.

I was casting around in my mind for another way of getting to the Battery and Stan must have been doing the same, for he said, "Well, this road is the only way up, and MacNamee's waiting." I looked at my watch. A shell burst in the road, and a splinter hit the stone house in front of us. Peanuts was fidgeting around, full of oats and crazy for action. Stan was watching me with a doubtful smile. A minute passed and, as my second hand reached 60, another shell landed, this time almost three hundred yards down the road.

"All right, Stan," I said. "They're coming just a minute apart. We'll wait for the next one and then go like hell." Stan nodded and gathered his reins. I chewed my cigar nervously, wondering if I'd ever smoke another. I heard the approaching whine and leaned forward in my saddle. Crash, and I gave Peanuts the spurs. With a rush we were on the road and galloping side by side. We went through the smoke of the last shell and over the fallen tree. Without slackening speed Peanuts avoided shell holes and broken branches. The rush of wind was filling my eyes with cigar ashes, but I didn't care. I chewed the butt and listened for the whine of the next shell. We were almost to the last shell hole when I heard it. Out of the tail of my eye I saw Curtis lying flat on his horse's neck. I felt a mile up in the air. If this one falls short, goodbye. There was a whistling scream and a crash behind me. I heard the angry sizzle of flying splinters. When I opened my eyes, Stan was still there. We galloped five hundred yards farther for luck before pulling down to a canter. Curtis was laughing.

"What the hell are you laughing at, you dizzy bastard?" I asked him.

"Look at your face," he gasped.

"What's wrong with my face?" I put up my hand and found that my cigar had unraveled, and I was plastered with the wet tobacco leaves. Only a ragged tuft remained clenched in my teeth.

When we reached the Battery we found the limbers waiting at the edge of the woods. All four guns were firing, but everything was picked up, and the cannoneers' packs were piled on the ground.

"Anything happened?" I asked Ritchie.

"No, but I think we're moving up most any time," he said. It seemed some gas shells had landed near without hurting anybody.

At about 7 p.m. several caissons of ammunition appeared, the guns were limbered up, and we pulled across the field and turned to the left on the Torcy road. Curtis and I rode at the head of the column with MacNamee.

# CHAPTER XL

*First three days of the Aisne-Marne offensive.*
*War in the open. More losses.*

"Lucy le Bocage, July 18, 8 p.m. Position unprotected in woods. July 19, killed Cunningham, Larry Williams. Wounded, Seth Eldridge*, Tyler, Dunn, Martin. (*died on stretcher). Left 10 a.m., July 21."

IT WAS STILL broad daylight as we turned right off the road through the little hamlet of Lucy le Bocage and entered a wide field of ripe wheat. I had a feeling of unreality to be riding a horse out here in plain sight of the Germans, where a few hours ago I wouldn't have dared show my head. I noticed several places where shells had exploded on impact, leaving great radiating stars of bare ground as their splinters had cut paths through the wheat. The fields were full of bright-red poppies.

We crossed to the edge of a wood and skirted it until we came to a point of small trees projecting into the wheat field. Here we un-limbered the guns, unloaded the shells from the caissons, and sent the horses back. While the gun crews were placing their guns in the edge of the bushes I led Peanuts about fifty yards into the woods, loosened his girth, took off his bridle, and tied him to a little birch tree. Then I took a look around the woods.

There were a good many mounds of fresh earth marked by a helmet on a rifle stuck bayonet down into the ground, and I found a few dead Germans in the bushes where they had been overlooked by burying parties. The odor was bad, as it was several days since the Marines had taken Belleau Wood. There were a number of foxholes made by the infantry, some of them roofed with logs and dirt, but most of them open. There were German potato-masher grenades in some of them. I noticed a shallow trench about sixty yards from the guns.

Our cooks had set up the buzzycot in a little clearing in the bushes near the wheat field, and I got a handful of hardtack on my way back to the guns. It was getting dark by this time, and the noise of firing was dying down. A few machine guns in front of us sounded very close. I took a last look at Peanuts to be sure he was safe for the night and then I opened my blankets and joined Woody under the water cart.

I woke up about sunrise and crawled out from under the water cart. There was more firing than last night. Most of the men were already up, and I could hear voices in the direction of the kitchen. I got my mess kit out of my saddlebags and walked down the path between the wheat field and the edge of the woods to get some breakfast.

There was a man on the path about thirty feet in front of me, but his back was towards me and I couldn't see who it was. He had a mess kit in his hand. To the left of the path I noticed a clump of heavy green grass and stooped over to pull some of it for Peanuts. Just as I stooped I heard a whiz and crash almost simultaneously. There was smoke over the path ahead. The man I had been following was lying on his back with the helmet over his face and his mess kit still in his hand. I went up to him and lifted the helmet. The face was a slate-gray color, and the eyes were open. I didn't know who it was. There was blood spreading onto the path from under him. My only feeling was a panicky desire to get away. I ran down the path to the kitchen clearing where the drivers were sitting around drinking coffee.

"That sounded close; where were you?" said someone. I tried to speak but my voice wouldn't work. I swallowed and tried again.

"Somebody's bumped off on the path," I said. "You better go see who it is." Then I got a cup of coffee. Two or three of the drivers stood up and walked over to the path.

"It's Phil Cunningham,"* they reported. "He got it in the back. Must have been a one-pounder."

* I went to school at Volkmann's with Phil Cunningham for four years.

166

MacNamee had finished his breakfast and was standing near the buzzycot smoking a cigarette. Suddenly the air was full of explosions. Without a warning sound, shells began to crash into the woods between us and the guns. I could hear the splinters cutting through the bushes. Everyone stood up uncertainly, holding their mess kits. The shells were still coming thick.

"There's a trench over there," said MacNamee, pointing with his bamboo cane. "Drop those damn mess kits and run for it." A shell exploded beyond the buzzycot. MacNamee never moved. As the men ran past him, he gave each one a slap with his cane, saying quietly, "Come on, come on, move fast." When we had all reached the trench, he followed us.

I still had a mess kit full of bacon and half a cup of coffee in my hand. I crouched in the trench and kept on eating. From where I was I could see the guns across a clearing. The woods were full of smoke, and above the racket of exploding shells I could hear cries of "Help," and "Stretcher bearer." The ammunition pile behind the fourth piece was on fire, and the smoke around it was full of the flashes of bursting high explosives. Some fool was dancing around trying to put out the fire with a bucket of water. MacNamee dashed over and pulled him off. I saw it was Charley Johnson. He later got the D.S.C. for it. I stood aside to let a stretcher go down the trench, carried by the Medical Corps man and one of our cannoneers. They had a little chap named Tyler on it. I got a glimpse of a cigarette between his white lips.

I don't know how long the racket lasted but probably not over twenty minutes. As soon as we dared we climbed out of the trench and approached the guns. There were still scattered explosions from the fourth piece ammunition pile, and the air was full of the bitter smell of powder. I found the birch where I had tied Peanuts cut off about two feet from the ground. Peanuts was grazing nearby in the bushes without a scratch on him. In the edge of the woods I saw someone lying on a stretcher on the ground. His face was so white I hardly recognized him as Seth Eldridge. The Medical Corps man had blood on his forehead and his glasses were broken, but he was busy putting bandages on Dunn and Martin. I went to get my blankets from under the water cart and found them torn to ribbons and still smoking. The cannoneers were getting back to their guns and clearing away the fallen branches and wreckage. I saw MacNamee strolling near them, still with his dapper cane in his hand. He beckoned to me and told me to saddle up and ride back to the echelon for the fourgon to carry back those who had been hit.

I was more than glad of the chance to get away from the devilish place and lost no time mounting Peanuts and heading for Lucy le Bocage. It was still early morning and the new sun on the red poppies and yellow wheat looked beautiful and natural. I thought of poor old Seth Eldridge and how enthusiastic he had always been about the beauties of French landscapes. He was an artist, and about as unfitted for "wallowing" as was Ives Gammell. I had often heard him explain with a crooked smile how he had enlisted "in an unguarded moment of misguided enthusiasm." Most of the Battery laughed at Seth and thought he was a little cuckoo. And Phil Cunningham, how quickly he had been wiped out. I had never liked Phil when I went to school with him at Volkmann's, and I was not particularly pleased to find him in the Battery at Boxford, but his sudden death gave me a shock.

At Lucy le Bocage there seemed to be a dressing station in a barn close to the cart road, where there was a wrecked ambulance in a ditch and, beside the road, a row of lifeless figures covered with blankets, all but their feet. I overtook and passed a straggling line of wounded doughboys walking to the rear with big yellow tags tied to their arms. Some were helping each other along but mostly each man was walking mechanically with no thought for anything but to keep moving. On the highway I passed a machine gun outfit going up to the lines with their little mule carts in single file at the side of the road. Paris Farm was silent and deserted as I rode past, and a few

168

minutes later I turned into the fields and reached the forward echelon in the edge of the woods. The drivers were standing around eating breakfast, and some of them were still asleep in pup tents. I gave my message, had a cup of coffee, told the news in monosyllables, and reluctantly rode back to the Battery.

In the open stretch between Lucy le Bocage and our corner of Belleau Wood there was a single stunted tree, and under this I found something that had not been there an hour before. It was a smashed ration cart. There was hardtack scattered all over the ground around it. I dismounted and filled my pockets. When I got near the Battery I saw that everyone was greatly excited and the guns were firing very rapidly. I galloped Peanuts to see what was going on. From my mounted height I could see over the rise of the wheat field before I reached the Battery and it was a remarkable sight.

Below our rising ground was a sunken road from which our infantry were trying to attack a low plateau, and on the plateau a company of German machine gunners were setting up their guns in shell holes. The whole thing was in plain sight from our hill. I could see the German officer giving directions and pointing with a cane as groups of men moved about in the field. Our guns were firing at them by direct observation and were making hit after hit, but what Germans were left kept doggedly at their job. Near our water cart I saw three pairs of boots sticking out from under a blanket covered with flies in the hot sun. Someone came running towards me yelling, but I couldn't hear a word till he got right up to me.

"Go back for more ammunition, and ride like hell," I finally made out.

"Who's under the blanket?" I yelled as he turned away.

"Seth Eldridge, Larry Williams, and Cunningham . . ." was all I heard as I wheeled Peanuts and touched him with the spurs.

So they got Larry Williams. I recalled that night at the armory when he had been playing the piano, and someone had told me his name. I galloped Peanuts all the way to the echelon without drawing rein and the first man I saw was Dinger Wheelwright, a cassion corporal.

"Got some loaded caissons?" I gasped. He nodded.

"Well, get them hitched and snap up to the guns as fast as God'll let you. I'll wait and show you the way." There was a flurry of action as mess kits clattered on the ground and drivers sprang to the horse line. I saw Dinger reach a long arm into a pup tent and pull out a lazy driver by the scruff of the neck. When the driver talked back, Dinger smashed him in the face* and he fell like a log. By the time Peanuts had his breath, the drivers were mounted and the caissons were swinging into the field at a lumbering trot.

"Gallop," I yelled as Peanuts dashed past the head of the column. As I reached the tree where the hardtack was spilled I looked back and saw them strung out about fifty yards apart, coming "on the loop," with the horses at a dead gallop and the caissons bouncing bodily into the air as their wheels struck rocks and stumps. No one paid any attention to a few shell bursts in the wheat field near the woods.

We were in time to see the Battery fire their last shell. There were still a few Germans manning the machine guns on the plateau, but with a fresh supply of ammunition our guns soon drove them off, and I saw scattered groups in khaki move across the plateau and disappear into the woods beyond.

In the afternoon the fourgon came up and went away with the three bodies. We worked hard digging shallow holes for shelter near the guns. After dark Ritchie and I crawled into neighboring holes and went to sleep.

The next day our gunners had to sink the trails of the guns in order to reach their targets, so we inferred things were going well with the infantry. When I rode back to the echelon I found that Divisional Headquarters had moved up to Lucy le Bocage. The roads were now

* Dinger lost his stripes for that.

## "Things were going well with the infantry."

Twenty-sixth Division infantry in the streets of Flaville. You can almost hear the whine of the shell from which these two doughboys are seeking cover. In addition this open space is probably under machine gun fire from the hill in the background. There may be German machine gunners still hidden in some of the houses. The tank is deserted as shown by its open manhole cover. Notice how the dead German's feet lie flat— an attitude seldom seen during life.

crowded with troops and wagon trains crawling towards the front. There were gangs of engineers filling shell holes, dragging away fallen trees, and mending culverts. Everywhere I heard the rumor that the Germans were pulling back. Ritchie and I had another peaceful night in our holes, and in the morning the Battery suddenly moved.

---

# CHAPTER XLI

### Into the enemy's country. Ferme St. Robert.
### "The Major's Promenade."

"Fme. St. Robert, July 21. N.E. of Epieds. Advanced all day behind infantry.
Position in edge of woods. Left July 24, 9 a.m."

---

I REMEMBER riding ahead of the column with MacNamee through the wheat fields to the shattered hamlet of Belleau, where the road was littered with German grenades, rifles, and packs, and rubbish from the shell-torn trees and houses. In a ditch beside the road I saw a pair of legs in gray-green breeches and heavy field boots. The upper part of the body looked like shapeless blackened rags. Turning to the right, we passed through Torcy and began climbing the side of the valley through open fields. We passed a lot of our infantry resting in a clump of woods. Small groups of wounded men were straggling back all the time. MacNamee kept sending me to make sure the column was coming in good order. It consisted of four guns and limbers, nine caissons and limbers, the water cart, and the soup gun.

It wasn't until we reached the Etrepilly Road that we began running into traffic. Ambulances, wounded men, and stragglers choked half the roadway, while the other half was a solid mass of artillery, ammunition trains, machine gun units, and French and American infantry all flowing eastward like a sluggish stream. At one place we passed a group of gutted houses still smouldering.

As the road led over the Etrepilly plateau the dead Germans became more numerous, lying in the ditch in grotesque attitudes and dotted over the fields beside the road. They were all bloated from the hot sun and crawling with flies. I saw a German wagon that had been hit by one of our shells. It was a splintered wreck lying on its side with the two dead horses in a tangle of harness and the driver on the ground a few feet away. There were rifles, overcoats, helmets, boots, blankets, broken machine guns, cartridge belts, potato-masher grenades, and a litter of rubbish strewn along the road, and ground into the dirt by the constant passage of troops and wheels.

Many of our cannoneers armed themselves with rifles and formed a sort of advance guard for the column. I saw some of our fellows running off the road to pick up German bayonets or helmets or pistols for souvenirs, but they soon tired of carrying them and threw them away.

At narrow places in the road where shell holes or fallen trees obstructed traffic there were interminable halts. From the top of the plateau several German balloons were visible. The column halted off the road, and MacNamee and I rode through fields skirting the edges of woods until we came to an abandoned German position in a little gully shaded by a row of trees. About three hundred yards to the left of it was a group of rambling farm buildings called Ferme St. Robert on the map, and less than a mile to the east was a row of trees marking the Bethune–Château-Thierry Road, where we could see shells bursting. MacNamee thought our infantry was probably holding that line. Beyond it were the German balloons. A haze of heat shimmered in the air.

I rode back and gave Kunhardt the message to make an echelon in the woods where he was, and to bring the guns up ahead. He rode up with me to see the way, and I remember he dared me follow him over a fallen tree that I had rode around before. While he was getting the guns I found a shorter way into the position through some fresh barbwire entanglements in the rear.

After exploring this position we decided it had been a German balloon base. They had rigged up a shower bath, and there were numerous shallow dugouts built into the hillside. The place was full of souvenirs and German magazines and letters. There were several cases of empty, long-necked wine bottles in straw covers. In one dugout I found a pair of soiled satin high-heeled slippers.

The guns were soon established under the row of trees, which was really a sort of thick hedge, and Ritchie, Beck, Peabo and company set to work stringing telephone wires while I rode over to St. Robert Farm where Battalion Headquarters was moving in. Lying across the gateway was a dead horse, a huge animal, but now so swollen that his appearance was extraordinary. The two legs on the upper side were stiff and pointed to the sky at an angle of forty-five degrees. Around his middle was a surcingle which had not broken as he swelled, so he had the effect of being almost cut in two by it. The odor was penetrating, pungent, and most offensive. Peanuts shied and almost landed me on my ear. For ten minutes I tried to get him past that dead horse, but he would plant his legs and stand shivering, with his eyes rolling in terror. I tried blindfolding him with my coat and leading him past, but just as I thought I was succeeding he would give a snort and tear the reins out of my hands. I had to give it up, tie him in the woods, and go the rest of the way on foot. In the barnyard were more dead horses which the Headquarters men were dragging away with long ropes. I reported A Battery in position and went back to the guns.

The horses had left, and MacNamee told me to follow them and help Kunhardt find the new ammunition dump, which the drivers said was on the move when they last saw it. It was getting dark when we set out. We struck cross-country over the fields in the direction we thought it would be. These fields were riddled with cart roads, especially along the edges of the woods, so the going was not bad.

At one place we heard a rustling sound in a dark clump of bushes beside the path. The light was too dim to see anything so we yelled, "Who's there?" There was no answer and the rustling stopped. Jack drew his pistol and fired a shot into the bushes. After waiting a minute we rode on. I never knew what it was; perhaps a stray horse, but it may have been a German, as our infantry didn't always get them all in their "mopping-up."

As soon as we came out on the main road we saw the dump. Four or five big trucks were throwing ammunition boxes down beside the road while a detail of men opened them with pickaxes and the drivers of three batteries fought to get their caissons loaded.

I have vague recollections of more riding in the dark, but I can't recall sleeping anywhere. One peculiar experience I remember. I was riding Peanuts at a walk beside some woods, and a single file of infantry was passing in the opposite direction. As the silent, dim shapes slipped by close to my horse in an interminable succession I felt myself getting dizzy. I tried shutting my eyes till they were past, but when I looked again they were still coming in endless line, and I found myself counting against my will. Hundreds went by; it must have been a battalion going into support. The ghostlike shadows came past like things in a nightmare and I kept seeing them whether I closed my eyes or not, and I couldn't stop the monotonous counting in my head.

My next memory of St. Robert Farm is of what happened the following night. The limbers came up and pulled the guns out of the hedge into a field where C and B Batteries were waiting in column. With our Battery in the lead, the Battalion column passed St. Robert Farm and slowly wound down a cart road towards the German flares. I noticed that the dead horse no longer lay across the gateway. On and on we went, through open fields under a starlit sky, and I heard strange rumors of our destination. One was that we were going ahead of the infantry to take up position in no-man's-land. My informant said it had been tried by the British, who found it very effective until the guns were captured or put out of action by machine gun fire. I believed it enough to feel pretty scared, I remember, and I think now it was really true.

After going a kilometer or more we turned to the right and halted in a hollow road beside a row of roofless houses. On the map I found this place marked as the hamlet of Chante-Merle. As soon as the column halted, shells began to fall around us, most of them exploding a few yards beyond the road. By their flashes I could see the individual stones of the wall under which I stood and some ivy growing near the top. I dismounted to be close to the ground. All the drivers were standing at their horses' heads. I knew we were fairly safe from direct hits, but if a shell knocked the wall down on us we were done. It was a miracle that none of them did, for they must have been just grazing it to land so close beyond the road.

This lasted about an hour. I heard another rumor that our infantry were falling back, and the Germans were attacking. Soon after, we got orders to mount. Leaving the shelter of the sunken road, the column wound out into the fields and made a wide circle to the right, then hit a cart road and followed it back to St. Robert Farm. We pulled the guns into their old places under the hedge, the horses went back to the echelon, and nothing more happened for the rest of the night. "The Major's Promenade" the boys called it, and it's a good thing he never heard some of the jokes about it.

At 9 a.m. the limbers came up again and we pulled the guns out and started across the field in column, just as we had done a few hours before.

# CHAPTER XLII

## *Crowded roads. Some green troops. Epieds.*

"N.E. of Epieds, July 24, 7 p.m. Evacuated this a.m. by Boches. Lots of dead horses;
not many bodies. Miles of allied artillery on roads. Epieds blocked with infantry
and machinegunners. Position in row of trees. Good dugout. Nobody hurt.
Left July 28, 9 p.m. Rain."

OUR BATTERY was part of a slowly moving river of artillery. From a hilltop I could see three roads winding away in the distance and above each hung a low, thin layer of dust beneath which the roads themselves seemed moving, so crowded were they with troops pushing up in the wake of the Germans.

At the foot of the steep hill into Epieds we halted for a long time. I rode ahead beside the column, past ditches full of dead horses and rubbish from freshly demolished houses. Below a bullet-scarred garden wall I saw a row of dead American doughboys partly covered with blankets and shelter halves. They lay on their backs with their feet turned out, and their faces were gray. In the village square there was a traffic jam, with columns of infantry and machinegunners trying to cross and their officers arguing and swearing around. One outfit was being fed at a rolling kitchen in an orchard. A staff car was drawn up beside the road, and I caught a glimpse of General Edwards in the thick of the snarl.

After a while our column began to move. We turned to the left in the square and took a cart road to the right between rows of hedges. Everywhere were dead horses, not yet swollen, but lying very flat and collapsed with their necks stretched out. I remember a clump of big oaks where a German battery had been in action a few hours before. The ground was littered with empty shell cases and the queer wicker baskets in which they kept their ammunition. There

176

were plenty of shell holes made by our guns, and some of the trees had splintered limbs hanging from them or lying on the ground.

So slow was our progress that it was 7 p.m. before we arrived at the place we were to go into position. Ritchie, Beck, Peabo, and I found a hole in the woods, covered with logs as big as telegraph poles, where we dumped our stuff. There were several similar holes nearby, probably built by the Germans not long before. The guns were placed under a single row of tall trees which ran parallel to the edge of the woods about fifty yards away. The rolling kitchen was in a tangle of bushes just off a cart road.

The Battery stayed here four days, firing most of the time.

I took several long rides back to the rear echelon and ammunition dumps, and the roads were always crowded with troops: infantry halted along the side to let a caisson train go by, the men lying back against their packs, artillery regiments bivouacking in fields, ambulances, supply wagons, water carts, ammunition convoys, all out in the open with no attempt at concealment from the enemy.

I remember seeing a German plane come down in flames about half a mile in front of our position. It left a trail of black smoke as it fell, and before it crashed I could see converging groups of Americans running towards the spot. Some of our boys ran over in the same spirit I have seen in children at the cry of "Kite broke away." They came back with the report that it was pas bon, no souvenirs, all burnt up. Even the aviator was just a charred mummy. They felt they had been cheated.

One night a lot of green infantry moved into the woods behind us and made themselves at home. They were two regiments from the 28th Division, who had never been at the front before. Peabo and I walked over for a visit and found them sitting around campfires as if they were in the Adirondacks. In the morning I saw them moving up in single file through the wheat fields. Whenever a shell burst in the same field with them they scattered in every direction. Later we heard they had been "wiped out," but we always thought they must have wiped themselves out. They left enough equipment behind in the woods to last us for the rest of the war.

By the length of time we stayed in this position we judged the infantry must be held up, but we were off the main road so we got no first-hand information. On one of my rides to the echelon a wounded man told me about a place called Croix Rouge Farm where his company had been "wiped out." This was a favorite expression with the doughboys and always meant they had suffered losses, but they used it to mean complete annihilation. It must often have seemed so to a man who saw all of his squad killed and was himself wounded.

On July 28th at 9 p.m. the limbers came up in a pouring rainstorm, and we pulled through the little hamlet of Courpoil and went onto the main road.

## CHAPTER XLIII

### *A crossroad in the Forêt de Fère. French cavalry. Scenes around the Croix Rouge Farm.*

"Ferme Croiz Rouge. July 29, 1.30 a.m. Fère-en-Tardenois–Charmel road; rain, dark. Guns in camouflage hedge; no protection. Fields full of dead Americans and French. Woods full of dead Boches. Roads lined with rotten dead horses. Stench. Left July 29, 9 p.m."

I HAD PICKED UP a poncho which I wore instead of a slicker and I was thankful for it now. I don't know whether it was a product of the French, German, or American army, but it shed the water and was long enough to protect my blanket roll and the saddlebags when I was mounted, which was more than the regulation slicker would do. The rain on my helmet sounded like hail on a tin roof. The night was dark, but there were frequent flashes in the sky, enough to show a momentary picture of the roadside or the shining flank of the horse in front.

After about three kilometers we passed through a town, as we could tell by the paved streets and the vague loom of dark houses. Later I found that it was called Beuvardes.

When the road entered a large wood—the Forêt de Fère—it was like going into a tunnel, except for occasional glimpses of sky overhead. The road ran straight as a ruler for several kilometers through the darkness. It emerged at a large crossroad where the air was poisoned by something rotting—a black thing on the ground. We turned to the right on a crossroad just discernible as lighter than its surroundings. Below us to the left were twinkling lights like fireflies, and we got the distant detonations of bursting shells.

At 1:30 a.m. our Battery turned in a sort of driveway and halted near some woods. Only the four guns and the rolling kitchen were with us as the caissons had been loading at the dump when we started. They had orders to follow along on the Charmel Road until met. I was looking for a place to sleep and, although sleepy enough, I was about despairing of finding one in the dark and wet when Mac-Namee found me. He said the caissons would be along anytime, and to ride back to the crossroads and bring them in when they came and for God's sake not to slip up because, aside from his needing the ammunition, if they should miss the turn in the dark they would ride into the German lines. Fortunately, Peanuts was still saddled so I mounted and galloped back without loss of time.

My only worry was that they might pass the crossroads before I could get there. I was reassured by finding everything dark and still. I tied Peanuts to a bush and sat down on the bank to wait. There wasn't a breath of wind, so the stench of the black thing in the road was inescapable. It made me sick at first, but after an hour I was almost used to it. Several infantry outfits straggled past at route march, the men's feet making a soft munch-munch in the mud, and once I heard wheels and ran down the road, only to find that it was an infantry kitchen.

During the long wait I found the corner very lonely. No shells fell

179

near it, but there was an air of expectancy and uncomfortableness that made me glad of Peanuts' company. There was something reassuring about the soft rustling noises he made in the bushes. As dawn came the rain stopped, and the black thing in the road began to take on definite shape. I saw that it was the rotting carcasses of three horses. Apparently all three of them had been killed by a single shell burst for they lay close together right at the center of the crossroad. The growing light brought out more and more detail, and I studied them as there was nothing else to look at. They were in the advanced stages of decomposition and lay flatter and more collapsed than newly killed carcasses. The hide was stretched like black leather over projecting bones where the hair had rotted off. They lay in a dark puddle of confluent liquid putrescence swarming with maggots. One of them was crushed where heavy wheels must have passed over it in the dark.

Suddenly I heard horses coming through the woods and strained my ears for the sound of toggle chains and wheels. I could see a couple of hundred yards down the tree-shaded tunnel of a road, but I knew it couldn't be my caissons even before the first horseman appeared around the bend. Under the trees at a sharp trot came a regiment of French cavalry in column of fours. Each rider carried a lance with a fluttering pennon at the tip. As they swept past I saw that it must be a crack regiment. Every strap and buckle was uniform, the horses were beautifully polished, the steel helmets were all worn at the same angle, and the ranks were kept compactly closed up so that the whole column moved as a unit without checking or change of pace. I stood lost in admiration until the last horseman had disappeared beyond the crossroad. Later in the day I saw the same outfit returning against the evening sky, the horses fagged, the men drooping with weariness, and about half the saddles empty, some with the dead men's lances thrust through the cantle rings.

About an hour after the cavalry passed I heard the welcome rumble of wheels and saw Kunhardt riding at the head of the caisson train. I mounted Peanuts and joined him.

"Anything happened?" he asked.

"No, nothing," I said; and then as an afterthought added, "Some Frogs just went by."

Although it was my third trip over this piece of road, it was all new to me in the daylight. A rolling slope of wheat fields dotted with farms and clumps of woods swept from the left edge of the road out of sight in a valley. On the right we were separated from the woods by the width of one field. The road was pocked with shell holes, and I saw a few dead horses scattered along in the ditch. The wheat near the road was trampled into paths or blackened where shells had exploded. Here and there I spied what looked like bundles of olive-drab clothes lying below the surface of the wheat.

We found the Battery in position under an artificial hedge which the Germans had made by stretching camouflage screens between tall poles. Most of the men were asleep in the woods or hunting souvenirs. I was getting a bite of breakfast when Storer told me to scout around and find a place to water the horses.

I stuffed a handful of hardtack in my pocket, mounted Peanuts, and rode off at random across the fields. The first thing I saw was a bare-headed yellow-haired American kneeling in a shallow pool of water such as cattle drink out of in a pasture. He was visible a long way off, with the wind blowing his hair in the sunlight. As I got nearer I saw that the pool was just right for watering horses. It had a low retaining wall on three sides, and the fourth side was open and sloped up to the level of the field. The man seemed intent on watching something in the woods about a hundred yards in front of him. He had a rifle in one hand, leaning against the bank.

"Hi, Buddy, what ya doing in the water?" I yelled. He never moved. I rode around in front and saw that he was dead. There was a little black hole in the center of his forehead. When I looked back I could still see the wind ruffling his hair.

Over near the edge of the woods I found a shallow, freshly dug trench with dead Germans and overturned machine guns every few yards. Some of the trees had crude platforms in their branches with machine guns mounted on them, and sprawled on the ground beneath were the dead German gunners. I saw a dead French chasseur in his horizon-blue overcoat lying half out of a trench. His helmet was still on. I wondered if he could have been one of the cavalcade I had watched pass the crossroads, but I thought not. They would be farther ahead by now. About half a mile away I found a big empty farm on the Charmel Road. There was a good watering trough in the barnyard.

Turning back across the fields I passed between groups of dead Americans lying in short windrows as they had been mowed down by the machine guns from the woods. Wave after wave had evidently assaulted from the ditches along the road before the survivors had obtained a foothold in the woods. They almost all lay face down with their rifles in front of them, as if they had been killed while running towards their objective. Some of their packs had broken open and I noticed letters and photographs from home spilled out onto the field.

Picking my way between the bodies, I reached the road and turned down into the valley. Luckily I met a Frenchman and asked him if there was a river down there where horses could be watered. He said yes, but he wouldn't advise me to try it as the Boches were still in possession of it; so I went back to the Battery and told Storer what I had found. Then I fed Peanuts and went to sleep. When someone woke me up it was getting dark and the Battery was pulling out onto the road again.

# CHAPTER XLIV

*Beck leaves the Battery. Esperance Farm. I search for the rear echelon. Some drivers killed.*

"Ferme Esperance, July 29, 12 midnight. Guns in open, in sight of Boches; no protection. Killed, July 30: Charlie Ellis, String Hooper, Snuffy Howland. Echelon south of Beuvardes. 3 Boche avions down. C Battery shot up. Fired 2080 rounds in one day. Left Aug. 3, 6 p.m."

THIS WAS ONE of those nights when in spite of the absence of moon and stars it was easy to see clearly for short distances. After a couple of hours of pushing along traffic-choked roads, we turned off into the woods about midnight, crossed a clearing near a farm, followed a row of gnarled willows along an open space, crossed a huge flat field diagonally and halted under the edge of some woods where shells were exploding just ahead.

A reel cart from Regimental Headquarters had joined us, and Beck and I were riding just behind it when we halted. A man rode down the column yelling for Sergeant Beck. Beck spoke up and asked him what the hell he wanted.

"Report to the adjutant," he said. "You've got orders to go to officers' school at Saumur." Beck dismounted, tied his horse to the reel cart and, without even saying goodbye, started back across the field at a run. I never saw him again in France.

At the time, I was more occupied by the shelling than by Beck's sudden departure. I could see the flashes of the shells through the trees and hear the calls of "Stretcher bearer, stretcher bearer." In a few minutes the column began to move, swinging to the right into open ground. For about five hundred yards we progressed over a billowy surface and halted under the sky in a bare field. The shelling was still going on in the woods.

While the limbers went back, taking Peanuts with them, the gunners set to work spreading camouflage nets over the guns and I helped Ritchie and Peabo with their telephone wires. All they had to do was tap in on the line the reel cart had laid and connect the guns with MacNamee's headquarters in a shell hole. Each section carried a camouflage net rolled tight and lashed to the gun trail, so there was plenty of work to get all four set up on poles and pegged down tight around the edges. Before it was finished shells began to whine over our heads and burst near a dark mass about one hundred yards away which I took to be a building of some kind. I looked around for a bit of shelter and ran into Kunhardt doing the same thing. We were too late though, for suddenly scattered shells started bursting near the guns. Kunhardt and I ran towards the building which was all quiet for the moment. When we reached it we turned a corner and lay down beside a low stone wall. We hadn't been there five minutes when a shell crashed into the building, causing a landslide of rocks and plaster.

"Let's beat it," gasped Kunhardt.

"Where to?" I asked him. There was no answer to that. He pulled out a tin can and began opening it with his knife.

"For Christ's sake what's that?" I said.

"Sausages," he replied. They tasted raw to me, but we finished the lot in silence. After about half an hour we got up and walked back to the guns, where I borrowed a shovel and dug myself a hole to lie in. Ritchie dug himself one next to it after I was through with the shovel. Then we spread our blankets in the holes and went to sleep.

In the morning I looked out of my hole and saw the guns neatly hidden under their four green nets about two hundred feet below me. My hole was on the side of a little hill, but that hadn't prevented an inch or so of water from seeping into it and soaking my blankets. Over at the farm I found some narrow German ammunition baskets and put them in the bottom to keep me out of the water. On the way over I passed a sort of round duck-pond with three tall elms shadowing it. The grass was short as if the place had been a lawn. Across a

184

"A letter and a box of cigars from my father."

". . . I wish to heaven that I were in your place. The great cause came to you and it came to my father, but I am left behind to nibble around these trees like an old rat. . . . But what difference does it make! Let each man take the part assigned him, and not merely act it, but *be* it. . . . Here's to peace through Victory. Thank God we've got the price, and are proud to pay it to the utmost. It's all in the day's work. As Admiral Lord Nelson remarked on his flagship, 'I wouldn't be elsewhere for millions of pounds sterling.'

Your loving father
Lucian."

stretch of rolling field I could see the woods where the shells had been falling when we halted. One of our batteries was firing from there now. Our own guns looked like four innocent grass-mounds and it's a good thing they did, for the sky was full of Boche planes and we were in clear sight of the German positions on high ground a few kilometers to the east. I could make out C Battery's guns about three hundred yards in front of ours and a little nearer the woods.

While I was arranging the baskets in my hole I noticed Ritchie kneeling down at the foot of the hill splicing a telephone wire. I heard a shell whine and pulled in my head. There was no explosion, so I looked out again. Ritchie was still kneeling in the same place, staring with fascinated horror at a round hole not three feet from him. The shell had been a dud. Poor Ritchie was so shaky that he was useless for the rest of the day.

Peabo yelled over to me from MacNamee's shell hole, where he had his switchboard, and I went over. It was a palatial residence, judged by the standards of the place. They had squared out a big shell hole and covered it with a tarpaulin off one of the caisson racks, and Peabo and MacNamee sat in there as snug as could be. MacNamee told me to ride back and find out what had become of the rear echelon. He thought it was around Beuvardes somewhere.

I followed a diagonal path across the field and found the drivers in a patch of woods with the horses and rolling kitchen. The cooks, Lorenzen and Snuffy Howland, were working about as hard as cooks ever wanted to work as, in addition to feeding the drivers, they had to send hot chow up to the guns three times a day. I noticed that they had the soup gun and a buzzycot both going. I made myself a piece of toast on the buzzycot before saddling Peanuts and starting back towards Beuvardes.

That ride was like a sight-seeing tour to me. Everything had changed with the fast-moving advance. The dead horses were gone, the roads were mended, and what I remembered as empty fields were full of troops in reserve, waiting their turn to go up into the lines. I rode through the whole of the Fourth Division and most of the 39th and 42nd. It seemed queer to see the strange insignia everywhere when I was so used to our own, and the sight of the familiar YD on a truck was like meeting a friend in a strange country.

I had no difficulty finding the way to Beuvardes, but once there my troubles began. It was a large town on a plateau surrounded by wooded hilltops, and the whole place swarmed with strange outfits. No one knew anything about our rear echelon and some of them even had never heard of the 26th Division. I spent most of the day riding from one clump of woods to another, following vague directions as to the location of some artillery outfit, or frankly wandering at random along the roads, and by a miracle I finally stumbled onto the echelon hidden in a sandpit halfway up the side of a hill.

Lieutenant Hommel* told me they had been fighting a tough war with traffic and the difficulty of drawing supplies and finding horses enough to move them. They had pulled up to Epieds July 25th and they had only reached Beuvardes a few hours before. Everyone called it Bo-var-dees. I told him our news, got something to eat, and threaded my way over the long road back to the guns.

When I got to the forward horse lines I found everyone very subdued. It seemed several drivers had been making toast on the buzzy-cot when a German shell lit in the fire and killed Charlie Ellis, a fourth section wheel-driver, String Hooper, caisson corporal of the eighth section, and Snuffy Howland, the cook. The drivers weren't used to casualties, and it took the heart all out of them.

The next day my visit to Beuvardes bore unexpected fruit. Hommel sent a ration cart up from the rear echelon with supplies and a bag of mail he had been carrying around for several days. The mail came up to the guns that night on the limber with our supper, and for me there was a letter and a package—a box of cigars from my father. I almost cried with joy. Ritchie and I sat smoking cigars at opposite ends of my hole till "far into the night."

* A *good* Plattsburger assigned to Battery A.

During our five days at the Esperance Farm position both sides were active with their artillery. We fired enormous schedules and the Boches shelled our woods continuously. It was only our being in an open field that saved us from destruction for the Germans pounded the hedges, roads, woods, and other likely places with which they were familiar from their recent occupation, but they apparently considered the fields unimportant. Even so, C Battery was badly shot up one day while they were firing. Among other casualties, Felix Knauth, one of their lieutenants, was hit in the leg, and a shell exploded in a hole where Jack Fallon and another man were sleeping. Their friends took one look in the hole and filled it up. Stray shells exploded around our position but we suffered no losses.

Ritchie and I used to sit in our holes smoking cigars and watching the German planes overhead. Great squadrons of them would come over and fly along our lines unchallenged except for the futile barking of the antiaircraft guns. Often they came low over the tops of the trees, firing with their machine guns at groups of our men. Once they bombed our caissons as they were crossing the big field. I saw three planes shot down in flames near our position.

On August 3d at 6 p.m. we dismantled the position, and the horses and caissons came up to move us ahead. The horses were pretty well fagged out by their continuous work, but Peanuts was still in good condition.

# CHAPTER XLV

## *Over the Ourq. The ridge west of Sergy.*

"Sergy Aug. 3, 11 p.m. Thru Château Nesle. Many dead; much equipment; bad smell.
Night in shellhole; rain. Left Aug. 4, 9 a.m."

BY THE TIME our column reached the River Ourq a fine rain was falling and it was almost dark. We passed a moss-grown building like a chapel nestling among thick trees on our left. While I was thinking how it really did nestle, I noticed a signboard that said Château Nesle and smiled at the pun. We seemed to be on no particular road. It was more like a cart track worn deep by much use. The Ourq was an alder-shaded stream not over fifteen feet wide with muddy banks partly hidden by rank vegetation. To the right of the low wooden bridge we crossed I saw a German, head downwards in the mud, with only his legs showing.

Beyond the Ourq the ground rose in shallow terraces which made difficult driving, especially since it was almost dark. For a long while we wound along the side of the ridge before climbing to a bare summit where we stopped. The flashes of guns firing were almost continuous.

Someone discovered that the soup gun was missing, and I was sent back to get it. The going was rough, it was pitch dark, and the noise from the unseen batteries was uncomfortably close. A heavy smell of putrefaction hung in the damp air. Every few yards Peanuts would shy and snort at something on the ground that I could not see. At last I found the soup gun mired in a gully with a broken wheel. There was nothing to be done, so I got back to the Battery as quickly as I could.

I found the horses and limbers huddled together a few yards down the hill from the guns and tied Peanuts to a limber wheel. It seemed as if there were batteries firing on every side. After telling Storer about the soup gun I went to sleep in a sandy shell hole without bothering to open my blanket roll. It must have been about midnight.

I was too wet and cramped to sleep much, so it was a relief to see the first light of dawn in the east. We seemed to be on the shoulder of a long, bare ridge with a shattered town below us to the right front. Someone said it was Sergy. The first thing I noticed was the great number of dead Americans on the ground. They lay in scattered rows as I had seen them in the fields around the Croix Rouge Farm. All down the side of the hill were shallow holes which the attacking waves of infantry had scraped out as they lay under machine gun fire between rushes. The ground was littered with equipment of every kind, and it lay so thick that a wagonload could easily have been collected in five minutes. The odor was not so bad by daylight, perhaps because a little breeze had sprung up.

I was famished for something to eat and I reluctantly followed the example of some of the boys who were gathering the emergency rations from the packs of the dead infantrymen.

Only a few batteries were firing, but the whole back side of the ridge was packed with American artillery so closely that the guns were almost hub to hub. We didn't fire at all. At 9 a.m. we limbered up and pulled around Sergy onto a crowded road.

# CHAPTER XLVI

## Last days of the drive. The Battery relieved.

"Chèry-Charteuve, Aug. 4, 9 p.m. No food; rain. Slews of dead horses. Boche smoke in sky; smouldering farms, roads choked. Peanuts hurt. Left Aug. 4, 11.30 p.m. Relieved!"

FOR TWELVE HOURS our column advanced over roads choked with artillery. It was our longest march during the whole offensive. We passed several small batches of German prisoners, but by the nature of the fighting* prisoners were bound to be few. Next to dead horses beside the road the commonest sight was a German machine gun with all its crew killed and belts of empty cartridges beside it.

By the time it got dark I was groggy for lack of sleep and food and I paid no attention to where we were going. Once when Peanuts was galloping to the head of the column he fell, stunning me and injuring one of his knees. After that he limped, but I had to ride him as we had no spare horses.

It had been overcast all afternoon, and around dark it started to rain. At 9 p.m. we pulled left off the main road into a bowllike valley with woods on the farther slope and set the guns in an orchard where most of the trees had been cut down by the Germans. It was on the outskirts of a village, but the road curved around some woods so the house belonging to the orchard was the only one in sight. In a garden behind the house I found some small turnips and tried to eat one raw without success. Ritchie and I decided not to sleep in the house after we found that it had no roof and had been used for a latrine, so we dug a hole near it and stretched our shelter halves over the hole to keep the rain out. I found a German officer's overcoat and we used it as a mattress. The epaulets were so pretty that I cut one off

* I.e., the Germans were fighting a rearguard action, using machine gunners who were ordered to sacrifice themselves in order to delay our advance.

190

and put it in my saddlebag. Peanuts was tied to a fence where there was thick grass for him to eat.

Ritchie and I fell fast asleep as soon as we lay down, and it seemed only a moment later that we were wakened by yells of "Everybody up. Harness and hitch." I couldn't hear our guns firing at all. We rolled our blankets, saddled our horses, and found the Battery in column waiting in a field. It was raining harder than ever but nobody seemed to mind because they said we were relieved.

It was 11:30 p.m. when the column headed to the rear and moved out to the road. Here we halted, apparently waiting for some of the other batteries to make a battalion column, and while we were waiting the Germans started to shell the fields along the right of the road. It seemed tantalizing to stand there and be shelled after we were relieved and might just as well be safe asleep miles behind the line. I felt like imitating Beck and lighting out. After about an hour of restless inactivity we heard the welcome "Forward," and the column pulled out onto the road, turned to the right, and pushed towards the rear. At one point on the road the shelling got very close, but we passed by without accidents and were not again threatened by anything worse than torrents of rain.

---

## CHAPTER XLVII

### *Exhaustion. Marching to the rear.*

"Outskirts of Beuvardes, Aug. 5, 3 a.m. Rain. Camp in mud;
little sleep. Good lunch. Left Aug. 5, 8 p.m."

---

THE BATTERY was a sorry sight as it plodded through Fère-en-Tardenois. By the feeble light of early dawn I rode along the column and looked it over, a spectator for the moment. A reaction had set in after many days of strain. The men sat their horses or plodded on foot through the mud in a stupor, saying nothing, noticing nothing, and feeling nothing. They were wet, ragged, dirty, and thin, with sunken eyes and unshaven beards. A few still carried German souvenirs, but most of this junk had long since been thrown away. The six-horse hitches had dwindled to four, and some of the horses were almost too far gone to keep their feet. The guns and caissons were thick with clotted mud. Our column had the road to itself all the way back and we needed it all.

At 3 a.m. we reached the outskirts of Beuvardes and halted in a muddy place under some trees. I tied Peanuts to a wheel, crawled under a paulin with someone, I forget who, and went to sleep like a dead man.

When I woke up it was about noon, and the first thing I saw was Lorenzen and the long-lost soup gun. Never had "Corned Willie" eaten in the rain tasted so good. There was a ration of oats for the horses too. The paulin was requisitioned to cover the kitchen, so Peabo and I put up a pup tent and lay smoking and drowsing while the rain beat on the roof. Sometime during the afternoon I summoned enough fortitude to clean the mud off Peanuts and give him a good rubdown with a piece of sacking.

It got dark early because of the rain and mist. If I had been running the army I would have used that night for a good sleep but after supper came orders to harness and hitch, and at 8 p.m. we splashed onwards through the dark. I heard someone mutter, "For Christ's sake, don't they know the war's over?" The remark was illogical perhaps, but it touched a sympathetic chord in my weary frame.

# CHAPTER XLVIII

## *A day in Château-Thierry.*

"Essômes, Aug. 6, 3 a.m. Rain, cold, mud. Billeted in garret. Slept in bed-linen. Loot. Wanton destruction by Huns in Château-Thierry. Left Aug. 7, 9 a.m."

I REMEMBER NOTHING about this miserable march but rain, cold, and mud. The nights could be cold even in August, and we were all wet before we started. The mud made an impression because I walked most of the way to save Peanuts' injured knee.

At 3 a.m. we felt a paved street under us and soon turned into a courtyard where we halted. I followed the crowd through a doorway, up some stairs, and found myself in a dusty garret lighted by a candle. There were some open chests and trunks with clothes and linen half-pulled-out and strewn around. We all wrapped up in whatever we could find and we went to sleep on the floor.

The next day was devoted to rest and grooming the horses. In the morning some of the boys got a laugh by appearing for breakfast in clothes they had found in the house. One had a suit of ladies' underwear over his uniform and carried a pink parasol. Another wore a high hat and green spectacles.

Essômes was a suburb of Château-Thierry. The inhabitants had fled at the approach of the Germans, and it was still deserted. This was our first chance to see the Germans' delicate touch so soon after they had passed. There were many fine houses in Essômes, and I went into several near our courtyard. I was impressed by the wantonness of the destruction everywhere; the slates of a billiard table cracked with a sledgehammer, curtains pulled down and polluted, furniture splintered with an axe, mattresses torn open, rugs burned, letters and photographs trampled by muddy boots, paintings slashed, even the children's dollhouse overturned, and the dolls broken. The German soldiers had evidently urinated against the wallpaper in a good many places, and I saw feces in most of the rooms. Brocaded curtains, lace, and silk dresses were the favorite substitutes for toilet paper.

In the afternoon the rain stopped, and some of us walked over to Château-Thierry. It was as the Germans left it except that the main streets had been cleared of rubbish to allow passage. In the residential sections everything was the same as in Essômes. In the business section all the shop windows were broken and the shops looted. Here the Germans had found more scope for their originality. I noticed a derby hat full of feces and, in a shoe store, a pair of ladies' dancing slippers full of urine. Many of the places had been burned, but not all.

We got back to Essômes in time for supper and I went to bed early and had a good night's sleep. The next day was warm and sunny. We harnessed and hitched after breakfast and got away in regimental column by 9 o'clock.

## CHAPTER XLIX

### Along the Marne. A week of rest.

"Mèry-sur-Marne, Aug. 7, 4 p.m. Along north bank of Marne through Azy, Nanteuil. Discipline, formations. New outfits. Vin, butter, sugar and milk in coffee. Left Aug. 15, 6 a.m. Entrained at La Ferté-sous-Jouarre. Through Èpernay, Chalons, Conarban (English aviation camp)."

IT WAS LIKE OLD TIMES, winding peacefully along the sunny, tree-shaded road with full stomachs and a night's sleep to our credit and no shelling to bother us. On our left lay the Marne, to the right were slopes of wheat fields and vineyards. In the little towns along the valley we saw wains and carts standing at every door piled high with household goods. The inhabitants were ready to fly at the first increase in the sound of the guns.

Through Aulnois, Azy, Bouneil, Saulchèry, Charley, and Nanteuil we passed, and at 4 p.m. we halted in the little town of Mèry-sur-Marne. The Battery was complete with all its men, horses, and rolling stock.

The Special Detail was billeted in a hayloft reached by an outside ladder from the street. Behind the house we dug a latrine against a wooden garden fence, and this was a very popular place both day and night, as most of the boys had diarrhoea, "the Japanese Spatters" as they picturesquely called it. The horses and rolling stock were parked on a huge grassy plateau overlooking the Marne. There was a supply of hay and oats so ample that the poor beasts must have thought they were in heaven. A few days of rest, grooming, good food, and gentle exercise brought them up amazingly. Peanuts' leg got well, and he regained his old-time fire. The men were slower in recovering.

One of the first things we did was to march over to Saacy, a few kilometers away, and get reoutfitted and deloused. We all stripped to the skin, bathed vigorously, threw away all our old clothes, and drew a complete new outfit. It was a relief to be free from the burning itch of lice, even for a few days.

Our duties for this week in Mèry were light. A formation morning and evening, grooming horses, leading to water, that was all. The rest was eating, sleeping, and swimming in the Marne. An attempt was made to revive the discipline which at the front had grown very sketchy. We were reminded that officers were to be saluted and certain other formalities observed. As for food, Joe Wilner and the cooks outdid themselves. There was milk and sugar in the coffee and seconds at every meal. We supplemented our rations with eggs, wine, and butter from shops in the town. Every evening the regimental band played popular music in the square, while we loafed around on the grass and smoked.

One day Elsie Janis came to entertain us. She was an actress from the States whose war work was going around entertaining the soldiers in France. I believe several of them did it. We rigged up a platform for her on the colonel's lawn and stood around while she sang and danced. "When Yankee-Doodle Learns to Parlez-voo-Français" was one of the hits.

Then one day we went over to Saacy to the Divisional Show. Early in the war a group of entertainers had been picked from the various regiments and formed into a travelling minstrel show attached to Divisional Headquarters. Two were taken from our Battery; Webster, a sort of natural clown, and Chapin, a Princeton man who played the banjo beautifully. There were about thirty of them, and they put on a pretty good show with a portable stage, scenery, costumes, and everything. It was the first time we had seen Webster and Chapin since June. In a way we envied them their soft life and in a way we despised them. I'm glad I wasn't offered their job, for I surely would have had a struggle to decide whether to take it or not and would have been sorry either way.

During this week I carved a pipe which I later sent home to my father. I was restless, and it soothed me to have something to be working on. One day Ritchie and I walked over to Saacy and had our pictures taken at a photographer's shop, postcard size. Mine looked like someone in the last stages of consumption and scared my family when they got it. I didn't realize how pathetic I looked.

While we were at Mèry old Joe Merriam appeared from Officers' School at Saumur, dressed up like a second lieutenant. He was just the same, and we sneaked off early one morning and went swimming. He told me all about his life at Saumur and his leave in Paris. I hadn't seen him since he left the Battery in April. He said he had been lucky enough to get assigned back to his own regiment, and was now in D Battery.

Pleasant and easy as life was in Mèry for the week after the drive, I don't remember seeing any enthusiasm among the men who had been through it, or feeling any myself. We all were indifferent to everything except food and sleep. When orders came to harness and

"I didn't realize how pathetic I looked."

Taken in August 1918 at Saacy-sur-Marne, just after the Château-Thierry drive. This is the picture I should never have sent home. The pipe is the one I was carving for my father. The boots were bought in Commercy while we were in the Toul sector.

"They thronged the roadside at the first sound of our wheels."
This scene is typical of all the daylight marches we made through inhabited country.

hitch at six o'clock one morning we took it as a matter of course, without knowing or caring much what happened.

After a march of a few kilometers we reached La Ferté-sous-Jouarre, a place we had seen before, and drew up to a loading ramp beside the railroad track. I remember only that it was very hot loading the troop train and I was glad to have it over and to sit hanging my legs from the door of a boxcar as the train gathered speed.

The track lay along the south bank of the Marne, so the river was always in sight and sometimes very close. We passed scenes of desolation and wreckage that showed how stubborn the fighting had been along this bank. There were sections of pontoon bridge, torn barbwire, shell holes, hurriedly dug bits of shallow trench, shattered trees, trampled ground, rows of fresh graves marked by wooden crosses and the litter of arms, clothing, and equipment with which we had grown familiar in the wheat fields farther north. At Dormans it was particularly bad. Here the French horizon-blue predominated in the rubbish, and the little railroad station was only a battered shell of masonry. Épernay and Chalons were big towns through which our train crawled. All that night and most of the next day we were on the train, jumping off at halts to water the horses, fill our canteens, or forage for wine or food as we did on every train trip in France.

At 4:30 p.m., August 16th, we pulled up beside a long ramp at a little station labelled Bar-sur-Seine and set to work to unload the rolling stock and horses.

# CHAPTER L

## *Training and reoutfitting behind the lines. Gomméville.*

"Gomméville, Aug. 16, 10 p.m. Training. Seine, bon. Left Aug. 30,
6 p.m., via Pothières, Bouix; dark, cold."

TWO THINGS I remember about the march to Gomméville. One
was the people in the towns through which we passed near sunset.
They thronged the roadside at the first sound of our wheels and
swarmed about us as the head of the column rolled into the village
street, laughing, crying, holding babies up to touch our hands, and
giving us flowers from the fields. We put the flowers in our helmet
straps. The people in this region had gotten the idea that we were
their preservers who had stopped the German advance from reaching their homes.

The other thing I remember was Jack Hart, the saddler, drunk as a
lord, and myself herding him along a moonlit road about a mile behind the column. He would run zigzag till he got well ahead of me
and fell into a ditch, from which I would pull him and start him on
another run. I finally got him to Gomméville, where he spent the
rest of the night digging a latrine.

Stan Curtis and I pitched a pup tent together in a meadow where
there was a long double line of pup tents already. I was thankful to
have Jack Hart off my hands and get some sleep.

Gomméville was above par for sleeping. A huddle of white-walled
houses under tall feathery trees beside a cool stream, that was Gomméville. And near the stream our meadow with its double line of pup
tents, and behind them picket lines full of horses basking in the sun
chewing their oats, and guns, caissons, and wagons parked in orderly
rows stretched level as a green carpet from the tree-lined road to the
tree-shaded stream. There was a deep pool at a bend where we rigged

up a springboard. We watered the horses in the town where the stream ran shallow over a wide pebbly bed, and there were baths taken here too, but involuntary ones, like the ones in the old Boxford days.

Our tent was next to Jopp's. Kenneth Jopp was the Battery dude. His ambition was always to be "doggily" dressed, and he would steal, swap, or buy any article of clothing that appeared to meet his requirements. It was his ruling passion and it was soon satisfied, as he was sent home to sell Liberty Bonds and tell his war experiences at society gatherings. He must have been resplendent then.

For two weeks we lived the Life of Riley at Gomméville. We settled down as if we were going to stay there forever. A school was started in the village schoolhouse to teach telephone work, signalling, figuring firing data, and several other things an artilleryman should know. Again we had formations: reveille, retreat, assembly, church parade, and we had practice marches and mock battles. Coöperation with airplanes was tried several times, the guns firing, the plane circling back and dropping the range corrections on a scrap of paper in a weighted pouch, and we talking to the plane by laying white cloth panels on the ground in different patterns. When the pouch came hurtling through the air and struck the ground all of us mounted men would make a rush for it and each try to be the first to scoop it up and gallop back with it to the executive officer. Much of the time we groomed horses, but we didn't mind getting up a sweat when we could spread our clothes to dry on the bushes and dive into the river afterwards.

The inhabitants were very friendly and long-suffering. I remember the stir there was one morning because two gendarmes complained to the colonel that Americans had given them black eyes and resisted arrest for stealing sheep. A serious offence, said the colonel, and did his best to find the offenders. I knew who they were and where they got the liquor, because I was one of an appreciative audience to hear the story of their adventure from their own lips at breakfast. They said they were returning from their convivialities, both full to be sure but no more than gentlemen should be, when they turned into what they took to be their gate, fell into a sort of bin, and immediately found themselves being trampled by a swarm of nervous sheep. Naturally they made a noise protecting themselves and trying to get out. The next they knew a couple of men with lanterns rushed them, and what was left for a gentleman to do? They did the best they could and eventually found their billet and went to bed which was all they ever wanted to do, but what the hell all this fuss was about they couldn't understand.

One of the best things about this time was the freedom from cooties. With our daily baths and clean clothes they never had a chance.

Soon leaves and furloughs began to be talked of. It seemed about time, as no one had had one since the Division had been in France. Towards the end of August the first batch of men received their leave papers. I think there were seven of them. Jopp was in great demand as they all wanted to borrow his doggy pants, but they might just as well have spared themselves the trouble. Before they could start, orders came suddenly to harness and hitch, march over the road to a place called Poinçon and entrain for the front. All leaves were automatically cancelled. I didn't care much. I didn't get one anyway.

# CHAPTER LI

## *Secret marches. Hiding in the woods.*

"Poinçon, August 30, 9 p.m."

"Nançois-Tronville, August 31, 3 p.m., detrained; via Tronville. Tannois, 5 p.m.
Steep hillside. Rain. Left Sept. 1, 8 p.m. Bois Longchamps, Sept. 2, 5 a.m. Woods, thick,
rain. Left Sept. 2, 9 p.m."

"Bois Courcelles, Sept. 3, 2.30 a.m. Left Sept. 5, 7.30 p.m."

THIS TRAINRIDE WAS like all the rest, with halts, hopping on and off, sitting in the doorways, and sleeping on horse manure just as we always did. It seems to me this was the very cold ride when it rained hard all night, and the roof of our car leaked so everyone got wet and half-frozen.

At all events we reached a place called Nançois-Tronville at 3 p.m. the next day and unloaded at a good cinder ramp beside a little station. I was sent ahead to look for Tannois, the village after Tronville, and I found it without any difficulty, leaving route markers along the way. It was the merest hamlet, just a clump of small houses with no shops or anything to redeem it in our eyes. We parked the rolling stock under the heavy foliage of a grove of oak trees and tied the horses to the wheels. We were supposed to be moving very secretly so didn't dare risk a long picket line which might be seen from the air. The only place for the men to sleep was a steep hillside which I took to be an orchard. I had never pitched a pup tent on the side of a hill before, and I had a long argument with Ritchie as to how it should go. I don't remember who won, but I know we pitched it so we slept with our feet downhill and kept slipping out from under the tent all night. Some of the tents were pitched crosswise and their occupants had a worse time, for after they had both sagged down into the lower wall of the tent the pegs came loose and the whole business rolled down the hill until it fetched up against something, a tree or another tent.

It rained a cloudburst all night, and everyone was glad when morning came. Not daring to travel by day, we hung around under the trees till 8 p.m. when we started off from Tannois on a long night march.

Our road lay almost due north. I don't remember just when we began to hear the guns. Except for its length it was an easy march as the road was good and we were in regimental column, so there was no reconnaissance for me to do. Towards morning I had the usual trouble staying awake, and alternately walked and rode.

At 5 a.m. we pulled off the road under some tall trees and unhitched. I could hardly keep my eyes open long enough to water Peanuts at a brook beside a rustic bridge about a mile away. Then I crawled under a wagon and went to sleep. Around noon I had some chow from the soup gun and groomed and fed Peanuts. We lay low under the trees until dark, and about 9 p.m. formed column again and resumed the march.

Our road now bore a little east of north, bringing the sound of the guns always nearer. We travelled more slowly and had more halts, so it was even harder to stay awake than the night before. Before daylight we came out on a wide macadamed highway and followed it some distance. I saw a big sign with VERDUN on it and remembered all I had heard about that place, which wasn't good. Apparently we weren't going to Verdun, however, for we left the main highway and followed a narrow wood road to the left for several miles. Then the column halted while each battery in turn swung off to the right and entered a tunnellike cart track in the woods. This led up a short, steep hill to a clearing. It was still dark in the woods so we tied the horses anywhere, pushed the rolling stock under the trees, and waited for daylight. It was only 2:30 a.m. but it seemed later.

It was devilish cold, as I remember, and a dreary fine rain was falling. When it got light we watered the horses in a brook at the foot of the hill. Peabo and I pitched our pup tent on a level spot, had some breakfast, and lay under the tent listening to the drops of water fall from the wet leaves overhead. We expected to pull out at night-

"We lay low under the trees until dark."

This may not be the Bois Longchamps
but it looks just about the same.

fall but to our surprise no orders came, and we woke up the next morning in the same place. It wasn't until the night of September 5th that we finally left.

In the meantime we lay low in the woods and rested. Some of the boys prospected around and discovered an aviation camp to visit, but I was content to sit near the small fires that were allowed us, thanks to the heavy foliage of the treetops, and take my ease. I remember one amusing thing that happened. Little Frank Tullo, the "Wop" barber, found some rum somewhere and got drunk. The boys were all sitting around after supper teasing him while he boasted about what a devil he was on a horse. As a matter of fact he gave horses a wide berth when sober. Of course the boys kept at him until he offered to give them a demonstration of horsemanship and someone led out old Lil, the seventh section wheeler, a mean horse that could be handled only by her own driver, Smith. Well, all horses looked alike to Tullo and he was soon boosted aboard. Italian vanity and rum kept him on for about two minutes while Lil bucked and the crowd yelled with delight. Then he flew into the air, turned two somersaults before landing on his back, and lay still. I thought he was done for, but the rum saved him and after a while he opened his eyes.

"Tullo musta fell offa dat damn horse, eh?" was his only comment.

---

## CHAPTER LII

### The Verdun Road. We enter the St. Mihiel sector.

"Rupt-en-Woevre, Sept. 6, 8 a.m. Bonell cuckoo. Interminable. Chills, fever. Left Sept. 8, 6 p.m. Wait in rain."

---

ALTHOUGH I SMELLED big trouble in the air I was good and sick of the Bois de Courcelles and was glad to leave. At 7:30 p.m. we slid down onto the road and took our place in the regimental column for another night march.

Meantime our Regiment had been assigned a new colonel, a man named Bonell, from the Regular Army. After this night's doings he was popularly known as "Cuckoo Bonell." All went well until we came to a place where the main Verdun highway crossed our road at right angles. A French camion-train was passing, a very impressive sight. No lights were showing so the camions were only shapes in the dark that sped by about ten yards apart, going at least thirty miles an hour. Their religion when carrying ammunition was to stop for nothing. If the engine went dead, turn off into the ditch and crash and leave the way clear for the ones behind. Rushing blindly through the night, the life of the driver counted for little compared with the safety of the convoy.

There were several sections in this convoy with about thirty trucks to a section and gaps between the sections. "Cuckoo Bonell" waited impatiently for one section to get by and then, in violation of all the rules, led his column across the road ahead of the following camion section. Immediately there was an uproar. The grinding of brakes, the swearing of truck drivers; and in the midst of it up whizzed a sidecar and out stepped a French general, asking for the ranking artillery officer. The general was wild. He asked Bonell if he didn't know the penalty for breaking an ammunition convoy at the front and swore he'd court-martial him. Curtis and I, who had been riding behind Bonell, hung along the edge of the crowd with our eyes hanging out. At last things quieted down. The damage was done so our column kept going until the last wagon had crossed.

Nothing more happened before daybreak when we were nearing our destination, a town called Rupt-en-Woevre. I saw Colonel Bonell afoot, raging along beside the column yelling, "Gimme a gat, I wanta shoota private," and a lot about the "goddamned militia." The burden of his song seemed to be that no one would obey him. He was all disheveled, out of breath from running, and sobbing with anger. I was aghast when I saw him. He sent the three batteries of the First Battalion up a hill in plain sight of the Germans. At this point some of the other officers thought it had gone far enough, and Lieutenant Colonel Goodwin took command of the Regiment. Cuckoo Bonell was led away swearing and weeping and the next day he was relieved of his command. I heard later that he was sent back to the States insane; syphilitic brain disease, I was later told.

By the time riders had been sent to rescue the three exposed batteries from their predicament it was day. The Germans did not shell us. By 8 a.m. the column rolled through the deserted streets of Rupt and up a wooded hill beyond, where we made camp under large trees.

It was raining and cold. There were one or two old sheds in a clearing where some of the men slept, but Jack Kunhardt and I took shelter under a sheet of rusty iron propped against a log. The horses were sent down to water in a muddy stream that flowed through Rupt. After some breakfast I rolled up in my blankets and slept. I felt sick, with chills and fever. It was a good time for it, as we stayed there two days doing nothing. All I missed was a reconnaissance to find good positions in the line east of Rupt.

The miserable weather kept up, a sort of rainy season. When the reconnaissance party returned, Curtis told me the place was packed with artillery and that they had had a hard time to find room for us. He said everyone was talking about the coming drive to wipe out the St. Mihiel salient, and if the Germans didn't know about it they deserved to be surprised.

It was raining hard at 6 p.m., September 8th, when we were ordered to harness and hitch. For about two hours we stood shivering in the dark before all six batteries were brought into column and we got word to move.

# CHAPTER LIII

## *The St. Mihiel drive. Old German trenches.*
## *Loot and souvenirs. I lose Peanuts.*

"Old French position behind Mouilly. Sept. 9, 6 a.m. Doughboys. Start drive. Fired 2300 rounds in 11 hours. Left Sept. 12, 11.45 p.m. Rain, mud, roads full. Hattonchatel, Sept. 13, 4 p.m. Echelon woods, guns reserve position under camouflage. Went after fourgon. Left Sept. 14, 10 a.m. Longeau Farm (near Billy) Sept. 14, 3 p.m. Reserve position under camouflage. Boche rations. Peanuts' seedy toe. Left Sept. 16."

"Ost Tranchée (on hill) Sept. 16, 11 p.m. Position under camouflage. Echelon in front of guns. Ritchie and I in puptent. Left Sept. 19, 11 p.m."

THIS WAS ONE of those dark nights when even the sky is black. We wound down the hill out of the woods, through the streaming streets of Rupt, and bore to the left into a ravine. Here the road began to climb and, after a couple of kilometers, the side-hills had closed in until we were travelling up a narrow defile. The wagons of all the batteries pulled off the road into a steep gully on the left, but the six firing batteries kept going. The road got worse and worse, with deep mud underfoot and muddy banks along the sides. Rain came down in sheets driven by gusts of wind. The column halted.

After shivering around for about an hour I rode up ahead to see what was the matter. I found D Battery leading the column. They were trying to get their guns up what amounted to a mud chute. The road had dwindled to a sunken path just wide enough so the hubs cleared the banks, and it mounted upwards under the trees that met in a tunnel roof overhead. One of their guns seemed to be partway up, judging from the noises I heard. I left Peanuts and worked my way through the tangled bushes along the top of the bank till I came opposite the sound. Just then someone lit a match. It was poor old Joe Merriam, squatting in the mud trying to untangle a mess of muddy harness. The match went out right away, but I saw enough to tell me

206

that we would have a long wait. All six horses were down, some of them kicking to get up, some lying still and panting in a bath of mud and sweat, the harness in a hopeless snarl, and a dozen men floundering around in the dark trying to get them straightened out.

Lieutenant Colonel Goodwin caught sight of me and ordered me to tag along and run errands for him. All I remember of the next three hours is scrambling through the bushes and sliding through the mud while Goodwin cursed and prayed and made suggestions and the rain soaked through my clothes. At last I gave him the slip, got Peanuts, and returned to A Battery. They were still waiting in no very pleasant state of mind. I told some of the drivers what they were in for which didn't make them feel any better.

Finally word came that all was clear and to go ahead. We did better than D Battery but we had trouble enough. A cannoneer named Bill Barry slipped off the bank and a caisson wheel crushed his ankle. This was our only casualty, which was surprising.

It was 6 a.m. before we got the last team up the road and came out into a level clearing where there was an old French artillery position standing empty and overgrown with weeds. There were trenches and dugouts everywhere, but most of them were crumbling in. I spread my blankets in a trench where a section of tole iron bridged it and went to sleep.

During the four days that followed there was no shelling from the Germans. Our meals came up on a limber from the echelon, and every night the caissons struggled up with ammunition. Towards the end the horses were so fagged that they could hardly make it. At the position we loafed around under cover and waited for the drive to start. There wasn't much to see. It was mostly mud, old trenches, weeds, bushes, and rusty barbwire. Occasionally bursts of machine gun fire sounded in the east and a rare shell whined over, but otherwise the place seemed dead. As I later saw, there were probably more troops crowded into that area than anywhere else on the western front.

It was the night of September 10th that the doughboys came in—

C Company of the 101st Infantry. Our men shared their dugouts with them and the next day entertained them with crap games and cards. At dusk the doughboys got orders to go down to their jumping-off trenches. It was rainy and bleak, and I didn't envy them, but they unconcernedly drew their issues of hand grenades, emergency rations, and ammunition, fixed their bayonets, and filed down a trench out of sight in the dark.

We hadn't long to wait. At 1 a.m. we started firing, and from every unsuspected corner came the flash and roar of guns. The voice of our Battery was drowned out as if it had been a mosquito in a boiler shop. It was like our first barrage at Ostel, but a hundred times bigger. The sky pulsated with light and the air was solid with sound. I could sometimes hear the shells from the heavies grumbling past overhead. It kept up the rest of the night and until noon the next day. Our Battrey fired 2300 rounds in the eleven hours. There was practically no reply from the Germans.

The horses were now waiting under the trees a hundred yards to the right of the position. In the afternoon we pulled the guns out of the pits and limbered up. At 6 p.m. the orders came to drag ahead. Our course lay at first across country where the going was almost impossible because of the mud. It was raining, and darkness was closing in earlier than usual. We pushed and hauled in the mud while the tired horses flopped around, and it was hours before the Battery moved a hundred yards. Then the going got easier but it was still so bad that we didn't strike the main highway into the salient, the "Grande Tranchée de Calonne," till daylight. This we found choked with traffic travelling at a snail's pace. With the greatest difficulty we found a gap large enough to get the Battery on the road.

All that day we plodded along the Grande Tranchée, with interminable halts every few yards. The sun was shining, and we had ample opportunity to examine our surroundings. It was a new kind of scene to me. This ground had been in the Germans' hands for almost four years, and they had consolidated it in their thorough way.

208

"There were great craters in the road being filled by our engineers."

This American shell must have annoyed the German gunners whose wicker ammunition baskets are piled in the foreground. It is easy to appreciate the traffic problem offered by a stretch of road cut up by holes like this. The country is similar to much that we had crossed in the Château-Thierry drive.

Everywhere were elaborate trench systems, concrete pillboxes, barb-wire entanglements, and luxurious dugouts. The place abounded in signboards carefully printed in German letters. The destruction of our bombardment had been terrific. In fact, we had churned things up so badly that it was interfering with our own progress. There were great craters in the road being filled by our engineers with dead horses, rocks, broken wagons, and everything that came to hand. The instant one was filled the engineers jumped to the next one, while the wheels of the long column packed everything down better than a steamroller could have done.

The Grande Tranchée de Calonne ran along the top of a sort of dike, so that we overlooked the country on both sides. Much of it was forests where there was nothing to see but splintered tree trunks. In the open stretches we saw acres of raw shell holes and battered trenches. I noticed a German tank lying half on its side in a shell crater. On the road itself there was much to see. Everything suggested that the Germans had been surprised in the act of withdrawing from the salient. There were many German trucks along the roadside with their drivers dead in the seat or on the ground underneath. In a patch of bushes on the left I saw a 77-millimeter battery that had evidently been rushed by our infantry. The gunners were all killed. As at Château-Thierry I saw many Boche machine gunners who had been killed before their long, webbing cartridge belts were spent. The American dead were surprisingly few.

Great batches of prisoners kept passing on the road, going to the rear under guard. They came shuffling along in groups of ten to columns of several hundred. There were many Austrians among them. The prisoners carried their wounded on their shoulders or in wagons pulled by hand. They were also put to use to evacuate American wounded. I saw one wounded doughboy on the seat of an old buggy, smoking a cigarette, nodding acknowledgements to the appreciative artillerymen and making believe the Germans in the shafts were horses. The prisoners on the whole were a seedy-looking lot.

Of course we made use of the long halts to go looking for souvenirs. We found everything in the dugouts as the Germans had left it in their hurried exit: half-eaten meals, unfinished letters, clothes and equipment in disorder. I was amused to see a hammock swinging between two trees with an empty wine glass and a half-smoked cigar on a stand beside it. We had been issued a War Department pamphlet warning us of booby traps, poisoned food, time fuses, and various other things the Germans often left behind them, but we found none.

In the late afternoon we halted in a deep forest. I explored a dugout on the right of the road that the Germans had used as a dressing station. There were many bloody bandages around but the wounded had all been evacuated or captured.

At about 4 p.m. we emerged onto a sort of hog-backed ridge along which the road ran to a town with high towers. From the ridge a great panorama of low country spread out to the east, with a line of burning villages showing the direction of the German retreat. The town at the end of the ridge was Hattonchatel, and it marked the center of the salient for which our troops had raced from the north and south. It was built on a sort of promontory overlooking the plains of the Woevre. The streets were full of Americans establishing headquarters and rummaging for souvenirs. I passed a large stable full of heavy draft horses which the Germans had been forced to abandon.

Below us to the south was another fair-sized town about two kilometers away. This was Vigneulles, a small railroad center. While the Battery was going into position in a field outside Hattonchatel, I rode down a winding road shielded on the American side by German camouflage screens. Vigneulles was full of American infantry. They told me they had just got there when a troop train full of Germans pulled in and started to get off at the station platform. They captured the lot. They said it was amusing to see the surprise of the Germans, who had just formed fours and were moving off when the

Americans took charge of them. I also heard that these same dough-boys had enjoyed a hot meal from a German rolling kitchen which drove into the square a few minutes too late to be of service to the German Army. The Germans had several quartermaster storehouses in Vigneulles which fell into the hands of the Americans intact. This was the source of most of the spiked officers' helmets which were sent home as souvenirs.

When I had looked Vigneulles over to my satisfaction I rode back up the hill and found the guns in position in an open field and the horses in some nearby woods. I pitched my tent near the horses, had some supper, and was just going to sleep when Storer found me and sent me after the fourgon, which was missing. I found it several kilo-meters back, pulled up beside the road. Whoever was driving it didn't know where the Battery was and welcomed me much more cordially than I did him. On my way back along the ridge I saw a huge light in the eastern sky that must have been a German ammu-nition dump blowing up.

Nothing happened during the night. We were ready to fire in the event of a German counterattack, but the Germans seemed to have no such intention. Early the next morning we took the horses to water at a little town at the foot of the hill on the German side— "Billy-sous-les-côtes."

Some of us couldn't resist the temptation to do a little exploring afterward. There was a row of tiny towns along the foot of the hill, all deserted, but some of them full of discoveries. We found several cages of live rabbits, some hens, some big tubs of honey, and a wa-gonload of good German fodder for the horses. The wagon was a beautiful light forage wagon which we appropriated just as it stood. We found some salt fish which we loaded in, and a lot of condensed soup in long cloth bags. This all helped our rations when Lorenzen got hold of it. We saw German hardtack here for the first time. It was like sweetened oyster crackers, very hard, but easy to eat, and came in little cloth bags. I tried some German tobacco but it was no good. It was black and wiry, more like coarse steel shavings than to-bacco, and burned my tongue.

In a town named St. Maurice we saw four heavy howitzers aban-doned on the railroad ramp for lack of time to load them on the train. One of them is on Boston Common now. In this town I made a gruesome discovery. There was a little square one-story building like a garage, with locked doors and boards nailed across the windows. I got one window clear and climbed in. Groping around in the dark, I bumped into something long on a sort of trestle in the middle of the floor. I lit a match. There was the body of a German soldier without any head. It was laid out neatly, the hands crossed over the chest, holding a spray of wilted flowers. I didn't wait to see any more, but before I got out I got the impression of several other figures similarly laid out, and racks of tools around the walls. In the same town we found a brewery and searched it thoroughly but found everything empty. We blamed the doughboys for that.

On the way back to the Battery we met a lot of doughboys in the woods. They were trudging along in single file, their rifles slung on their backs, and they were hung all over with souvenirs. They were loaded with the little bags of sweet hardtack. Some carried German helmets in a bunch, like carrots, and some had several pairs of Ger-man field glasses hung around their shoulders. They were willing to sell or swap anything they had but preferred to wait until they got behind the lines where they could get good prices from the Y.M.C.A. secretaries, MP's, and others. However, I saw a Luger pistol that I liked the looks of and, as they were very popular and hard to find, I bought it for a few francs.

When we got back to the position we found the Battery hitched up and ready to move. The column turned back along the Grande Tranchée de Colonne, the way we had come. I noticed a company of infantry asleep in a field beside the road. The men were lying in the mud with their packs on and nothing over them, dead to the world in spite of the cold. About noon we took a wood road to the right where there was a sign, "Pioneer-weg au Longeau." There were Decauville tracks and engineers' supply dumps in the woods. This road took us out to some open fields where we went into position. This was at 3 p.m., September 14th.

We stayed here for two days. The camouflage nets were rigged over the guns and everything made ready for firing but nothing happened as the Germans were out of range on the plain below. I made several trips to Billy and the other towns, which were quite near, and I tried out my Luger pistol with some German ammunition I found. The horse lines were in the mud under some trees. To my great grief Peanuts went lame in the forefoot and I found he had developed seedy toe. This meant paring out the hoof, packing it with tar and oakum, and using another horse until Peanuts was fit to be ridden. I'm glad I didn't know I was never to see Peanuts again. The horse I got was a fool thing that Allen had discarded and it made life miserable for me.

On the 16th we moved to a new position nearer the infantry lines, relieving D Battery of the 102nd. This proved to be another dud, as we did no firing for the three days we occupied it. As for being shelled, no German shells had come near us during the whole drive. Ritchie and I slept in a pup tent under some bushes. The horse lines were in a clearing of the woods near a cart road. There were several old German dugouts and concrete huts where some of the boys slept. Near one of the dugouts was a German grave with an elaborately carved wooden cross bearing the date 1914. We watered the horses at a stream about a mile away on the back slope of a hill. The nights were getting pretty cold, and it was cold on rainy days, as all three of these days were.

On the night of September 19 we were all waked out of a sound sleep by orders to harness and hitch.

# CHAPTER LIV

## *The plain of the Woevre. Life in Herbeuville.*

"Herbeuville, Sept. 20, 1 a.m. Ruins, shelled, Wadonville. Hammonville, 'diversion'
for attack north of Verdun, i.e., 'Argonne drive.' Fox gassed. Lived in cellar. Wet.
Left Oct. 3, 1.30 a.m."

IT WAS STILL RAINING, and felt all the colder for coming out of
warm blankets. Silently we hitched up and took the road past the
horse lines. The cooks, mechanics, and spare drivers stayed in bed as
the echelon was to be left where it was.* The rest of us came out of
the woods onto a crossroad sheltered by a long camouflage screen.
This was about halfway between the towns of St. Rèmy and Dommartin, neither of which I ever saw.

We turned to the left, passed some fields, and turned to the right
down a steep hill. From here down, the road was a series of hairpin
turns, each stretch leading to a lower level. About halfway down we
passed an outfit of mule-drawn machine guns camped beside the
road. At the bottom of the last grade we were almost forced off the
road by some E Battery caissons coming in the other direction. Our
leading gun missed going into a shell crater only by masterly driving.
After a few hundred yards of level road we came to the main street of
a town. Everything was deserted and silent. We passed a little park-
like square with ornamental iron railings, bore to the left, and halted
near buildings.

Although the rain had stopped, it was too dark to tell much about
our surroundings. Two of the guns were boosted across a yard littered with fallen masonry, and the other two were pushed into some
prickly bushes across the street. The caissons were then unloaded and
the horses went back. It must have been three o'clock in the morning

---

* This was an incongruous position, as the guns, horses, cannoneers, and drivers were all
together in the same place, which was both an echelon and a firing position.

by the time we were ready to turn in. I crawled under some bushes behind a wall and slept until morning.

Herbeuville was the name of this town on the plain of the Woevre. Memories crowd so thick around it that I hardly know how to put them down. The focal point was the kitchen. This was on a dirt floor under a large, leaky tile roof surrounded on three sides by ruined buildings. On the fourth side was a garden through which a muddy footpath led to an apple orchard. Two guns were in the edge of the orchard and were left there, but the other two had landed in a less favorable spot, so they were moved to a ruined house beyond the orchard on the right. One was dragged onto the ground floor of the house behind a gap, and the other was placed in the front yard in an angle of the stone wall beside the house.

We were on the forward edge of the town, the only building in front of us being a tiny red-roofed railroad station. The road ran past it into the level plain and out of sight in the distance. About two kilometers away a heap of rubble marked the site of Wadonville. To its right a larger heap was Hannonville, and to its left still a third was Saulx. Beyond them we could see the rooftops of the line of German villages, Marcheville, Riaville, and St. Hilaire. Above the horizon floated German observation balloons in a curve. On the horizon itself several smoking factory chimneys could be clearly seen at Conflans, not far from Metz. We thought Metz was our next objective, and the Germans doubtless thought so too.

On sunny days we lay in the vineyards at the edge of Herbeuville and watched the German shells exploding on the plain. Hannonville, Wadonville, or Saulx was sure to catch it every day, and sometimes all three at once. We were like spectators in orchestra seats. We could hear the distant grunt of the heavy gun behind the German lines, then the approaching crescendo of the shell and, while the sound was still growing louder, we would see a billowy geyser of white dust rise lazily above the battered town. There was an appreciable pause before the double slam of the explosion reached our ears. With

215

steady regularity this would go on hour after hour, till it was no wonder that nothing was left of these towns but rubble.

One day I walked out to Wadonville to see what it looked like close to. The streets were almost obliterated by the fallen walls of masonry and it was hard to separate individual houses in the confluent heaps of plaster and stone. I was surprised to find groups of our doughboys living in deep cellars. They said they slept there daytimes and at night patrolled the fields between the towns. There were no regular first-line trenches. In one of the cellars they had some wounded men waiting for night when an ambulance could come out for them. I heard their cries and groans from the street. There happened to be no shelling during my visit, but it started again as I reached Herbeuville.

We had troubles of our own in Herbeuville. As I remember, they started the second night. About a dozen of us, including Ritchie and Peabo, were sleeping in a row on a wooden platform like a piazza which ran along the foot of a solitary house-wall and was sheltered by a tin roof. It was in a sort of yard where the Germans had left a store of lumber, engineers' supplies, and other odds and ends. I woke at the first crash and lay still, listening to stones rattle down on the tin roof. It was raining and cold, and I was comfortably warm in my blankets. In a minute I heard the familiar, unhurried sound of another heavy shell approaching. This time the crash shook us.

"The bastards'll be knockin' that wall down on our heads if they don't look out," remarked an indignant voice.

"What do you say," Ritchie asked me, "shall we drag ass?"

"Oh, let's wait for one more," said Peabo. He was always a bear for sleep. The next one landed in the street right beside our lumber-yard. A splinter tore away part of the tin roof overhead. The air was full of choking fumes that made my eyes water.

"Come on!" yelled Peabo as he made a break for the gate, dragging his blankets behind him. No one needed any urging. After a short sprint through the dark I found myself in MacNamee's cellar, a few houses down the street from where the shell landed. We finished the night crowded on the mud floor, listening to the muffled explosions of shells outside till we fell asleep. The next day we found a cellar of our own and rigged up bunks in it with material from the engineers' dump across the street.

During this process I discovered a can of kerosene. My cooties had been getting pretty bad, so I thought this was a good chance to kill them off. I undressed, went all over the seams of my clothes with kerosene, and for good measure rubbed myself down with it. By the time I had my clothes on again I was in agony. The stuff burned like fire, and for the rest of the day I roamed around like a dog with a can tied to its tail. It didn't kill the cooties either.

From this time on, Herbeuville was shelled at irregular intervals about every day, but there were so many corners to dodge around and cellars to duck into that no one took it very seriously. A little of the playful atmosphere of our first position on the Chemin-des-Dames returned. Most of the shelling was of heavy caliber like those that used to land in the swamp at Ostel, and we could hear them coming a long way off. The trouble was, these heavy shells did terrible damage when they landed and no dugout or cellar in Herbeuville was proof against them.

Because of the low ground, it was an ideal place for gas. I don't remember any bad gassings, but some of the boys who lived in a cellar near the first platoon got it bad one night. I think six of them were evacuated. Fox, our favorite cook, was the worst off, but he recovered. He was replaced by a new man named Archibald Frank, who made up in brilliance what he lacked in reliability. He was partial to unexplained disappearances, in some of which the mess fund was thought to have participated, but his cooking was so good he was always forgiven.

Meanwhile the echelon was enjoying life on the top of the hill near Dommartin. How I hated to ride up there. After leaving Herbeuville there was no protection all the way up the zigzag road, and the German artillery seemed to be getting more active every day. There was one place near the top that I especially dreaded—a crossroads on a bare little plateau which was often shelled by 77s.

One day I found a new way to go up. By following another road out of Herbeuville I could cross some rough fields and climb a rocky path straight up the side of the hill to the big camouflage screen. By cutting a hole in the screen I got onto the zigzag road about three-quarters of the way up, above the machine gun echelon, and cut off a long and dangerous detour. The only trouble was the fool horse I had to use. He always fell down when he stepped on a loose stone, and once he got his hoof caught on a piece of wire in the camouflage hedge and almost broke my neck. It was just the place I needed Peanuts' dainty footwork.

At last the clumsy brute got so on my nerves I wanted to lose him. Each evening I hitched him in the place where the most shells had fallen during the day, but in the morning he was always intact and stupider than ever. Finally, one morning I found his halter shank tied to a tree in the orchard, and no sign of the foolish horse. I joyfully reported him "lost in action," but before night he was back. He had somehow got loose—perhaps I forgot to fasten his halter strap—and wandered halfway up the hill to the machine gun echelon where he had spent the night among the mules. The machine gunners promptly returned him to us.

On one of my rides up the hill I found the echelon in confusion. A shell had landed among the horses, killing one and wounding several, and a splinter had wounded a driver named Apollonio who was asleep in his pup tent. The drivers dug a hole and with much labor buried the dead horse. During the night another shell exploded on the hole and exhumed the horse. The drivers were properly discouraged about it.

I think we had been less than a week in Herbeuville when the practice started of taking roving guns out on the plain at night. One or two guns with their crews would be pulled a kilometer or more into the open plain towards Wadonville or Saulx and the horses sent back. Then they would fire what ammunition they had and before daylight cover the guns with bushes. The next night the horses would go out and move them to a new place where they would do it again. It was intended partly to make the Germans think we had more artillery than we had, and partly to distract their attention from Herbeuville. Poor old Ritchie and Peabo and the telephone detail had an awful job to keep wire strung out to them. The gun crews didn't like it very well either, because they were liable to have a German patrol walk into them at any time. In one way the scheme failed, for Herbeuville was shelled worse than ever.

I spent most of my time keeping track of ammunition and riding back and forth to the echelon. No more exploring was done in the direction of Billy, for the German artillery was too much on the job. One day a Red Cross man brought a load of chocolate and cigarettes into Herbeuville in a sack on his shoulder. Unlike the Y.M.C.A., he gave them to us free. I remember that Peabo, Ritchie, and I took our cigarettes into our cellar, lay on our bunks, and chain-smoked them all to make sure of them.

We didn't have Herbeuville quite all to ourselves. There were some infantry platoons in reserve, who lived in cellars and had their kitchen beyond the square near the church. We seldom saw them as they slept daytimes and went up to the line at night. Sometimes a burst of German shelling would bring some of them into one of our cellars, but they were a changing population and we never got to know them well.

Towards the end of our stay in Herbeuville we received orders to fire in a big demonstration against Marcheville and Riaville. The rumor was that the Allies were going to start a big drive farther north, but the Germans were supposed to think we were starting a drive against Metz and so concentrate their reserves in the wrong place. Whether it worked I don't know. After dark the infantry who had been sharing Herbeuville with us lined up in the street for the attack and filed out onto the plain. This sight always made me feel queer for I knew that many of them would never see the next day.

The attack started at 1 a.m. We began our schedule of fire at 6:30 a.m. and kept it up off and on all day. With field glasses I could catch glimpses of small groups of infantry moving on the plain. Once I saw some German troops just before they disappeared behind a wall. The white bursts of our shells were plainly visible. All day the wounded doughboys straggled back through Herbeuville. They said their losses were enormous. Around noon we heard all the objectives were taken. There were several American planes directing our artillery fire. One of them was flying low towards our lines when a German antiaircraft shell exploded under its tail and it dove down onto the plain in flames. That night the doughboys came back to their old line of Hannonville, Wadonville, and Saulx, and we shortened our range accordingly. I could hear a terrific bombardment in the north, which I judged to be the beginning of the real offensive.

For the next few days the Germans retaliated by shelling Herbeuville unmercifully. They blew the remaining tiles off the kitchen, but none of our men were wounded.

On October 2d our infantry attacked again, and that afternoon we got orders to move back to a position on the hill where B Battery had been.

## CHAPTER LV

*Shrapnel fire. Cold weather. Fed up with the war.*

"Near St. Rèmy (north of Dommartin) Oct. 3, 3 a.m. Cold. On hill. Lived in tiny
dry dugout with Allen. MacNamee went to Coëtquidan. No firing. Pleasant.
Left Oct. 10, 6 p.m."
"Rupt-en-Woevre Oct. 11. Bivouac. Left Oct. 11, 6 p.m."

WE REACHED the new position about three o'clock in the morning.
It was in a field just behind the crossroads I disliked so much. While
we were crossing the field to the edge of some woods where the guns
were to be, shrapnel began bursting over our heads. This was the
only time we were under shrapnel fire during the war. They burst
with a metallic clang above us, and we could hear the balls rattling
into the woods. We scattered and ran for cover. My place of refuge
was behind a big tree. The shelling stopped in about ten minutes, and
we finished our job of getting the guns in position, unloading the
ammunition, and stringing telephone wires.

Most of the gunners slept in tar paper shacks in the woods, but Allen and I found a tiny concrete dugout with two bunks which we appropriated. It wasn't really a dugout so much as a box about six by
six by four feet in size, built in a hole, so its roof was level with the
surface of the ground. It was entered by a steep flight of narrow steps
cut out in the mud. Here I was comfortable for a week, having practically nothing to do. Our battery did no firing in this position.

Two days after our arrival MacNamee was ordered back to the
Artillery School at Coëtquidan. Everyone in the Battery felt like
crying when he left. He had come to us a stranger, and in the six
months of his command he had won the respect and affection of
every one of us. I can still recall the emptiness of that day. I think my
being fed up with the war started then. There was a tune the band used
to play at Boxford about "A long, long trail awinding into the land

of my dreams" that was very sad and plaintive. I remember that parts of it ran constantly through my head, but the words I heard were, "Nights are growing colder. This war's got to end." One rainy afternoon especially, I reduced myself to a very low state of mind with it while riding slowly back from watering my horse alone. It was the same old horse I couldn't get rid of.

The weather was getting colder and the rainy season was setting in. Allen and I used to lie in our cozy bunks smoking and reading letters from home. About this time I got another box of cigars from my father.

The kitchen was in a gully on the back side of the hill. Here Frank treated us to the best of his cooking. He used to make prune pies in mess kits which sold for a franc apiece and tasted delicious. He claimed the money went into the Battery mess fund, but I always suspected that was a myth. Near the kitchen was an empty German artillery position with a litter of wicker ammunition baskets on the ground.

We were relieved by a battery of the 113th F.A. on the night of October 9th, and the next night we pulled out onto the road. I don't remember anything at all about this march except that it was cold and dark and tiresome. We reached Rupt-en-Woevre in the early morning of the 11th and lay low in the woods all day. The other batteries of the Regiment were doing the same thing. We saw some of them to speak to when we watered the horses at the same muddy little stream in Rupt.

At 6 p.m. we left Rupt in regimental column, travelling north.

# CHAPTER LVI

## Introduction to the Verdun sector.

"Baleicourt, Oct. 12, 4 a.m. Rear echelon. Heavy forest, mud."
"Charny (near Verdun) Oct. 15, 6 p.m. forward echelon.
Left Oct. 15, 8 p.m."

THIS WAS ANOTHER of those very black nights and it was the coldest yet. The long column wound through the dark with everyone thinking his own thoughts. Mine were gloomy ones. I was getting sick of the whole business and I couldn't get my mind off of home.

I remember seeing a signpost with Verdun on it, perhaps the same one we had passed on the way to Rupt in September, but this time we were going the way the sign pointed. As the first suggestion of gray came into the sky we passed a place where tall buildings loomed above the road. Then came more stretches of barren road.

At 4 a.m. we crossed a railroad track, went through some soggy bare fields, and climbed a steep hill to the edge of some woods. I remember galloping around with Storer and then going back to bring the Battery through a cart road in a grove of very tall trees growing in black mud. Here we halted and unhitched. There was an empty Adrian barrack under the trees, where we spread our blankets and went to sleep.

When I woke up a few hours later the rain was coming down in a fine drizzle. I fed my nasty horse and got some breakfast myself. Then I rode back over the way we had come to find a place to water the brute. There were a good many troops in the woods through which I passed. Down on the railroad track I saw two huge guns mounted on special railroad cars on a siding. Someone told me they were 16-inch naval guns manned by sailors. Around the foot of the hill to the right I found the town of Baleicourt. It wasn't much of a town—mostly wooden barracks, shacks, and French canteens. At one of these I bought some tasteless gritty chocolate before going back to the Battery. I watered the horse at the foot of the hill. The woods we were in were called the Bois de Sartelles. When I got back to them the drivers were grooming the horses in the rain. I could hear the distant sound of artillery.

We expected to move any minute, but nothing happened for four days while we sat around in the rain. One night there was some talk about the war's ending at six o'clock, but I didn't take any stock in it. It was disturbing just the same and made me feel bluer than ever. The next day some of the boys went over to Baleicourt to see the Divisional Show. I don't remember whether I went or not but I remember hearing that some infantryman had been killed by a shell on the way back.

On Tuesday, October 15th, at 2 p.m. we left the heavy wagons in the Bois de Sartelles and, with the rest of the outfit, took the road north across the railroad tracks on a main road. It was raining and bleak. The road led through flat country with very sparse vegetation and no buildings. There were shell holes and rusty wire as far as I could see on both sides of the road. About 6 p.m. the column halted among some crumbling ruins on the bank of a canal. The name of the place was Charny. To the left were several large field hospital tents. The rolling kitchen pulled into a marshy field at the right of the road and served bread and coffee.

By about 9 p.m. it was dark enough for our purpose, and still raining. The guns, caissons, and water cart pushed on up the road, leaving everything else at Charny for a forward echelon. We soon reached another ruined town called Bras, where great camouflage curtains were hung across the street like election banners at home. We turned to the left on this street. Everything was quiet. After a few kilometers the road got rough and muddy. There was a low embankment on the right, where I noticed the doors of several dugouts reinforced with sandbags. A little beyond this we turned sharp to the right. I don't know who was leading the way, but he seemed to know

224

where he was going. The three firing batteries of the First Battalion were in column, so it was probably the major. Someone said this corner was Samogneux. I couldn't see any signs of a town anywhere. We were now travelling northeast. The road was getting narrower and more muddy. About midnight we halted in the dark.

---

## CHAPTER LVII

### *Death Valley. The breaking point.*

"Position south of Haumount. (Ravin d'Haumont-près-Samogneux) Oct. 16, 5 a.m. Huntington back. Death Valley. Driving rain, cold, no protection. Muddy shell-pitted hill to push guns up in the dark. No path. Hopeless. Bunch gassed. Woody badly hit. Bunch of horses killed. Left Oct. 23, midnight."

---

THERE WAS an almost perpendicular bank about four feet high on the right of the road and above it a hill rising in rough terraces. Some of the cannoneers got picks and shovels off the limbers and broke a gap through the bank, but it was still too steep for the horses. After several attempts to make them pull the first piece up, we unlimbered and, with everyone pushing that could get a hand on, we practically lifted it up the bank. The other three guns went the same way, and we spent all the remaining hours of darkness pushing them to the top of the hill, two or three hundred yards from the road.

Time and again it looked hopeless, as a gun would slip down a dozen feet that it had cost us half an hour's work to gain, inch by inch. Everything was so muddy that it was almost impossible to get a foothold, and only a few men at a time could get an efficient grip on the gun. The rest were in the way, and we were hampered also by the darkness. Often everyone would fall and let the whole weight of the gun come on one or two men. After an hour of it most of us were sobbing with weakness, and only one gun had been pushed to the top of the hill.

I remember sinking down in the mud to my knees and being too weak to move. Leaving my feet stuck, I lay on my back and let the rain fall on my face. Ritchie stumbled over me and produced a little bottle of rum* from his pocket. We each drank half. Ordinarily it would have burned the skin off my throat, but I didn't taste it at all. Soon the warmth returned to my feet and began creeping up my body. I dug some of the mud out of my sleeves and wallowed over to join the straining mob around one of the guns.

With the help of long ropes manned by cannoneers from the other two batteries, we finally got the last gun up. It was none to soon, for the first gray of morning was showing in the east. While the gunners were getting their camouflage nets spread, I noticed a group of men standing behind the guns. One of them was Freddy Huntington, spick and span in a clean uniform. A German shell racketed high over our heads. Freddy was the only one to duck, and everyone laughed at him.

As the light grew, I saw more and more of our surroundings, but it wasn't much to look at—barren, shell-scarred hills in every direction, with not a living bush or tree in sight. The road we had followed ran up the valley out of sight between two hills. The fringe of dead trees along their tops formed our horizon towards the front. It was too late to get any sleep but I recovered my blanket roll from the mud and carried it up the hill, looking for a place to leave it. Near the top I found Peabo and Ritchie installing the telephone switchboard in a shell hole. I chose one near it, levelled off the bottom, and pegged my shelter half across the top. Then I got out my mess kit and went down the hill to the kitchen for some breakfast.

Lorenzen had set up his buzzycot in a shell crater about fifty yards from the road, and a dozen wet, cold men were standing around watching him cook steaks. Without warning, shells began to explode in the road, the splinters sizzling over our heads. We all crouched in the kitchen while Lorenzen went on cooking. Instead of letting up, the shelling came closer. When a shell exploded on the

* "Rhum Negrito" bought in Rennes while we were at Coëtquidan.

"Someone said this corner was Samogneux."

Twenty-sixth Division wounded coming out of the trenches near Samogneux. The stretcher bearer is wearing his gas mask at the "alert." Notice the old telephone wires along the wall of the trench, and the mud in the bottom of it. Study the faces if you think war is fun.

"It wasn't much to look at."

Where I lived at the first Death Valley position. Peabo's telephone central is under the more pretentious arrangement a few feet to the right. Our guns are a few yards farther up the hill, and are not shown in this picture. The road runs up the valley towards the German lines, which are at right angles to the valley, and just over the low ridge in the background below the arrow indicating my residence.

"Soon I came to the sandbagged dugout entrances."

Some walking wounded from the 103rd Infantry resting on their way back to the dressing station.

hill a few yards above the kitchen we all dashed across the road and crouched in a crumbling old trench that ran up the other wall of the valley. Most of the boys stayed where they landed, but I walked up the trench till I had climbed to a high level.

From this point I could look down the valley to the rear. There was an infantry kitchen at a turn of the road about half a mile back, from which smoke was rising. The only moving object was a water cart drawn by two horses. While I watched, a shell exploded beside it. One of the horses struggled to get up, but the other horse and the man lay still in the road. Later I learned that the man was Woody. After ten or fifteen minutes the shelling stopped, and I came down to the road. I found the rest of the boys sitting in the trench eating steaks. It seems Lorenzen had dashed back to the kitchen to rescue them while the shelling was still going on. People have got the Croix de Guerre for less.

All our ammunition had been dumped beside the road, and now we had to carry it up to the guns. Each man took four shells in a sandbag and, with frequent halts for breath, climbed the hill with them. We worked ourselves out without making much impression on the pile of shells beside the road. I hated to think of the load the caissons would bring from the rear after dark. That afternoon I got permission to get six spare horses from Charny.

Allen's plug I had left tied to a piece of barbwire in a shell hole around the angle of the hill. I saddled him up and rode back down the valley. Everywhere the country was the same—bare, dismal, shell-torn, with no vegetation. There were many troops bivouacking in shell holes beside the road. At the corner I looked for the town of Samogneux. It was an area of masonry rubble, nowhere more than six feet high—the most complete ruin of a town imaginable. After I passed I noticed that the land on the left of the road was growing higher till it sloped up in a bare hillside while on the right of the road lay level fields. These fields were full of American artillery. Beyond them I saw the line of the River Meuse marked by dead trees. Soon I

227

came to the sandbagged dugout entrances which I had noticed in the night. They were dug into the side of the hill and housed Regimental and, I think, Brigade Headquarters. Vacherauville was a heap of ruins little better than Samogneux. At Charny I found the drivers and the rolling kitchen.

Back at the Battery with the six horses, I put my plan into execution. Tying two blankets together by the corners, I swung them across a horse and put six shells in each side. This made a load of about three hundred pounds which a horse should be able to carry up the hill. The weight broke the blankets and the shells fell to the ground. With five shells on a side the blankets held, and with all six horses working we got the shells up the hill before supper time.

It succeeded so well that I decided to picket the horses in shell holes for the night and use them again the next day. Their drivers had brought some oats, and on my way to Charny I had noticed a huge shell crater full of water where I thought we could water them. It was a few hundred yards straight back from Samogneux. When we got them there we found the walls of the crater were very steep and the edge crumbling. The water level was about three feet below the level of the ground. Two of the horses fell in and for a while I thought we had lost them as the sides were too slippery and steep to offer them any foothold and the water was fifteen or twenty feet deep in the center. Some French soldiers saw our fix and brought a long piece of rope with which we were able to drag them out more dead than alive. We watered the others at the Meuse, about half a mile farther away. Then we took them up the valley and tied them in shell holes near the road.

During the night there was heavy shelling all down the valley but none of the bursts came near the top where my shelter half was. In the morning I went down to see how the horses had made out. One was killed, one strayed, and all the rest were wounded. Allen's old plug had a shell splinter through the lungs. When I saw him standing with his head between his knees and bloody froth coming out of his side at every breath I repented of all the mean things I had said about him. It wasn't his fault that Peanuts was brighter than he.

Well, that ended the horse business, and we went back to carrying shells by hand. We made a rule that every man who came to meals had to carry four shells back up the hill and, as there were about twenty-five of us eating three meals a day, this plan accounted for three hundred shells. In the eight days that we were there we fired less than 2000 rounds, so with what the horses had carried up we got along all right.

I think it was the next night that I had a peculiar experience. I had made myself comfortable in my shell hole with a couple of salvaged blankets for a mattress and a sweater rolled up for a pillow. About thirty feet away was a shell hole that all of us who lived near there used for a latrine. I woke up during the night and, having diarrhoea as most of us had, I left my bed and went down to the latrine. The Germans were shelling the road as they did every night. When I got back to bed I found a piece of hot iron the size of my hand on the pillow and a jagged hole in the shelter half.

C and B Batteries of our battalion were in positions in front of us, a little to the right and much farther down the hill. There were two batteries of the 322nd F.A. to our left front. They moved out one night, and in the morning I walked down and salvaged several trays of fuses they had abandoned. They must have had a stormy time in that position for we frequently saw it shelled and heard their calls for stretcher bearers. A few days after they left, a German shell hit one of their ammunition piles and the whole business blew up.

We slept high enough to be fairly safe from gas, but one night our guns were badly swamped by gas shells mixed with high explosives. One of the guns was hit but not put out of action, and none of our men were killed. Six of them were gassed, however, and had to be evacuated, including Lorenzen, the cook, and McCann, who had been wounded at Bernècourt in May but had rejoined the Battery.

Every day the shelling was getting worse so we were under a constant strain. Some single shells came over, but usually they came in bunches suddenly, like rafale fire. New troops had been moving in behind us all this time as if for an attack, so the valley had a fairly large invisible population, and wherever a burst of shelling landed it was pretty sure to be followed by calls for stretcher bearers. One afternoon I was out alone repairing telephone wire in the waste of shell holes behind and to the left of our position when I heard faint groaning. I found two doughboys in a shell hole. They had been sleeping there when a shell exploded just inside the shell hole, blowing off their legs. They had done the best they could with first-aid packets and tourniquets but they were moribund when I found them. There was nothing I could do. The same night I found a dead stranger in the trench leading to our kitchen hole. The back of his head was crushed in, I suppose by a large shell fragment. All this was beginning to get on my nerves.

On clear days we could see the German observation balloons over the hill to our front. One morning I noticed some queer-looking bunches on the side of the hill that I didn't remember having seen before. With field glasses I saw that they were tanks under camouflage.

On one of our last days in this position I went up to the infantry lines with Freddy to register the guns. He must have thought he was still at Chemin-des-Dames. There was no registering done, and we were lucky to get back with our lives. We found the infantry just inside a strip of shattered woods. There were no trenches; the men lay in the mud about five yards apart. They wore slickers saturated with mud, and the whites of their eyes were the only clean part of them visible. They had burlap covers on their helmets to prevent the light's glancing on the metal surfaces.

In a deep old German dugout we found the infantry captain. He was dressed exactly like the men except for his small collar insignia, and looked worried to death. He was smoking cigarettes as fast as he could light them. He told Freddy of a place to try for an observation post, and we went outside to find it. There were two or three infantry runners hanging around the dugout entrance. One of them told me they were having a hard time getting their wounded out and their supplies in. They made no attempt to evacuate their dead. He pointed to a row of muddy bodies half covered with blankets. I could see they were dead by their feet. He said the ration detail had been shot up three nights running, and they hoped to get relieved before they starved.

Freddy and I walked some distance bent over, to a gap in the tree trunks. We could see a bare hillside opposite, fringed at the top, like ours, with dead trees. Just then machine gun bullets began to snap above our heads and we dropped flat. We wormed our way back in the direction we had come and returned to the Battery.

On October 23d our infantry attacked, and we fired our share of the preparation and barrage. Late in the afternoon we got orders to move the Battery farther forward up the valley. Freddy Huntington took Peabo with him to pick out a place for the guns. It was dark when they returned. Peabo said the new position was about a kilometer up the road the other side of Haumont, and there would be no trouble getting in if he and Freddy could again find the lane through the heavy barbwire entanglement beside the road. They had marked it with a white stone.

The limbers were due at midnight. The next few hours were spent in packing and getting everything down to the roadside. We got the guns down the hill without much trouble. I kept expecting to see the road shelled, but nothing happened. It was a cold night with large masses of clouds drifting across the moon. After everything was ready we sat beside the road waiting for the limbers. I had no horse now so I was packed light. I had left my Luger pistol under a wet blanket in my shell-hole bed, thinking to come back for it later, but at the last minute I went up and got it. The holster I left behind however, and never saw it again.

After waiting for about two hours we heard the limbers coming up the road.

# CHAPTER LVIII

*We move up the valley. Disaster. Seven days of torment.*

"Position north of Haumont, Oct. 24, 1 a.m. Horror. Peabo killed. Priebe mangled. Ammunition train men and horses slaughtered. Foster and I in shell hole. Gas shells all night. Found dugout. Gas. Many killed and wounded. Nightmare. Left Nov. 1, 9 a.m."

THIS IS A CHAPTER I hate to write.

When the limbers came up we saw that, in addition to our own caissons, there were six or eight from the Divisional Ammunition Train. The park wagon, a clumsy thing drawn by three horses and driven from the seat, had also come along to transport the kitchen stuff, telephone equipment, and odds and ends. Some of the caissons were empty so we loaded them from the ammunition pile along the side of the road. This was soon done, the guns limbered, and everything packed and ready to start. It was about midnight.

There had been no shelling from the Germans. As the column started, each carriage waited till the one ahead had gone about fifty yards so that a shell landing on the road would not be likely to get more than one. As I remember it, the park wagon led with Rodliffe and Knox on the seat, then came the four guns, then our caissons, and the A.T. caissons last. The cannoneers walked, carrying their packs. I was walking about opposite the second gun, well towards the head of the column.

We passed the remains of the position vacated by the 322nd and, a little farther along, drew aside for an ambulance coming down the hill from beyond Haumont. It was too dark to see more than a few yards. As we advanced up the valley the road got still narrower. When the head of the column halted I thought we had reached the place. On the left there was a high bank with a shell hole near the bottom and another a few feet above it. On the right the land seemed

"We suddenly got orders to pull back from the valley."

One of our caissons by daylight on the Death Valley road. It is headed towards the rear. A four-horse hitch is being used because of the shortage of horses. Note the pitiful condition of the ones in this picture. This is the place we got caught on the night of October 24th. Clarence Smith on lead horse. Wheel driver not recognized, a replacement I think.

level, but I could make out that a dense tangle of barbwire came right up to the road.

After we had stood halted for a few minutes I sensed that something was wrong. The carriages behind were closing up, and I heard calls for Captain Huntington and Sergeant Peabody from the head of the column. It was then that the German shells began to fall on the road.

There was a whine followed by a glare of light and a splintering crash. I jumped for the shell hole at the edge of the road. Explosion followed explosion in quick succession. A cloud was over the moon, but by the light of the shell flashes I could see what was happening. The park wagon was wedged across the road with one of the horses down and both Knox and Rodliffe wounded. The other carriages had crowded up into a compact column and the shells were exploding among them.

In one flash of light I saw horses rearing in terror. Someone was trying to drag the body of a driver from under their hoofs. Everywhere I looked was confusion. In the dark intervals between explosions I heard shouts and the whistling sound that terrified horses make, mingled with cries for stretcher bearers and for Captain Huntington.

Our one chance was to get off the road, but only two people knew the location of the gap through the wire. There was no possibility of turning around in that narrow space, and the way ahead was blocked by the park wagon. By the next flash of light I caught a glimpse of Peabo running towards the head of the column. A second later another shell exploded and I saw him fall. In the darkness that followed I heard a groan just over my head. Crawling up the bank to the next shell hole, I felt something soft in it. Just then the moon came out.

I saw a man named Priebe lying in the shell hole. His face was the color of ivory, his coat was soaked with blood, and there was a hole the size of my fist in the right side of his chest below the shoulder, from which blood was pouring. I ripped open his first-aid packet and plugged the hole with gauze. It didn't stop bleeding, so I used my own packet and then tied my belt around his chest to keep the packing in. Then I pushed him to the bottom of the shell hole where he would be less likely to get hit again and went down to the road. My hands were sticky with blood and my nose was full of the smell of it.

I found a little group of men doing something at the side of the road. They were building a barricade of blanket rolls around a man who lay on the ground. By the moonlight I saw it was Peabo. Ritchie got up and walked past me.

"Is he all right?" I asked him. He shook his head.

The worst of the shelling was now down the road where the Ammunition Train caissons were, but single shells kept exploding in the field beyond the road and higher up on the bank above our heads. Apparently Peabo had succeeded in locating the gap through the wire, for some of the gun teams were pulling into the field past the park wagon, which had been dragged aside. Men were cutting the dead horses out of harness and clearing away the wreckage at top speed. My job was to see that the ammunition reached the guns, so I ran across the field to where the first piece was unlimbering and tried to pick a route through the barbwire entanglements which seemed everywhere in the dark. When I got back to the road they were putting Peabo into an ambulance. Someone said he was dead. I led the caissons that could still move, into the field and through the tortuous gaps and lanes of barbwire to the guns. The ammunition from the disabled caissons was thrown beside the road.

Meanwhile the shelling had gone down the road in the direction of our old position. The horses started back, spaced well apart. The cannoneers worked at getting their guns set in and hidden under nets. Ritchie had taken charge of the telephone detail and was working like a tiger. No one would recognize him now as the bashful recruit I had first seen at Boxford.

I was helping carry in ammunition from the road when the Germans started shelling again. This time I jumped for a big hollow on the bank behind a ledge of rock. I found a cannoneer named Foster there ahead of me. A shell exploded just above our shelter, showering us with a landslide of sand. I recognized the strong smell of gas and yelled to Foster to put on his mask. I wanted to get higher up the bank, away from the gas, but shells were landing so close outside that I didn't dare to move. Foster and I lay on our backs in the dark, breathing through our masks. I began to feel sick to my stomach and had a crazy impulse to pull my mask off for one breath of air, but I resisted it.

The next thing I remember is opening my eyes and seeing daylight through the windows of my gas mask. I took it off and smelled the air. There was still gas around, but not strong. I sat up and shook Foster. We had both been unconscious for some time, but it may have been partly natural sleep. We could hear no shelling now so we crawled out of our hole and looked around.

On the road at our feet were the fresh shell holes and wreckage of the night. Beyond was a maze of rusty barbwire strung between stakes in an irregular pattern through a field which sloped gradually upward. The guns were under their camouflage nets about a hundred yards in from the road. Beyond them was the beginning of a shallow gully that got deeper as it reached the top of the rise. I crossed the road and made for this gully.

In the upper end of it I found Ritchie and some of the Special Detail shoveling excreta out of a wooden-floored dugout built in the bank. It was a good enough dugout but it faced the wrong way, so shells could come in the door. We lived in it for the six days we stayed in this position.

The kitchen was set up in a shell crater near the guns. A new man named Harrington came up as cook. He was not a cook by nature, but a hard worker, and he had squared out the shell hole to make a level floor. The next day a German shell spoiled all his work and all his cooking too, but he dug it out again and served what was left of the meal with the sand right in it. I always had a great admiration for him. He was a stocky little bearded man from somewhere in Missouri.

It seemed as if the Germans were shelling this part of the valley all the time. There were some troops across the road about half a mile away where a Decauville track ran up a gully. We could hear their cries for stretcher bearers after each bombardment.

We had very little shelter where we were. The gunners dug big holes behind the guns to live in and covered them with logs and paulins. The kitchen was another place to duck into, and there were shallow shell holes scattered between these and my dugout. I slid into one of them when a shell surprised me carrying my dinner up from the kitchen and found I was sharing it with a dead man who was only partly buried.

There was a dead infantryman lying beside the road just opposite the kitchen. One day someone covered the face with a slicker to keep the rain off, but the next day the wind had blown the slicker away. He was still there when we left.

All I had to do was look out for the ammunition and occasionally help Ritchie with his telephone wires. As I remember, the men in our dugout were Pete Murray, Martin Joyce, Willie Saindon, Ritchie, and myself. One of them tended the switchboard, one or two were always out over the lines, and the rest slept.

One night I had a call to go down to the captain's dugout right away. It was really a shell crater built up with shell boxes full of dirt and roofed over, but he called it a dugout. It was pitch dark, raining, and the Germans were shelling quite close to the position. I expected his message would be mighty important. What it turned out to be was an order from Brigade Headquarters demanding an exact list of the shells and fuses we had on hand, immediately. I stumbled around to all the ammunition piles, feeling for the shells in the dark. Counting them was out of the question and, as for the fuses, I couldn't even find any. All the time shells kept exploding near enough so the splinters came overhead. In disgust I made up an imaginative list and gave it to Freddy. It seemed to satisfy him all right.

236

I think it was the day after this that we heard definitely that Peabo was dead. There was no news of the others. Ritchie and I were the hardest hit by it, as we knew Peabo the best.

During the last three days and nights in this position the Battery's morale reached its lowest ebb. No one smiled and nothing seemed funny. Everyone went around with a furtive look, watching for a place to jump for when the shelling began. Even Chandler, the sergeant of the fourth gun section, the most reliable, hard-working, sane human I ever saw, and a giant of a man, admitted that he had "lost interest in the war." I remember writing a letter home about this time, full of jokes and artificial optimism. It is a ghastly document as I read it now. I thought my time was about up and I didn't much care.

On November 1st, out of a clear sky, we suddenly got orders to pull back from the valley. The limbers came up at eight o'clock in the morning in broad daylight. Like crazy men we worked to drag the guns out to the road and pack everything up. What ammunition we had left, we piled beside the road. Then, with everyone walking except the drivers, we got out as fast as we could.

After we reached the first turn in the road we heard shells landing in the old position. Allen found that he had forgotten one of his instruments and went back after it. When he rejoined us he said there were two dead infantrymen lying beside our ammunition pile.

# CHAPTER LIX

*Out of Death Valley. A good position. The armistice.*
*Celebrating without fireworks.*

"Position near Fort Douaumont, Nov. 1, 1918, 2 p.m. Heaven. Quiet after the storm.
French position. Comfort; life; hope. Rolling barrage up to 10.59, Nov. 11, then peace.
Left Nov. 13, 4 p.m. on perm."

WHEN WE GOT BACK to Bras I was sent ahead on a borrowed horse to learn the way into our new position while the Battery went on to Charny for a rest and something to eat. Instead of turning to the right at Bras, I kept straight, following a good road that wound between bare hills.

About five kilometers out of Bras I was met by a French artilleryman at a little bridge. He took me up a long, rough road to the top of a large hill, where there was a battery position occupied by the Ninth Battery of the Sixteenth French Regiment. He said the place was called the Forêt d'Haudromont, but no trees were visible. All I saw was a wide panorama of bare hills pocked with shell holes.

The Frenchmen were cordial, gave me a meal and all the pinard I could hold, and showed me over the position. It was a very old one, with deep trenches, dugouts, sappes, protected gun pits, and everything for comfort. There were even ammunition racks built into the side of the trenches, so there was no need of going above the surface of the ground for anything. They said there was no danger from gas, the hill was so high.

In the afternoon I explored around to see the best way for the guns to come up. The main road curved around the foot of the hill, but only went to a quarry about three-quarters of the way up, and from here to the position the ground was too steep and rough for anything on wheels to negotiate. While I was riding at the foot of the hill a few shells exploded up the road, and I took cover in a big partly fallen-in dugout. I was soon convinced that the first way I had seen was the only practicable one, so I went over it again, noting carefully the worst places. One was a narrow log bridge over a culvert, and another was a mean combination of deep shell holes which might prove disastrous to a carriage in the dark. Then I went down to the Bras Road and waited for the Battery.*

It was dusk before they came along, and dark before we reached the position. We had brought only two of our guns up, so the French sent two of theirs back, leaving the Battery half-French and half-American until the next night, when the relief was completed.

Ritchie and I slept in the telephone dugout with the men of the "cinquieme pièce," as they called their Special Detail. It was a beautiful, large, dry dugout with wooden floor and walls. We sat around smoking, swapping lies, and drinking pinard with the Frenchmen till about midnight, when we turned in and slept soundly till morning in comfortable wire bunks.

The next day Ritchie and the French telephone men went over the lines, and I tagged along to see where Battalion Headquarters was. It was in some big dugouts built into the side of a gulch in front of our hill.

Many of our telephone calls came through a French central, and our telephone men had a hard time to understand. At first they thought the central was run by a man named Deedan because the Frenchmen all said "Dis-donc" so often over the telephone.

Our kitchen was in a cave the size of a ballroom, about three hundred yards down the hill to the right of the position. It was approached by a deep trench whose walls were full of crumbling dugout entrances. Near the kitchen was the Grande Carriere, a big stone quarry where a battalion of French Colonial troops lived, and where the French telephone central was located. It was a rabbit warren of rooms and corridors, all hung over with camouflage nets on the out-

* A lonesome place with intermittent 155s falling on the hillside above.

side. Our kitchen was manned by Fox and Frank. The ration carts and even trucks could drive right up to it on the main road, so we never lacked for provisions, and Frank again flooded the market with prune pies at a price, somewhat to Fox's disapproval. I don't think the officers ever knew about it.

If the position had a fault it was that it swarmed with rats. We used to shoot them with our pistols. I killed one with my boots at the turn of a trench. They ate all the candle ends at night and ran over us while we were asleep.

Except for the rats, the life was much like that at the Chemin-des-Dames. Daytimes we sat around watching the planes in the sky and the German shells exploding on neighboring hills. The one behind us was Fort Douaumont, which was shelled every day by heavy guns. We would listen to the great projectiles drone far over our heads and see the lazy geysers of black earth rise in the air when they landed. Sometimes we heard shells passing in the other direction, from our railroad guns at Baleicourt. Occasionally some 150s landed around the position, but we didn't pay much attention to them, we were so secure. At night the caissons came up with ammunition, which we "hopped" from hand to hand as we used to do at Ostel. The guns fired a good deal, but not enough to interfere with anyone's sleep.

I think it was on November 6th that we got orders to pack up and be ready to move forward. The cannoneers pulled the guns out of their pits to be ready when the limbers came up, but they didn't come. Then we were told the move was postponed, and we settled down again.

The next day I walked over to Battalion Headquarters where I found that the attack was called off. On my way back, I yelled the good news as soon as I came in sight of the gun pits. The cannoneers swarmed out and danced around, yelling with joy. Someone lobbed a big stone in my direction, and to be funny I tried to catch it on my helmet. I leaned forward, my helmet fell off, and the rock dropped on my head. I sat down with my eyes full of blood. Some of the boys took me down to the French dressing station in the quarry, where a few stitches were put in my scalp.

On the 8th, some of us started forward on a reconnaissance party to find advance positions, but we got only as far as Battalion Headquarters, where Freddy had a long talk inside, resulting in our turning back. The next morning there was a lot of firing, and we heard that the attack had started and the infantry had taken Flabas but could go no farther. We got packed up again, and again the limbers failed to show up.

On November 11th Ritchie was at the switchboard when a call came through from Battalion to suspend fire at 10:59 as an armistice was to go into effect at 11. Although we all were interested, I don't remember that anyone took it very seriously. I thought it might mean some kind of a temporary halt, to last a few hours or perhaps a day.

At 11, all sounds of firing stopped. A few minutes later we heard church bells ringing at Verdun. We decided that if there was anything to celebrate we would do our share, so we dug out all the Very pistol cartridges we had and fired them off. None of them would work. I remembered how Bird, Joyce, and Murray had taken them out in front of Bernècourt to warn us of the tank attack, but I kept quiet about it.

The next two days we loafed around the position waiting for something to happen. I noticed nobody discarded his helmet or gas mask, and the caissons came up with ammunition at night just as usual.

On November 13th Ritchie and I got our furlough papers, threw away our helmets, and hopped a truck for Verdun, en route for Aix-les-Bains.

# CHAPTER LX

## *Ritchie and I go on leave.*

"Aix les Bains, Nov. 17, 5 a.m. Left with Lyell Hale Ritchie on permission for Aix. Verdun to get new clothes and bath. Baleicourt for travel orders. Favresse, St. Dizier (pas bon), Dijon (bon hotel, good food, etc.). Villa Gabrielle, Alps, bicycles, theatre, afternoon teas, etc. Left No. 25, 6 p.m."

"Lyons. Changed trains on the run."

"Dijon, Nov. 26, 3.30 a.m. Hotel de Paris, bon. Left Nov. 26, 3 p.m."

"Is-sur-Tille – changed."

"Langres – Marne – Nov. 26, 11.30 p.m. Night on floor in Y.M.C.A. Left Nov. 27, 5 p.m."

"Paris, Nov. 27, 8 p.m. '12 hour' pass from station. Hotel de Londres et d'Anvers. Gare de l'Est, Boulevarde St. Denis, Rue des Italiens, de l'Opera, Place de la Republique, Hotel de Ville, Notre Dame, Place du Havre, Arc de Triomphe, George V, Clemonceau, Champs d'Elysees. Left 8.30 p.m., Nov. 28."

"Montigny-le-Roi, Nov. 29, 7 a.m. Meuse, Provenchere, left with L.H.R., Horne, Lane. Rain. Marthe Silvestre (14½), Agnes Jeanne Rose Cecile (12½). Rue Camille Flamarion, Montigny-le-Roi, Haute-Marne. Therese (4½). Hot chocolate, pommes frittes. Left Dec. 23, 1918."

THE MONTHS after the armistice are an anticlimax, but to complete the story I must say something about them. As I look back on it, the time falls into four periods: the seven-day leave that Ritchie and I stretched to six weeks, the time spent in billets at Varenne, the two months at Mayet, and finally the trip home and my discharge from the army. Each period will just about make a chapter.

When Ritchie and I got our papers from Storer for a seven-day furlough we packed up, shouldered our loads, and ran down the trench to the kitchen to hop a truck for Verdun. Frank had two prune pies which we bought and ate. It took us only a few minutes to get tired of waiting, so we started down the road on foot. At the bottom of the hill a truck passed and we tried to hop it but failed because our equipment was in our way. We had blanket rolls, overcoats, slickers, gas masks, spare boots, mess kits, meat cans, condiment cans, toilet articles, canteens, and souvenirs, all but the last charged against us on the Battery books. My Luger pistol I had stuck inside my pants in anticipation of what was to happen. We had walked about a mile, carrying these loads, when we saw another truck overtaking us. It showed no inclination to stop, so we threw all our stuff into the ditch and climbed over the tailboard on the fly.

At Verdun we got deloused and drew new uniforms and underclothes from a quartermaster store. Then we hopped a truck to Baleicourt, where we got our health certificates stamped and our furlough papers signed by the personnel adjutant. We were told to report to the officer in charge of the divisional leave contingent on board the special leave train which started from Baleicourt day after tomorrow. Ritchie and I agreed that it all sounded too formal, so that night we hopped aboard a slow-moving French civilian train and found an empty third-class compartment. We didn't know where the train was going, but we took off our boots and puttees, rolled up our coats for pillows, and went to sleep on the seats.

We were put off at a station called Favresse sometime in the night. The train left us standing in our stocking feet and shirtsleeves on a cinder platform in the rain and dark. Fortunately another train came along after an hour or so and took us as far as St. Dizier. Not having tickets, we dispensed with the formality of entering the station and dropped off when the train slowed down at the edge of town. St. Dizier did not appeal to our holiday mood as there were too many American Military Police in the streets, so we got a meal in a café and took a train out. We were careful to keep travelling south.

We got to Dijon in the evening, found it a good town with no Americans, and blew ourselves to an expensive dinner. Towards midnight we tried to get a room in the swellest hotel, but there was nothing doing, so we put up at a little third-rate hotel near the station. In the morning we took a train to Lyons, where we had a meal, and then took a train for Aix-les-Bains.

We arrived in the station of Aix-les-Bains at 5 a.m., more than

243

twenty-four hours ahead of the leave crowd from the 26th Division. The American Provost Marshal stamped the date of arrival on our papers and turned us over to a bus driver who took us to a hotel named Villa Gabrielle. The next day the crowd arrived, with two friends among them, Harry Horne and Ed Lane.

The place was overrun with American soldiers on furlough, but they were given a fair amount of freedom and seemed to be enjoying themselves in a mild way. The famous Casino was turned into a Y.M.C.A. building where "group games," milk chocolate, and educational talks had replaced roulette, liquor, and sporting ladies. Ritchie and I went there only once. We took a sulphur bath, went on bicycle rides, spent a day going up an Alp in a cog railway train, loafed, and shopped. I bought some carved wooden figures and a picture to take home to the family, and when the storekeeper suggested sending them parcel post, I asked him to send my Luger pistol too, which he did. The pistol is on my mantel now.

On November 25th the authorities told us our seven days were up and we would have to move on. At first we felt insulted, but on thinking it over we saw pleasing possibilities in the situation. Instead of being herded back to the Regiment with the crowd we would be turned loose on the country. We agreed to return to the Regiment in a fairly roundabout way. That night Ritchie and I took a train out of Aix-les-Bains.

At first we had no particular destination. We changed trains at Lyons and headed for Dijon, which we knew to be a good town. We landed there at 3:30 a.m., put up at a hotel, spent the day seeing the sights, and took a train out in the afternoon.

We evaded our fare by jumping off in the trainyards wherever we could. This time we almost ran into disaster. Our train started to slow down and we got ready to jump. To our horror we saw an M.P. beside the track, and a minute later the train had stopped inside a barbwire stockade full of soldiers. We were taken off the train and herded into the stockade. We found the place was called Is-sur-Tille, and was a replacement depot where stray soldiers were held pending assignment to various organizations. When questioned by the authorities we showed our papers and said we were coming home from leave. We were then asked where our Regiment was stationed, and we had to admit we didn't know. Luckily for us the authorities didn't know either, so we were given travel orders to Langres, where we could report to the A.P.M.* office and get transportation to our Regiment. A leave train would be through in the morning which we could take. After dark we slipped through the gate in a crowd of soldiers being hustled aboard a train and left Is-sur-Tille with them.

We didn't know where they were going but we wanted to get clear of them the first chance. This came about midnight when the train slowed down at a station. We dropped off unnoticed and found ourselves in the rain with no signs of life anywhere. The only road led up a long, steep hill, and at the top we saw lights in a Y.M.C.A. hut. The secretary was closing the counter with padlocks for the night. He refused us permission to sleep on the floor and went on closing his shutters. All the lights were out except one behind the counter, so the place got darker with each shutter he closed. We stamped to the door, gave it a bang, tiptoed back into the room, and went to sleep under a table.

In the morning we set out to find a meal. We found we were in Langres after all, and it looked like a bad town. The streets were swarming with American officers as there was an army school there. Also there were many M.P.s around. Except for them we appeared to be the only enlisted men in the place. We were afraid to go into cafés or restaurants where we might get arrested, so we kept moving. By noon we were hungry and decided to report to the A.P.M. office and get transportation back to the Regiment.

We marched up to an imposing stone building, told our business to a guard, and were ushered up a flight of stairs and into a small room. A hard-boiled major sat at a desk interviewing a private who

* American Provost Marshal.

was standing between two armed M.P.s. Ritchie and I were in time to hear the major ask how it happened that this soldier was travelling on an unauthorized train without travel orders. Ritchie and I looked at each other. When the soldier failed to produce an answer he was led away by the two M.P.s. The major cleared his throat, looked at us, and then to our surprise, he got up and walked through a doorway into an adjoining room. We could hear him talking to someone in there. I saw a closed door in the opposite wall, and at the same time heard the M.P.s coming back. Ritchie and I quickly crossed the room, opened the door, and found ourselves in an empty hallway. At the end of it was a flight of stairs, and it didn't take us long to get to the bottom. We opened a door and looked out into an alley. There was no one in sight. We ran down the alley, walked rapidly across town to the railroad track, and hopped on the last platform of a slow-moving train.

This proved to be a Paris train. We found ourselves in the corridor of a first-class carriage crowded with people sitting on their luggage. Most of them were French, but we saw an American Red Cross girl and sat on the floor beside her. She gave us some chocolate and made friends with us very readily. Her object apparently was to make us talk about the war, so we made up stories for her. She expressed such admiration for a briquet of mine that I had to give it to her. I hated to see it go. One of the French artillerymen at Ostel had made it for me out of parts of German shells.

As soon as the crowd thinned out, Ritchie and I moved into a compartment with a French major. He talked with us all the way to Paris. Among other things he asked us how we expected to get in without papers. We had no ideas, so he offered to get us in through the French gate. At 8 p.m. the train stopped in the Gare de l'Est, and the major told us to stick close to him. There were two gates leading to the street, one with "American Provost Marshal's Office" over it, and one with the French equivalent. The major went through the French gate, showed a card to the poilu on guard, and walked on into the street. I tried to follow him with Ritchie at my heels, but I was stopped by the poilu's bayonet point against my stomach.

"Par la-bas les Americains," he said, indicating the other gate. I protested something about being with the major, but he only repeated his tiresome suggestion. He seemed quite inflexible about it, so Ritchie and I backed up and went over to the other gate, where we took our places in a line that moved slowly past a ticket window. By the time I reached the window I had considered every possibility and was resigned to a couple of weeks in a Paris jail followed by court-martial proceedings. The officer behind the window asked for my papers. I passed up the old leave card. He looked it over, smiled, and said, "Did you know this expired November 25th?"

"Yes, sir," I said politely, "but we are looking for our Regiment, which was north of Verdun when we went on leave."

"Did you expect to find it in Paris?" he asked. Ritchie was pulling me by the coat. I suppose he thought the officer was planning to shoot me. I didn't have the face to make an answer. I probably blushed.

"Well," said the officer unexpectedly. "Go ahead in, but you will have to take the 8:30 train to Langres tomorrow morning. Here's a twelve-hour pass. Next."

Ritchie and I found ourselves on the sidewalk in a state of stupor. Before we had decided which way to walk we were joined by the French major, who congratulated us on getting through and apologized for the failure of our original plan. He said he would take us to his own hotel and see that we got rooms. On the way there I thought I saw two familiar forms across the street and gave them a yell. It was Horne and Lane. They said they had escaped from the leave train the day after we left Aix-les-Bains and had just reached Paris themselves. They joined forces with us, met the major, and we were soon installed in two large double rooms on the Boulevard Magenta.

We spent a few minutes slicking up, and spent the evening seeing the sights. There were plenty to see, but I won't go into much detail. The streets were full of soldiers in the uniforms of all the Allies, and the prevailing mood was festive. Taxis whizzed by with Australians dancing on the roofs or sitting astride the hoods. The Australians were the wildest. Everyone on the sidewalks went arm in arm regardless of whether they spoke the same language or not. The cafés were doing a rushing business. The lights were all blazing after four years of darkness. Lane and Horne got lost in the crowd before we had gone a block. Sometime after midnight Ritchie and I located our hotel and turned in. Sleeping between sheets was a novelty.

When we woke up it was eight o'clock. Horne and Lane were still sleeping, so we woke them and held a council of war. Our train left in thirty minutes, and we felt we would be doing Paris an injustice if we left so soon. At the same time we had no desire to see the inside of a jail. We examined our passes and noticed that it would be easy to change the a.m. to p.m., so we called for pen and ink and gave ourselves another twelve hours.

In the afternoon we saw George V and Clemenceau ride under the Arc de Triomphe. The Champs Elysees was lined by chasseurs on beautiful horses. The long double line of lances tipped by pennons stretched out of sight under the trees. Between them passed some of the immortal regiments of the French and British armies, while the crowds wept, laughed, and cheered. Afterwards we got together with Lane and Horne and found they had enjoyed many adventures, including a taxicab wreck. They said Paris was the place they had been looking for and they had no idea of leaving it. Ritchie and I had had several harrowing collisions with the Military Police during the day, and we were about ready to drag out. We had a rousing supper together, paid our hotel bill, and said goodbye to Horne and Lane. Their last charge was, "If you see Storer, tell him we're still looking for the Regiment."

Then we walked over to the Gare de l'Est, gave up our passes at the A.P.M. office, and took the 8:30 out. We didn't wait for any travel orders for fear of embarrassing questions. We sat down in a compartment with two French officers who told us the train went

"A picture to send home to the family."

Taken in November 1918, while on leave at Aix-les-
Bains. A comparison with the first picture shows the
effect on one's age of a few months of war.

through Langres, and they supposed we were going there as it was quite an American town. We were disgusted at this news and vowed we'd never go to Langres again while there was a jump left in us. We were amusing them with a story of our successes against the Military Police when one of them pointed to the little round window in the partition between our compartment and the next. To my horror I saw an M.P. examining the papers of some American officers. The Frenchmen laughed heartily at our panic, but at the same time suggested a way of escape. The train was travelling rapidly through the suburbs of Paris and it was dark outside. The Frenchman opened the door, we climbed out onto the running board, and the Frenchmen shut the door again. We crouched low to be out of the light from the car window, and prayed that no passing train would rub us off. In a few minutes our friends opened the door and told us the M.P. was gone. The rest of the night passed pleasantly. We talked, slept, and helped the Frenchmen drink their wine, but one of us stayed awake in case another M.P. should come through. At 7 a.m., the train slowed down and we dropped off.

The place proved to be a small town called Meuse, and there seemed to be some Americans in it. We saw a mess line under some trees behind a shed, picked up a couple of stray mess kits, and joined it just as if we belonged. The cooks never knew the difference, but handed out stew, bread, and coffee which we ate with satisfaction. Then we washed our mess kits and walked over to a big barn near the tracks where some soldiers were sitting around smoking. From them we learned that Meuse was a newly established railhead to supply a division which was moving into billets in this area, and they were part of a large work detail assigned to unloading the freight cars as they came into the siding. Later, trucks would distribute the supplies to the different towns where outfits were billeted. The men were from different outfits themselves, strangers to each other, and that explained why no one had noticed us in the mess line. They slept on straw in the big barn. Ritchie and I found an upper loft reached by a ladder, where we made ourselves at home. During the day we salvaged some blankets, and after supper we turned in and had a beautiful night's sleep. We liked it here and stayed about two weeks.

One day Lane and Horne blew in with a long story of their life in Paris and how they had got out just ahead of the police by taking a taxicab to a suburb and hopping a train. They had evidently hit on the same train we took, and their anxiety to avoid Langres had brought them to the same place. The four of us lived a quiet life of complete independence till it got too unpleasant. Every day we walked over to a fair-sized town called Montigny-le-Roi where there were cafés and friendly French people who treated us like distinguished guests. We slept in the barn and messed with the railhead detail, but after a while the sergeant in charge began to notice our presence at meals and our absence from work. One night he tried to get us up with the rest when a freight train came in, so the next morning we took our blankets and moved to a farmhouse about a quarter of a mile away on the other side of the track.

Here we each paid a franc a day for board and lodging, slept in fresh hay, and felt very secure. We helped the farmer around the place a little, but there wasn't much to do at this time of year. I borrowed his shotgun and went crow hunting once or twice. The farmer's wife kept us supplied with hot water for shaving and fresh milk. We took walks to the neighboring villages, making friends with the inhabitants, who always entertained us, usually ending up at the Silvestre's house in Montigny for a bowl of hot chocolate.

Some days there was a little snow on the ground but it never amounted to much. American army trucks were getting more and more numerous on the roads. I developed a genius for hooking rides, much to Ritchie's discomfiture, for he was conspicuously weak in this department. One day a YD dispatch rider appeared at Montigny. He told us the Division was moving into this area with headquarters at Montigny and the regiments scattered around among the neighboring villages.

In a few days Montigny was turned into an army town with a Y.M.C.A. hut, Military Police, and all the discomforts that went with it. Ritchie and I considered moving farther south, perhaps to the region of Bordeaux, but we decided not to. We were getting a little fed up on bumming, our money was running low, and we wanted to get our arrears of mail. Also we wanted to find out how we stood with the authorities after our long absence. So on December 23d we hooked a truck loaded with bread at Montigny and after a ride of a few kilometers hopped off in the main street of Varennes-sur-Amance, where we were quickly surrounded by a crowd of inquisitive friends.

## CHAPTER LXI

### *Varenne-sur-Amance. A Christmas eve party.*

"Varennes-sur-Amance. (Haute-Marne). Dec. 23. Bon billet. Well received. Couldn't knock on a door without coming in and having a 'goutte.' X-mas eve. Rum, cognac. Malade with L.H.R. Rabbit dinners. Foot-drill. Hikes. M. and Mme. Garnier-Morlot. Rose 18, Germaine 11. Jeanne (Lisette), Yvonne, Marguerite. Sad farewell.
Left Jan. 22, 1919, 6 p.m."
"Vitry, Jan. 23, 2 a.m. Entrained. Cold, footsore after a 30 k. hike with 40-lb. packs. Wait in cold. Eau-de-vie. Bonne sensation!"

AT VARENNES there were several surprises waiting. The biggest was that we were not punished for our escapade. Our story about looking for the Regiment was accepted at its face value and nothing more ever came of it. The next thing I noticed was that most of the horses were gone, among them Peanuts. This made me think that the war was really over.

I found the Special Detail living in an empty house which contained some chairs and tables and had its own garden, approached through numerous sheds and outbuildings. Ritchie and I made straw beds on the second floor of a barn which was built onto the back of the house. We could get to bed by going upstairs and walking through a back hall or by way of a ladder from the barn floor. There was a tremendous pile of mail waiting for us, including Christmas boxes. It took us about all day to get settled and read our mail.

The next day was December 24th. To celebrate Christmas eve the Special Detail planned a party, and we all laid in a stock of rum, cognac, and wine. I borrowed some glasses from Madame Garnier next door. Seven of us sat down to the celebration right after supper. I happened to be corporal of the guard that night, but it didn't interfere with the party. As a warning to anyone who has never tried celebrating with cognac I might add a few details.

I remember feeling called upon to tell the captain I was still corporal of the guard and getting out into the street. After a few steps I fell over a conical pile of crushed stone, and spent a long time trying to get away from it. With my body at an angle of forty-five degrees and my hands on the stone pile, I kept walking round and round without being able to regain an upright position. Someone pulled me off it and took me inside again. Later I felt ill, so I started for the back garden. In one of the sheds I fell over Ritchie lying with his head at the foot of a short flight of stone steps. I shook him and asked him what he was doing. "They die outside," was all he could say. I called some friends and we started to carry Ritchie to bed. I had him under the shoulders. About three steps from the top of the staircase I suddenly got dizzy, and my last recollection is of falling downstairs in a tangle of arms and legs.

I woke up with the sun shining in my face. I was partly undressed. One boot was beside my head and I had been sick in it. I got dressed and went out. The sight of a row of empty cognac bottles on the table made me sick again.

As I spoke French I was given the job of collecting wine for the Battery's Christmas dinner. It was the most unfortunate occupation I could possibly have been given. With a wheelbarrow and two men I went around from farm to farm. At each place the farmer insisted on my sampling his wine before buying a keg. Often I was able to get rid of it when his back was turned, but some samples I had to drink. It made me sick each time. The lovely Christmas dinner was a hollow mockery to me. After four days I was able to eat again, and inside a week my headache was gone.

Varennes consisted of a main street without sidewalks, crossed by half a dozen cartroads leading into fields each side of the town. There were about a hundred houses lining the main street. A few large farms stood at varying distances from the town. Each house had a square manure pile covered with chickens in front of it, and a small garden approached through outbuildings behind. The country was hilly, with meadows, woods, and brooks.

There was nothing for the men to do, so we were taken on hikes and made to do infantry drill. This was a bore for everybody. We saw in a newspaper that the 26th Division was part of the Army of Occupation, so we kept expecting to go into Germany, but on January 17th the guns and the rest of the horses were turned in, so then we didn't know what to think.

For Ritchie, Allen, and me the Garnier family next door was a godsend. Almost every evening we called on them to play cards, talk, and listen to old man Garnier play the flute. Often they invited us to dinner. All the families in Varennes had their special soldiers that they had adopted. The night we left, the Garniers gave us a farewell supper. They helped us put on our packs in the kitchen, buttoned our overcoats under our chins, stood near us when the Battery lined up in the main street, and cried when the column marched away.

This was on January 22d. It was a long, cold march to the railroad at Vitry, where we entrained.

## CHAPTER LXII

### *Mayet. Mère Martin's hospitality. I go on leave again and meet a lady.*

"Mayet 5 a.m., Jan. 25, 1919. Billeted D Bat'ry. Cognac. Slept on bench. Cold. Found room with Knox. Vielle femme seule (Mère Martin-Leclou). Boar-hunt, Forêt St. Hubert. Eccomoy. Butter 7 francs la livre. Rifles. Julia, Juliette, M. Maufras (precepteur). 'The World and Thomas Kelly,' Arthur Train. 'The Hon. Peter Stirling' Paul L. Ford. 'The House of Mirth' Edith Wharton. Eggs 6 francs doz. 'King Spruce' Holman Day. 'The Common Law,' 'The Yellow Crayon.' Feb. 19th review by Pershing of whole div. 'Les Landes.' Mud, rain, cold. Marched 10 κ. Stood 6 hrs. 10 κ back. Perm. Left Feb. 27, 9 p.m."

"Le Mans (Sarthe) 10 p.m., Feb. 27. Y.M.C.A., dark. Left 12.30 a.m., Feb. 28."

"St. Malo (Ille et Vilaine), 9.30 a.m., Feb. 28. Hotel Victoria. St. Servan. Andree Bougan 3 rue Le Fer, Villa Castelmar. Bon weather. Y Janes, dance, Russian, Belgian lady (Theda Bara) Boston, room 10, Leonarde (gamine). Left St. Malo March 4 (ἐξελαύνω) 5.30 p.m."

"Mayet, March 5, 1919. Bon letter from Ros. and KWR. AD 174. Cootie baths, embarkation, inspections, equipment, cooties, etc. Rumors of leaving. Start B't'ry history, 'editor in chief.' Left noon, Mar. 27."

THE TRAIN JOURNEY lasted about thirty-six hours. We marched past the Mayet railroad station and halted in a place beside the tracks, where the men fell out and made themselves comfortable on the grass. It was drizzling, cold, and almost dark. I was one of a group ordered ahead to do the billeting. For several hours I slept on a bench in the railroad station. Then I remember walking through the streets of Mayet with an officer from D Battery. We passed lighted shop windows, cafés, tall impressive buildings, and once we crossed a wide square with a statue in the center. Then I lost the officer somewhere, in a café probably, and went looking for the mayor's house. After many inquiries I found it up a dark street at the far end of town. He proved to be a maker of wooden shoes, and a very good sort. Over a bottle of brandy we discussed the billeting possibilities, and I left with a list of citizens' names in my hand and bells ringing in my head. I have a vague recollection of showing the D Battery officer various houses in dreamlike streets, and of ending up in a hayloft where I slept soundly, thanks to the mayor's eau-de-vie.

Mayet turned out to be the largest town we had lived in, with hotels, cafés, shops, a business section, and many fine houses. The Special Detail was quartered in the hayloft of a stable belonging to a considerable estate. There was a large, formal garden with tall trees, gravel paths, and a high vine-covered wall. All the houses had gardens behind them, but from the street the house fronts presented an unbroken line. It was only on opening a carriage gate that the gardens were visible from the street.

To our consternation we received a truckload of rifles packed in long boxes and covered with a heavy grease called cosmoline. A rifle was issued to each man, together with a bayonet and infantry pack. The rumor was that we were going to Russia as infantry. From then on we had daily drill in close order and the manual of arms.

I got sick of the leaky hayloft after a few days and decided to live somewhere else. Picking out a small house at random on the main street, I knocked on the door. It was opened by a very old woman with shrewd, gray eyes. I decided I liked her at the first glance and asked her if she wanted a lodger. She took longer to reach a decision, but we finally made a deal, by which I was to have a room for a franc a day. Moving in was a simple matter, as I left everything but my razor and toothbrush in the hayloft to indicate my official place of residence. Mère Martin-Leclou was the old lady's name.

Her house had two rooms on the ground floor: a front one into which the street door opened directly, and a back one slightly smaller. They both were low-studded, with heavy black beams and tile floors. The front room was the living room–kitchen. It contained wooden chairs and tables, a fireplace on which all the cooking was done, and rows of pots and kettles against the wall. In the back room was a double four-poster bed piled high with feather puffs, some chairs, and a huge piece of furniture full of drawers where the linen was kept. A door opened onto a narrow garden between high walls, against which rabbit hutches were built on one side and bundles of faggots piled on the other. At the foot of the garden, open fields stretched away to a patch of woods. The house had a second story but I never found out what it contained.

Mère Martin proved to be a most motherly soul after her first distrust had worn off, and she spent most of her time thinking of ways to make me comfortable. Always when I came in from drilling on cold days she made me change my socks and drink a cup of café-kirsch. She insisted on mending my clothes and doing my laundry, such as it was. Although she knew I was supposed to eat at the Battery mess, she asked me every morning if I would be "home to supper." If I said yes, she would answer, "B'en! Va pour des faagots avant d'partir-moi, j'vais tuer un lapin." After supper she would sit knitting beside her lamp and regale me with personal reminiscences of the Franco-Prussian war. Her favorite story, about how she had escaped from a patrol of Uhlans on the Eccomoy Road without breaking one of the eggs in her basket, I must have heard twenty times. At first I had trouble understanding her broad provincial accent, but I soon caught on to it, and I often made her laugh by mimicking some of her expressions.

Sometimes her cronies called on her in the evening. They would sit around the fire gossiping for hours, while I wrote or read unnoticed in a corner of the room. Except for an occasional phrase, they might have been talking Spanish for all I could understand. Invariably on entering or leaving the house they would pause on the threshold, bow, and say, "Bonsoir, messieurs-dames!" in a measured cadence, without a particle of expression, and they paid no attention to the fact that the old lady and I were their only audience. They all were partial to snuff, which they brought in little triangular paper packets, but it was very dear and hard to get because of the war. The old lady used to grind up Bull Durham and mix it with her snuff, which made her supply inexhaustible.

Whenever Lorenzen's back was turned I took the opportunity of adding a can of Karo or a bag of sugar to Mère Martin's larder, much to her delight. She would hoard it all up and chuckle over it like a miser with so much gold. She had a bucket that for years had been the bane of her life because it leaked, so one day I got her a new one at the Commissary Store and put it in the old one's place under the table. The old one I hid under some faggots. Then I sat down with a book to enjoy her surprise when she should come in and see the improvement. It was the first thing she saw when the door opened, but her reaction was not just what I had counted on.

"A new bucket," she cried, "where is my old one?" The house was kept beautifully clean and neat. I can still see the lacelike tracery of scrollwork on the tile floor that she made with water from a tiny, long-nosed watering can, before getting the fat besom from its place behind the door.

As the winter passed we got to be great friends, and I became very fond of the old lady. Several times she urged me to bring some friends home to supper, and when I did, she produced delicious civet-de-lapin, with vegetables, dessert, wine, and café-noir. She seemed to eat nothing herself. Towards the end I invited Knox to share my room, also at a franc a day, but as he spoke no French, he never got to know the old lady well.

Meanwhile the Battery went on drilling in the mud and snow and rain with the devilish rifles. Storer conceived the idea of writing a Battery History, and made me editor of it, so I was excused from afternoon drill.

Many of the boys were "living out" as I was, and by visiting around at each other's houses we got to know a good many of the townspeople. I was sometimes sent into the country to buy vegetables for the cooks, and there was one farm I particularly enjoyed visiting. Besides a huge manure pile and a savage dog, there was a most amiable old farmer and two buxom daughters. After our business with "des navets" or "des choux" was finished, the old man would take me shooting rabbits in the fields, and then we would sit by the fire, drinking some of his favorite vintages and playing cards with the girls until it was time for me to start back. On market days I would see them in the square at Mayet and get their advice on whose butter was best to buy. It came in big, squat pats, wrapped in fresh vine leaves.

One day, just after a light fall of snow, the Colonel arranged a boar hunt in which the Regiment was to act as beaters. All day we ranged through the Forêt de St. Hubert, where the trees were planted in rows and there was no underbrush. Afterwards I heard that one boar had been seen, and one hare killed. That evening Mère Martin told me about what boar hunts she had seen "dans le temps," which was her expression for "the good old days."

There was some kind of lending library where I got any number of trashy books to read, and I spent a good deal of time writing up the History. On February 13th there was a big Divisional review at Eccomoy. It took place on some level plains called "les Landes." I shall never forget the superb sight of thirty thousand troops moving in time to the stirring cadence of the "March du Sambre et Meuse"* while the flags of the regiments floated above the moving sea of bayonets. A few days later Lane and I drew passes for a furlough in the Brittany area, and on February 27th we started.

The train landed us at Le Mans at 10 p.m. We spent a couple of hours in a Y.M.C.A. building listening to someone play the piano, and at 12:30 took a train out. There was snow on the ground when it got light enough to see. I remember changing trains at Dol, and seeing a railroad employee dead beside the track with both legs crushed. I remember wondering if he had survived four years of war only to meet his death in this silly way. The Brittany countryside looked familiar, with its rough fields, hedges, and holly. At 9:30 we arrived at St. Malo.

It was a small place, with none of the formality of Aix-les-Bains.

* Played by the massed bands of all the regiments in the Division. The air shook.

We got our papers stamped by the A.P.M. and left the station. There were very few American soldiers about. A dilapidated cab took us to the hotel we were assigned to in the neighboring town of St. Servan. I have no intention of describing so well known a place, but will confine myself to the story. For a week Ed and I walked around the beaches, explored the ramparts, docks, and historic buildings, and sampled the cafés.

One night we went over to the Y.M.C.A. hut in St. Malo, which was the casino in peace time. We found a dance going on. I soon sickened of the professional sweetness of the "Y. girls," and gave it up for a bad job. While I was idly watching the dancers and waiting for Ed to break away and come home, I saw a little French girl of exquisite grace and beauty, dancing with a redheaded soldier. She was obviously a finished dancer, and her partner was obviously the reverse, and also handicapped by a load of cognac, so I promptly cut in. It was a success from the start. Andrée said she had been wondering how to shake the redhead, but found her English didn't cover the emergency. I said I hoped she wouldn't remember the right expressions for getting rid of partners now, and she said she had stopped trying to. We danced and danced till poor Ed got tired of waiting and went home alone.

I asked Andrée how she happened to be there, and she said the organization in St. Servan which corresponds to the Vincent Club in Boston had agreed to take turns attending the soldiers' dances at the Y.M.C.A. with a chaperone. By the time we were fairly started on learning each other's business the party was over, and Andrée told me to come and meet her mother. This I did, and found that she was the wife of the mayor of St. Servan, spoke English, and had friends in Boston. The musicians were folding up their music stands, and someone was putting out the lights. I saw that I must be "bloody, bold, and resolute," so I asked if I could call the next day, and was rewarded by an invitation to dinner. We parted with emotion on both sides, ecstasy on mine, and, I dare say, consternation on Madame Bougan's.

The next day I was in a flutter till seven o'clock came. Ed was disgusted, and said so. At seven o'clock I slicked myself up for the last time and sallied forth to find the Villa Castelmar, 3 rue Le Fer. I was feeling that I had bitten off more than I could chew, but it was too late to turn back. I soon found the place, and gave a pull on the iron ring, hanging by a chain from the high wall. A bell sounded somewhere in the distance. I was thinking there was still time to run for it, when the gate opened and a maid showed me into the parlor. Here I saw Madame Bougan and Andrée, who greeted me with formality and introduced me to M. le Maire and Mlle Hèlene. Hèlene was about nineteen and was attractive, but without Andrée's style. I have neglected to say that Andrée was seventeen. The mayor was also the town's doctor, ran the hospital, and for four years had been doing the work of the doctors of all the surrounding towns, who were in the army. He was a big, bluff, cordial man with a black mustache. Dinner was an affair of many courses, with much politely manufactured conversation. Afterwards, M. Bougan retired to his study, and the rest of us sat in the parlor, where the young ladies played the piano and sang. Then we played word games, and card games, and laughed about each other's bad French and English, and by 10:30 Madame Bougan looked restless enough to make me feel that the party was over. We arranged a promenade on the cliffs for the next afternoon, and I found my way back to the Hotel Victoria and told Ed all about it. From his caustic comments I judged that he was jealous.

It wasn't that at all. He was only waiting for me to stop talking. After I had unloaded my story about Andrée's perfections, he announced that he had not been idle either. As we were the only Americans in the hotel, he had felt the full responsibility for keeping things lively, so he had enlisted the help of a Belgian lady from Boston who looked like Theda Bara and played the piano, got the manager's permission to move the piano into the dining room, and staged a dance, to which the waitresses and guests were all invited. It had been such a success that the manager was going to repeat it the next night.

"I go on leave again and
meet a lady."

"A 'cootie incubator' had been installed in the town."

The clothes were rolled in tight bundles and placed in the machine, where they were exposed to steam under pressure. On emerging, they were shrunken and wrinkled beyond recognition. This was a sad blow to anyone just going on leave, when he would want to look most dapper.

When I went to get Andrée for the promenade on the cliffs, I found that the whole family intended to come. This made a dreary start, but once on the steep paths Andrée, Helène, and I outdistanced the old people, and made good progress in advancing our friendship. Helène was "fiancée," so she put on superior airs which Andrée tried to squelch by uncomplimentary remarks about the young man. I had very little talking to do. We explored an old tower where somebody I should have known about was imprisoned in the thirteenth century, saw the harbor and the River Rance, inspected the château recently bought by some rich "embusqué," and finally ended up at the Bougans' house.

The next day was to be my last at St. Servan. Ed's dance at the hotel left me cold. I was wondering how I could possibly tear myself away from the charming Andrée. She really was charming, even allowing for the effect of going eighteen months without seeing a girl to talk to. There was a daintiness about her way of speaking and a graceful playfulness of mind that exactly suited her delicate but pert type of beauty.

The next afternoon I made a farewell call on Madame Bougan, and found her at home. While Andrée drifted around in the background, Maman showed me over the house, pointing out particularly fine pieces of furniture that would be Andrée's on her marriage, going into the details of Andrée's dot, and dilating on her own Boston connections.* I found it distinctly embarrassing, but Andrée seemed perfectly at her ease. It's probably just as well it was my last day of leave. I thanked Madame Bougan very sincerely for her kindness, left my respects for the doctor and Helène, and grabbed my hat. Andrée came as far as the gate, where we agreed to write to each other, she in English and I in French, in order to improve our foreign languages. At 5:30 I found the train pulling out and Ed waiting for me on the station platform in no sweet frame of mind. Our journey back to Mayet was uneventful.

A strange change had come over the place in our absence. Every-

* Thorndikes.

one was talking about embarkation points, transports, and going back to the States. All kinds of inspections were being held, and a "cootie incubator" had been installed in the town for delousing our clothes. In the next few weeks great rivalry developed between the batteries as to which could report the fewest lousy men at roll call. Lousiness had become a disgrace, and the culprits were now scorned, even by their friends. This was all because of a Divisional order that no organization containing lousy men could be taken on board a transport. Some of the sections got flat irons, and worked over the seams of their clothes at night to kill the cootie eggs, others relied on kerosene, and others thought soap and water the most effective.

The fad gradually died out, and we plugged along in our routine of hiking and close-order drill. I lived happily at Mère Martin's, working on the History and lying low at drill hours as far as possible. When I told the old lady about Andrée, she was very unsympathetic, and took an aversion to her from the start. Whenever she saw me writing a letter she laughed at me and made scurrilous comments to which I pretended to pay no attention.

One rainy night there was a knock at the door, and there stood Tom Proctor in a captain's uniform and a broad grin on his face. He had heard we were at Mayet, and had walked all the way from Le Mans to pay a call. Mère Martin was thrilled to learn that he was an old friend that I hadn't seen since leaving home, and she showered him with hospitality. About midnight he borrowed my slicker and started back in the rain.

Towards the end of March there was a sudden revival of rumors about home, and another drive on the cooties. Again there were interminable inspections of everything, and at noon on March 27th we made our packs and marched down to the railroad. My leave-taking at the old lady's house broke me up, as I had no idea she was so fond of me. I remember the way she looked, standing in her doorway with her apron crumpled up against her chest, as our column moved down the street. I shall always remember her with grateful affection.

# CHAPTER LXIII

## *Home.*

"Brest, March 28, 1919. 56 in box car. No straw. 'Meal car.' Froze all night. Arrived
Brest 11 a.m. 'Embarkation mess hall,' rest camp, pyramidal tents like Boxford.
'Pontanezon.' Lay-out. Rain in torrents all night and day. Money changed. Inspection
and bath at 'the mad-house.' Rumor we board 'Agamemnon' 10 a.m. Sunday.
Equipment inspection, Sunday a.m. 2 inches snow."
"S.S. Agamemnon (Kaiser Wilhelm) March 30, 1919. Cold. 4 mile hike to pier. Lighter,
Agamemnon. Packed in close. 4 tier skeleton bunks. No room to move or place for stuff.
Sunday night in harbor. Top bunk. Slept well. Up 6. Breakfast. Waited in line 3 hrs.
'Up anchor' 1 p.m. Last look at France through rain. Rumor we are going to Odessa!"
"Tues. Apr. 1. Heavy swell and roll. 'Undecided,' verging on 'sick.' Better towards night."
"Wed. Apr. 2. Fair, warm. Not sick. 1 ship, porpoise."
"Thurs. Apr. 3. Calm. Uneventful. Crowded. Warm."
"Fri. Apr. 4. Storm, rough, all sick, lost breakfast, held lunch. Wet to skin. Calmed in p.m."
"Sat. Apr. 5. Calm. Uneventful. Later rough."
"Sun. Apr. 6. Calm. Fog. Feel low."
"Boston, April 7, 1919. Fog, Boston Light, Minots, reception, Commonwealth Pier.
Night on ship."

O UR LAST RIDE in France was in boxcars, and crowded as we had
never been before, but we didn't care, because we were almost sure
that home was a possibility at last. There was always the chance of
Russia, or some foreign port for further service, but the fact that we
had turned in the wretched rifles was against it.

At 11 a.m. the train stopped at a big, raw encampment, and we all
got out and formed column. "Embarkation Mess Hall" was the sign
over the gate we marched through. Here we went along runways
between wooden railings, like cattle in a slaughterhouse, but instead of
getting slaughtered we got fed. Then we marched two or three miles
to a tent city on the mud called Camp Pontanezon. The tents were

Sibleys, like the ones we had at Boxford. Each tent had a stove in it with a stovepipe going out the top, but there was nothing to burn. We were marched to mess in some distant barrack, and marched back to our tents like convicts. Everyone said that getting assigned to a transport depended on good behavior. There were stories of outfits being kept two months at Brest because they straggled when they marched, or were shy the proper number of tent pegs per man. We believed everything we heard.

After a very cold night we woke to find two inches of snow on the ground. That day the Battery went through a place known as "The Mad-house." It reminded me of "The Pit" at the Nantasket Beach amusement park. With our packs we entered a large wooden building in single file, and were steered into a bath department, where we took off all our clothes and threw them away. Then we filed into a sort of steam chamber where soapy water fell on us from the ceiling. In the room beyond we were painted all over with some white disinfectant by men with large whitewash brushes. Then we progressed to a shower room, after which we were given towels and told to use them. At the door of the next department the towels were taken away from us and we were given a complete new set of clothes, with no regard for our different sizes. After getting dressed, we were herded into a large hall where we found our packs waiting for us. We then lined up, took distance, and opened our packs, each man laying out all his worldly goods according to a prescribed pattern. We had been drilled in this at Mayet. Strange embarkation officers made a minute inspection and pulled out a few men who were deficient in something, a cake of soap or a can of dubbin or a fork. I never knew what happened to these unfortunates. I was too busy watching my own stuff to see what went on around me. When it was over and our packs made again we were marched out into a torrent of rain. It rained all that night.

The next morning we had our French money changed, were inspected again and searched for unauthorized possessions, which meant

264

anything not issued by the Government,* and at last we lined up for our march to the pier. We were on our good behavior every step of the four miles from Camp Pontanezon to the water. I didn't dare believe it was true till we crested a hill and I saw a great transport lying in the harbor. At the pier were delays and formalities, with checking over of lists and answering to names, but at last I found myself walking down the gangplank to the deck of a crowded lighter, and a few minutes later I was on board the *Agamemnon*. Even now we kept our mouths shut, because of a story about a whole regiment's being taken off a ship and sent back to Camp Pontanezon when one man yelled "Who won the war?" at an embarkation M.P.

We were herded down several decks into the hold, where we found wire bunks four deep, with such narrow aisles between that we had to walk sidewise through them. I got a bunk next to the top and threw my pack and overcoat into it, saving my mess kit out. We messed in what had been the ship's ballroom. It was divided in two by a partition about ten feet high. We walked between counters behind which stood kitchen police who splashed oatmeal, rancid stew, and coffee into our mess kits, and on emerging from the line we walked up some steps over the partition and down some steps on the other side. We were then in the larger half of the hall, where long tables hung from the ceiling by chains. These were the proper height to use standing up. After eating, we dipped our mess kits in a trough of dirty water and climbed back on deck, still being herded. There was none of the freedom of the old *Adriatic*. This ship was alive with troops, so there never was room to sit down anywhere. That night we stayed at anchor, and I slept well in spite of the close air. My bunk was so near the ceiling that I couldn't roll over in bed.

The next morning there was some mistake about which battery messed first, and we stood in line, mess kits in hand, for three hours

* My Luger pistol has been for some weeks on the mantelpiece in my fathers' study at home thanks to the honesty of an Aix-les-Bains storekeeper.

before being herded below. At 1 p.m. the anchor was raised, and the *Agamemnon* steamed out of the harbor. I thought we were going home, but a lot of the men knew on good authority that we were bound for Odessa. Through a veil of rain we watched the outlines of France fade into the distance.

I won't add much to the notes about the voyage. We had no life preservers or abandon-ship drill, but there were other things. The mess hall on a rough day deserves a word. We would walk unsteadily down the aisle, waving our mess kits, while the servers would try to put food into them. I always gave them credit for trying. Then we would tackle the double flight of stairs, which had no handrails and needed none, as no one could have used it while holding a full mess kit in one hand and a full coffee mug in the other. The combination of the pitching ship and the slippery stairs was disastrous to many, and there would be another spectacular fall and another addition to the pools of lost lunches, eaten and not eaten, that paved the floor. The blasé kitchen police wouldn't even smile, as it was all old stuff to them. If a man negotiated the barrier safely and could bear the odor of the eating place, he would put his food on a swinging table and try to keep near it as it moved back and forth.

There was plenty of food on the floor of the sleeping quarters, but it was all second-hand food. Wire wastebaskets had been provided at the corners of aisles, and even if they had been buckets they wouldn't have met the demand when everyone was seasick. I won't insist on describing all the details of our life on the *Agamemnon*. I kept my health fairly well, considering, but I often thought of poor Jock Mc-Sweeney, and how he had vowed to walk home through Siberia. He was in a bunk somewhere on board, but I never saw him during the voyage.

On April 7th we were going half-speed ahead through the fog, when a tugboat came alongside with a band playing. Everyone crowded on deck as the news spread. Soon the *Agamemnon* was the center of a flotilla of small craft loaded with welcoming committees.

People threw food and gifts to us, but they all bounced off the side of the ship into the water about twenty feet below the rail. As we passed the Boston Light and Minots the small boats increased in number. There was everything from rowboats to ferries. They all were crowded with people who had come to see their own soldier, and it was pathetic to see their efforts at locating him in that solid mass of khaki. On some of the boats were banners displayed, saying, "Chelsea welcomes Oscar Pearlstein," or with just a name to attract the attention of some particular soldier. When a family had located its soldier, there were frantic wavings and shoutings until some other boat cut in between.

With bands playing and all the whistles in Boston harbor screeching, the *Agamemnon* nosed up to Commonwealth Pier and made fast. I had a good place near the rail. Through all the tumult of cheering and bands I saw Peabo's face as I last remembered it, and the windrows of American dead in the wheatfields around the Croix Rouge Farm, and I thought of their families sitting at home. A gangplank was lowered to the pier, which was crowded with people jostling to get nearer. Suddenly I saw my father, and behind him my mother and sister and the hard-working Ros.

By persistent efforts I made them look my way, and we saw each other. There was too much noise to hear anything so we just looked and made foolish signs. They seemed to be trying to tell me to do something. I noticed several soldiers going down the gangplank and mixing with the crowd. Pretty soon I heard my name being paged from behind, and I squirmed my way back from the rail till I found an officer, who told me I was wanted at the gangplank. Through some friend on the official reception committee, my father had got permission for me to go ashore for five minutes, and I walked down the gangplank to where they stood. There was so much to be said that I couldn't think of anything to say. As I remember, they said they were glad I was back, and I said I was glad to be back. For the rest of the five minutes we didn't speak at all. Then I went back up

267

the gangplank, and when I had succeeded in squirming to the rail again they were gone.

That night we slept on the ship, and the next morning we filed down the gangplank and onto a train, where we sank into the plush cushions of a luxurious daycoach. At all the towns through which our train passed on the way to Ayer there were cheering crowds on the station platforms. When we marched up the road into Camp Devens, the first man I saw was Priebe, in a campaign hat, and with one arm shorter that the other. He didn't see me. We were installed in big wooden barracks with running water, heat, spring beds, and mess halls where we sat down to eat.

Two weeks later we had a parade down Commonwealth Avenue, with the whole Division in line, and four days after that we were mustered out of the service. I turned away from the adjutant's office with my discharge paper in my hand and found my father standing in the road behind me. Arm in arm we walked over to the waiting automobile.

Printed at
The Stinehour Press
HAEC OLIM MEMINISSE JUVABIT